The Palgrave Lacan Series

Jacques Lacan is one of the most important and influential thinkers of the 20th century. The reach of this influence continues to grow as we settle into the 21st century, the resonance of Lacan's thought arguably only beginning now to be properly felt, both in terms of its application to clinical matters and in its application to a range of human activities and interests. The Palgrave Lacan Series is a book series for the best new writing in the Lacanian field, giving voice to the leading writers of a new generation of Lacanian thought. The series will comprise original monographs and thematic, multi-authored collections. The books in the series will explore aspects of Lacan's theory from new perspectives and with original insights. There will be books focused on particular areas of or issues in clinical work. There will be books focused on applying Lacanian theory to areas and issues beyond the clinic, to matters of society, politics, the arts and culture. Each book, whatever its particular concern, will work to expand our understanding of Lacan's theory and its value in the 21st century.

More information about this series at
http://www.palgrave.com/gp/series/15116

Yuri Di Liberto

Being and Contemporary Psychoanalysis

Antinomies of the Object

palgrave
macmillan

Yuri Di Liberto
University of Calabria
Rende, Cosenza, Italy

The Palgrave Lacan Series
ISBN 978-3-030-18475-9 ISBN 978-3-030-18476-6 (eBook)
https://doi.org/10.1007/978-3-030-18476-6

Cover illustration: morkeman/gettyimages

This Palgrave Macmillan imprint is published by the registered company Springer Nature Switzerland AG
The registered company address is: Gewerbestrasse 11, 6330 Cham, Switzerland

To Elvira
…and to all the blue flowers out there

Acknowledgements

This book wouldn't have been possible if it wasn't for the creative environment of the University of Calabria and its doctoral program. The courses, seminars and dialogues of the past two years all led to this book. It is with the Lacanian seminars held by Felice Cimatti and Fabrizio Palombi that the germs of this book were put. I would also like to thank Carlo Serra for our talks during these years.

My friend and colleague Claudio D'Aurizio doesn't know perhaps, but our walks in Cosenza were essential. As well as our endless dialogues about philosophy and psychoanalysis.

I'm also thankful for everything that didn't have a direct impact on the book but that nonetheless nourished my ideas indirectly. All my friends and colleagues from Bologna, Rome and Palermo that have been supportive—one way or another—of my works.

I'm deeply thankful to Francesco La Mantia. It is by sharing our ideas that I could refine some of the arguments of this book. And I also would like to thank Francesco for the hints and suggestions that here and there helped me enriching some of my arguments.

I have to mention the indispensable help of Fernando Armellini and thank him once again for the Hebrew terms I mention in Chapter 3 of this book. I'm very thankful to Adrian Johnston, whose works helped me in enlightening some crucial aspects of ontology and psychoanalysis; also, I have to thank him for supporting the overall project's idea since the start.

I would like to thank Robert N. McKinley, Brendan Rome and Justin M. Pearce from the University of New Mexico for their terrific work while helping me during the review of the manuscript.

Furthermore, this book wouldn't have been possible if it wasn't for Joanna O'Neill and her patient work.

Finally, I'm very grateful to Calum Neill and Derek Hook for believing in my project and welcoming it; I am very proud to be part of their series at Palgrave.

Introduction

It is historically evident that psychoanalysis was born from philosophical premises. It was born through a refinement on the philosophical questioning of being and subjectivity and their relationships. Inasmuch as philosophy covers the possibility of theorizing about Being as such, psychoanalysis entered the scene as an attempt to reintroduce subjectivity in a scientific fashion. That was, at least, Freud's plea for a clear theory about how civilization shapes the subject in the early stages of its history.

It is with psychoanalysis that the pathological regains its space, this time acknowledging its own intrinsic logic. The symptom is not an out-of-the-norm; it is instead a quintessential element of the human animal.

With Jacques Lacan, this basic derangement of civilization becomes a matter of *how* and *to what extent* language shapes the subject in its bodily existence. Or, to put it another way, Lacan's often rigorous re-reading of Freud has led him to focus on the operations of language and how they shape (and are shaped by) the subject itself.

Because of the acknowledgment of this linguistic agency in subjective life, it has become fashionable to portray psychoanalysis as a kind of language-centered idealism. It is not surprising, indeed, that already Freud had to face similar accusations.

At a first glance, it would seem that psychoanalysis cuts off the Real: 'objecthood' is itself determined either by fantasies or by plain hallucinations.

This is what various forms of philosophical realism are arguing when it comes to psychoanalysis.

The accusation of linguistic idealism lies next to the attitude to portray psychoanalysis as an idealistic dimension. A subject is what is represented by a signifier to another signifier, to recall Lacan's famous diktat. Subjectivity lies in the middle of a mismatch within the realm of words. Subjectivity, in this view, has to do (or coincides with) an *attempt*: it is an attempt to fit into the order of meaning (or of Meaning with capital 'M').

Yet psychoanalysis, if closely explored, states that it is by *interpretation* that one access the body. The unconscious is, in this view, the result of the ancestral interpretation pursued by the caregiver(s) upon the bodily events of the infant.

The corollary of a subjectivity as a locus of a de-naturalized nature lies next to the thesis of representation. The baptism into the realm of language constitutes an active and a passive dynamic all at once: the body is 'semiotized' and in turn equipped with the possibility of re-signifying its surroundings. It is a passage from a lacking first nature often characterized via the fantasy of the mother-child whole, to a second nature which is already, so to speak, a signified one.

Moreover, it is a nature endowed with negativity: the body which speaks gives rise to a subject that desires. Because of that, for Lacan subjectivity is an object which doesn't correspond to itself.

Psychoanalytical 'speculation' starts by acknowledging this basic element of subjectivity. The scenario of the speaking animal is the one in which «after a need is satisfied, and the subject gets the demanded object, desire continues on its own; it is not 'extinguished' by the satisfaction of need» (Zupančič 2011: 18).

Lacan adds a positive element to this play of negativities: object small *a*, an object which is set to feed and renew this dynamic itself. As Zupančič has pinpointed: object small *a* «can be understood as a void that has acquired a form. In Lacan's words: 'Object *a* is no being. Object *a* is the void presupposed by demand…'. "*That's not it*" means that, in the desire of every demand, there is but the request for object *a*» (Ibid.).

The emphasis must be put here on the 'formed' nature of this remainder. In its propelling force it nonetheless determines—by using signifiers—a specific and idiosyncratic Real. It is a Real which calls for the recognition of one's own *hic et nunc*, one's own facticity.

For this reason, Neurosis is nothing but the name psychoanalysis gives to subjectivity when it is viewed under the effects of this very facticity: the fact that there's language. Thus, the object of subjectivity is first and foremost caught in its idealistic default position: it is an object which posits its own objects. It is not a surprise that these same objects are linked to bodily representations. In a passage from Giuseppe Berto's *The Obscure Illness*, which describes neurosis, there's a line in which he portrays his suffering as a «malign influence» coming from the «loculus where, so to speak, the father was resting» (Berto 2016: 186). The dead father is not the buried one, but it is instead an object which takes a specific place within the phantasmal anatomy of the subject. That is the power of language: to enrich (for better or for worse) one's access to his own body with objects whose agency is to cut the subject from its supposed nature.

Hence, Lacan's emphasis on language is not to get rid of the bodily *tout court*, but instead to acknowledge the existence of subjectivity as a hybridized object stuffed with signifiers and their power to derange enjoyment.

It has become fashionable in latest philosophical returns to Realism to put a lot of emphasis in a supposed incompatibility between psychoanalysis and the theorization of a philosophical Real. It is an incompatibility often suggested by both Lacan-oriented authors and realist philosophers (transcendental materialism, object-oriented ontologies, etc.).

For example, in a quick and explicit remark made by Slavoj Žižek, he says that «[…]there is no place for the subject in OOO [object-oriented ontologies]» (Žižek 2018: 61). To be clear, he laments the fact that philosophies centered on the Real of objects tend to dismiss the Lacanian Real as too anthropocentric (and therefore too idealistic).

That is, this view on subjectivity as a hybridization of matter-and-language seems to give us little room for reflecting on the reality of being as such: the Real of the subject seems to be all too subjective to come close to the Real of being.

The dream of such philosophical projects is either to place subjects amongst objects or to get rid of the subjective element of being so that one can access a Real without the bias of the subjective point of view.

Despite their supposed incompatibility, I wouldn't portray the relation between the Real of philosophical speculation and the Real of psychoanalysis as totally separate. Indeed, throughout the book I try to suggest that they have much to share and much to gain from each other.

In doing that, I tried to implicitly stick to another philosophical call made by Žižek: «We reach the Real only when we reflect on how we fit into the reality of objects around us» (ibid.). I took this statement as an underlying guide for my argumentations: it is only by exploring objects (whether they are subjects, objects broadly taken or their entanglements) that both philosophers and/or Lacanian scholars can re-define the Real.

And indeed, there's plenty of room in the Lacanian corpus itself to characterize a Real of subjectivity which is regarded as a 'thing' but without falling prey to a plain objectification of it.

In order to reach the trope of the Real as another way of access to subjectivity, I emphasized some basic differences between the philosophical Real and the psychoanalytical one.

For that matter, I tried to cover the question of the Real in its double philosophical and psychoanalytical articulation in the first chapter. There, I focus my attention on a possible comparison between the Real of philosophical speculation (as in Quentin Meillassoux) and that of psychoanalysis.

In doing that, I suggest that when it comes to the philosophical category of 'Being', one doesn't have to fall too easily into philosophical fantasies of the whole. That is, I tend to align myself to psychoanalysis as it is (also) an attempt to deconstruct theoretical or second-order world-view(s) often pursued through specific conception of matter of being.

I do also re-engage with the question of the relationship between nature and language. Indeed, I tend to defend psychoanalysis against the accusations of correlationism: the idea according to which we can have access only the relation between subject and object, and not the object in-itself.

This trope would constitute the issue of 'fantasy' as the default-mode implemented by the subject when dealings with everyday objects. Against the idea of a psychoanalytical reductionism to the play of fantasies, I defend during the chapter the idea according to which the Real of psychoanalysis is something which acts differently in regard to the Real of speculation. But in any case I argue for a fruitful parallel between the two.

In order to do so, I suggest that the Real of psychoanalysis has to do with a basic reconfiguration of the notions of 'Nature' and 'Temporality'. That is, despite maintaining the reciprocity of the two types of Real, I make a plea for a close rethinking of the difference which lies at the center of the Real taken from its subjective side.

After having clarified the main features of the Lacanian Real and have them compared to the Real of speculation, I develop a tripartite characterization of objects on the model of Lacan's Borromean topology. This is what I do in Chapter 2 of the book.

I argue that when it comes to objects, one should be able to distinguish between three modes of existence: that of 'values' (Symbolic), 'gestures' (Imaginary) and 'events' (Real). As some scholars may notice, during Chapter 2 I tend to align myself with other object-oriented ontologies (such as Levi Bryant's). Indeed, I agree on the possibility of theoretically isolating objects along the lines of a *typization* into symbolic, imaginary and real ones.

However, much like Chapter 1, 2 also sets some fine distinctions between objects of speculation and the 'thing' (or thing-body) of subjectivity. That is, I suggest that in isolating these objects, one is always facing the peril of missing the key role (and asymmetry) played by the Real of subjectivity.

That's why after delineating the tripartite or Borromean account of objects, I develop the argument about the anti-philosophical stance of Lacan. I tried to suggest the idea that being forgetful about the 'libidinal element', so to speak, is the gateway to fetishize objects in general.

But, once again, I take this very possibility as something already acknowledged by psychoanalysis and I put it within a comprehensive account which acknowledges the role of sublimation in the experience of thought.

The concluding part of the second chapter bridges the issue of objects (in their tripartite aspect) with the third chapter, which is a chapter on the Real of the body. Indeed, I conclude Chapter 2 with a reformulation of the very concept of the 'speculative'.

I defend a realist account of subjectivity as an object in which the 'speculative' doesn't take the shape of a subject-to-object relation, but instead the one of a coincidence (Hegelian, one might say) between subjectification and objectification.

In other words, I envisage the possibility of thinking subjectivity as the 'Thing' of psychoanalysis: it is a Thing which is, because of its constitution, already imbued with the 'speculative'. Here, I tend to portray this 'speculativeness' of the psychoanalytical Thing as indicating the possibility that language *plus* the body give rise to a crucible of forms.

It is only with Chapter 3 that I fully develop this trope of a living and creative Real of subjectivity. In order to do so, I focus on the Real of the body. As the reader may notice, I reengage here with a question which was left open in the end of the first chapter. There I suggest the possibility of re-thinking psychoanalysis as having to do with a realism of subjectivity, but I left open the possibility of giving whatsoever positive account of such a Real.

Chapter 3 develops this possibility left open by Chapter 1 by drawing on some elements of Chapter 2 (especially the arguments about 'differentiality' of the Symbolic register and 'simulated gestures' of the Imaginary).

In doing this, I give an account of how language enters the scenario of the corporeal. In order to do so, I draw from some key concepts of psychoanalyst Didier Anzieu. I try to show that, despite their divergences, Lacan and Anzieu help us defining a way in which enjoyment takes specific and singular expressions in subjective life.

The reader could here have a feeling of a metapsychological model based on Lacanian categories. In fact, while developing the arguments I tend to open up this possibility. Against the odds of falling prey to the metapsychological temptation, I would rather say that Chapter 3 is an attempt to clarify *how* the Real of the 'speculative' has to do with enjoyment and its bodily incarnation. That's why I end up suggesting the idea that enjoyment is diagrammatized. I borrow the concept of the diagram (mainly) from the works of mathematician Gilles Châtelet and leverage it to describe the workings of fantasy, enjoyment and the Lacanian 'sinthome'.

I conclude the chapter by proposing the idea according to which it is only through a transformation or a repositioning of the subject in regard to its own diagrams that the 'sinthome' (or the Real) is reached. The Real of psychoanalysis has to do, then, more with an acknowledgment of what was 'already there' than it has to do with a supposedly state of being to be reached.

References

Berto, G. (2016). *Il male oscuro*. Vicenza: Neri Pozza.

Žižek, S. (2018). Marx Reads Object-Oriented-Ontology. In *Reading Marx*. Cambridge: Polity Press.

Zupančič, A. (2011). *Ethics of the Real: Kant and Lacan*. London: Verso.

Contents

List of Figures

1

The Real: *From Ancestrality to Actuality*

1 The Problem of the Real

In his book *After Finitude*, the philosopher Quentin Meillassoux draws a new departing point for contemporary philosophy. His work marks the beginning of what it is now known as Speculative Realism. In fact, many of the forms this Realism has taken (transcendental, object-oriented, etc.) all start from an inaugural critique of what Meillassoux calls correlationism. By correlationism he means «the idea according to which we have access only to the correlation of thought and being, and in no way to one of those terms taken separately» (Meillassoux 2008: 17). According to this definition, then, he calls «*correlationism* any current of thought which establishes the insuperable character of this correlation» (Ivi).

Accordingly, the Realist move to get rid of correlationism has to do with the (often) hypertrophied importance that twentieth-century philosophers gave to language, language games, discourses, etc. It seems that much of what we call philosophy became trapped in the idea according to which, due to our inevitable finite and linguistic nature,

Y. Di Liberto, *Being and Contemporary Psychoanalysis*,
The Palgrave Lacan Series, https://doi.org/10.1007/978-3-030-18476-6_1

we can never have a knowledge of a real beyond our language games or our mortal minds.

The *Linguistic Turn*, Kant's transcendentalism, post-structuralism, (etc.), all seems to have merged into the idea that everything that exists is always correlated to the knowing mind, that is, to the subject. The correlationist is doomed to live a *claustrophobic* reality in which the Real *an sich* is structurally and inevitably forbidden. This is because we can never escape the subject-to-world relation; we can never say something about the world as an independent reality because we have *language* (Foucault, Lacan, etc.), because we have access only to *phenomena* (Kant), or because *life* is a co-product of matter itself (Deleuze).

Meillassoux' plea is then to reengage with the possibility of a thought which is capable of saying something *true* about the Real before (and independent from) the human-to-world correlation. A thought which is then devoid of correlationism in all its forms.

Accordingly, realists have put Lacanian psychoanalysis among the descendants of correlationist thought. Shaviro, for example, asserts that «Lacanian psychoanalysis [...] fails to make enough of a break with correlationism. Indeed, it posits a Real that cannot be correlated with thought» (Shaviro 2014: 7). Even Lacan is unable to escape the claustrophobic cage of correlationism, because «even when correlationism *does* posit some sort of "exteriority" to thought»—as the «Lacanian Real»—«this exteriority still remains "relative to us"[...]» (ibid.: 109). Even if Lacan envisages psychoanalysis as a having the «encounter with the Real» (Lacan 2003: 52) as its object, it is always nonetheless a Real from the perspective of a human subject.

Levi Bryant has made a similar point as well when he states that Lacanian psychoanalysis is a «variant of correlationism», because in focusing on the relation between «language and being» it implicitly defends the idea that «being cannot be thought apart from a subject» (Bryant 2015: 46).

One point is to made clear. What Meillassoux is advocating is *not* a strict denial that our ordinary access to the world is more or less carried through linguistic categories or that language does have an agency in shaping human activity as such; rather, his anti-correlationist position stands for the idea that there are some type of (scientific) enunciates that are capable of saying something *true* about the world even before the advent of any knowing subject. Meillassoux calls this Ancestrality: «Thinking ancestrality is equal to thinking a world without thought: a world without the giving of the world» (Meillassoux 2008: 43). Thinking about the truthfulness of scientific enunciates implies the idea that «thought can have access to the non-correlated, to a world capable of existing without being given» (Ivi). The aim of (realist) speculation is therefore to think of an *Absolute*. The idea of a state of affairs with is not dependent on human thought or on the phenomenal giving of it to a human subject.

What I would like to suggest is that: (1) although Lacan (and psychoanalysis more generally) may fall into the category of correlationism, he envisages correlational thought as a trap to be overcome rather then a mere state of affairs, (2) Realisms can easily fall prey of a *subjectless* account of history and may, therefore, consider the real effects that language plays on subjectivity formation as irrelevant, (3) Speculative Realism and Lacanian psychoanalysis do share a lot of their respective fundamental ideas if properly examined, and, finally, (4) both Speculative Realism and Lacanian psychoanalysis can work as correctives of each other.

Now, a point which is worth underlying here is that both the concept of ancestrality and the absolute explicitly aim at the problem of historicity. When Meillassoux underlines the capacity of science to say something true about a pre-human (i.e. not-yet-human) world, he is thinking about the reality of «Arche-fossils». These are, in turn, prehistoric materials; that is, real traces of a materiality of being before the advent of a knowing subject. To be more precise, arche-fossils are even witnesses of a world in which there was no precondition of life itself. Scientific knowledge tells us something about a pre-historic history. Or, to put it in another way, it tells us a *history before history*.

It is at this exact intersection that contemporary realism is split into two. For one part we have Meillassoux' Being as *Absolute*, for another—namely the object-oriented philosophers—history (and human history in particular) is made *part* of the philosophical investigation as such. In this second scenario it is objects (rather than Being with capital 'B') which are investigated in their own regards. It is their independency from a knowing subject and their capacity to exert concrete agencies which are made subject of investigation. Hence history is often portrayed as made up of *assemblages* (such as in the case of Manuel De Landa) or machinic concatenations (Levi Bryant).

Now, far from denying the agency of materiality as such in shaping history (both human and non-human), I would also like to pinpoint that against the background of objects and their flows there's still room (and necessity) for the idea of subjectivity portrayed by Jacques Lacan.

Moreover, I will suggest that Being *qua* Absolute (or *qua* objects) falls into the category of fantasy (in the psychoanalytical sense) if it is not able to account for the role and place of subjectivity. I will now sketch out a fantasy of historicity. Although I'm not opposed to this general account, I will also suggest that Lacan's idea of subjectivity counterbalances this materialist picture. Nonetheless, I also find that Lacanian psychoanalysis can re-join the realist philosopher when it comes to the necessity of scientificity.

2 History and the Fantasy of the 'Material Swarming'

Since Meillassoux' realism involves a problematization of historicity, I would like to sketch out an idea of history which takes materialism and object-oriented thought as its theoretical starting points. I will call this general picture the 'material swarming' account of history. I will then argue that although Lacan sticks to some extent to this idea, he nonetheless counterbalances it by introducing the idea of the split subject. Also, I suggest that without introducing the split subject the whole picture falls into a mere fantasy.

If we look back at the history of the world, we find ourselves compelled to choose between two types of history. There's an official one which is made of great names, influential figures, national narratives, wars, revolutionary turning points, etc. Parallel to this official history we can find an unofficial one. If we follow this second type of history, we find out that (official) history is rather sub-determined by the sibylline dynamics of material flows, capitals, technologies, discourses, molecules, and so on. That is, once we abandon the official character of names and nations, we find out that there's a deep history—to use Smail's parlance—made of material assemblages and the microscopic/macroscopic organizations they allow for. History is, in this sense, conceivable as a continuous *material swarming*. It's the swarming of objects and subjects alike, the swarming of linguistic and discorsive entities, semblants and immaterial entities. Sometimes, a compound organization emerges as a local vortex of stable synergies, synergies that may in turn give rise to more complex emergent entities.

In the exchanges and compounds which make up this material swarming, subjectivities, desires, fears, and relationships arise. Grammars and linguistic objects such as "I", "We", etc., are already at work in this swarming, carrying out moral and anthropogenic operations upon us in every stage of our lives. From the birth on, we are already caught in these hybrid flows and organizations made of discorsive, moral and material entities.

History-as-swarming already comprises in itself the continuous production of a thermodynamic entropy, a living and uncanny Real which psychoanalysis calls the unconscious. If we were able to take the position of an all-seeing Laplace demon we could somehow trace out a map of the swarming, but we would nonetheless recognize the presence, at each step, of a subtle remainder which follows its own logic and structures.

Moreover, this unaccountable remainder of unconscious formations is nonetheless a key element in humanization, and it also plays a key role in the welcoming of the infants into social realities.

That is, the human environment presented to the newborns is already (and necessarily) made of demands and linguistic entities, without any clear-cut distinction between vital needs and recognition by the other human peers.

In the swarming, objects do exercise a modeling operation upon human organization. Objects are not mere inert entities, but they act upon human lives in all sorts of manners. For instance, Levi Bryant envisages 'rice' as a type of «bright object», an object which inevitably shapes the lives of the humans harvesting it: «The rate at which it develops, how it is planted, how it is harvested, [...], all contribute strongly to the organization of people's lives that rely on rice» (Bryant 2014: 203).

Rice is an example of an object which shapes the lives and habits of a local community. People have to organize their lifestyles according to the rates of growth and necessities of a given object.

The historian Fernand Braudel described rice as a «tyrannical» plant (Braudel 2006: 118). By ascribing real «responsibilities» to it—Braudel underlines—, for example, how the relations between country and city in China increased due to the farmers' need to get fertilizers from the city markets. In short, a given object—rice, in this case—manages to shape the concrete lives and habits of a given context, both economically and geographically. The swarming we're talking about inevitably hosts "demands" and transforms contingency into necessity. Humans harvest rice and, in turn, are harvested by it. In short, that's the point at which the material becomes economical. Or, more precisely, where the boundaries between these two dimensions merge into a continuum.

Within the material swarming of unofficial history there's also the necessity for moral prescriptions and proscriptions. The lexical tokens we use to ascribe our actions into their ethical acceptability or unacceptability already find their place into the material-economical organizations of the swarming.

For example, Antonio Gramsci, in his analysis of the Fordist mode of production, argued that «puritanism» was understandable only under the theoretical acknowledgment of the new working methods, which demanded a certain degree of abstention from sexual *loisirs* and alcohol consuming (Gramsci 2014: 2167). To make it clear, workers had to abstain from alcohol—and uninhibited sexuality—in order to maintain their psycho-physical equilibrium and avoid physiological collapse. "Puritanism" was the linguistic token which collected the prescriptions/proscriptions of a given piece of the social field: in order to maintain productivity, an immaterial machinery of normative entities had to be put to work. So far, then, we could say that it is not just the case of a transformation of the material into the economical, but also the case of a transformation of the economical into the ethical. All of that happens without any clear-cut ontological distinction: for a period of time these compunds work by their own logic. Moreover, the swarming implies all sorts of mashups. As Alliez and Lazzarato argue, it's not only that human action is inseparable from that of non-humans, «but also that humans are subject to formatting processes of subjectivity which are, historically, deeply different [...]» (Alliez and Lazzarato 2016: 409). However, the philosopher or the social scientist could take here two different paths. On the one hand, we could envisage history as *just* the set of entanglements happening at the "swarming" level (as Latour does), or we could try to see how the ungraspable remainder of these workings happens to shape the lives of subjects in their deep idiosyncratic ways.

It is this second path which psychoanalysis seeks to uncover. In a forceful passage from the Seminar XXIII, Lacan seems to undeniably stick to the 'swarming' account of history:

> Life chances pushes us left and right while we make of them *our destiny* - because we weave it in a particular way. We make of it *our destiny* because we speak. We believe we say what we want, instead it is what the others wanted, in particular our family, which speaks to us. The *us* must be conceived as direct object. We *are spoken*, and that's why we make life events, which pushes us here and there, something *plotted*. (Lacan 2006c: 159, our italics)

The swarming is always and already active at all levels, from the micro to the macro, or, to use a more vivid expression: from molecules to markets. Let's take an example. Recent studies on the effects (and correlations) of steroid hormones on decision-making in the financial markets has shown that different concentrations of testosterone and cortisol hormones do effect the decisional—and supposedly rational (!)—behavior of traders in the domain of High-Frequency trading. In particular, it seems that higher levels of testosterone are linked to high-risk/impulsive behavior (hazardous gambling), while cortisol effects decision-making by avoiding risky actions. Plus, it was also noted that testosterone is *addictive* and its production increases in a positive feedback loop that goes from "wins" to "higher-risk taking" which in turn may lead to other "wins". The reward mechanism is a loop of addiction to winning. Thus, the most reasonable conclusion to draw from these findings is that «economic agents are more hormonal than is assumed by theories of rational expectations and efficient markets» (Coates et al. 2014: 459).

It wouldn't be a surprise to find out, if it was possible at all, that some of the financial crisis occurred in our history were also the products of "grown up" adolescents with suits and ties too much high in testosterone.

It is reasonable to do such a conjecture, for «a trader's interpretation of information may not be stable: a trader with high levels of testosterone may see only opportunity in a set of facts; while the same trader with chronically elevated cortisol may find only risk» (ibid.: 459).

The ups and downs of financial markets may be in fact «steroid-induced shifts in confidence and risk preference» (ibid.: 459–460). This fact alone should already discourage the fine feelings of the humanist, especially the one who equates *anthropos* with rationality or *logos*, or the one whose dream is to portray high cognitive capacities as autonomous from the hormonal 'swingings' of our bodies.

All of this should in no way imply as a consequence any eliminativism considering consciousness or morality, especially when they are understood as a prerequisite for our actions. However, it is undeniable that these incursions into neurobiology or the modeling properties of the swarming should at least shed some doubt on our anthropocentric exclusivism, a lesson which is *consistent*—at first glance—with the psychoanalytical framework of Jacques Lacan, especially if we recall the overall tone of the "swarming" quotation above.

Within history-as-swarming one can't aprioristically divide the *micro* from the *macro* when it comes to causality. The swarming of the molecules creates vortexes and vicious (or virtuous) loops, leading to all sorts of outcomes, both historically and biographically. What is history from the point of view of a hormone? What is history from the point of view of a molecule?

Of course, if we "zoom out" from these entities, we end up with the full body and consciousness of the living human being. However, when and where we should suspend this "suspecting attitude" is in no way clear. The world seems to be split into two: there's the swarming, with all its rules, emergentisms, autopoietic assemblages, ethico-logistical constructs, etc. But there's also the reality of the *cut*, of the *parlêtre*: $ (Lacan's formalization of the speaking subject). Or, to use an expression suggested by Kiarina Kordela, there's also (even before the advent of capitalism) an ontological *surplus* (Kiarina Kordela 2017: 45). Moreover, this body who takes a place and a position in language activities is first and foremost what is caught in its *mistakes*, which are not merely momentarily cognitive impairments of speech; instead, they are rather revealing short-circuits of the unconscious. The line of the 'I' is continuously broken; the daylight of social molecular-institutional adaptations alternates with the nightlife of an upside-down world in which objects are paradoxical, language lives its own incandescent existence, etc. This summarizes into the Freudian—and Lacanian—idea that *knowledge* is to be placed in the unconscious rather than in the putative awareness of conscious' rationality.

The material swarming has just one rule: *everything happening in the swarming remains in the swarming*. One could easily catch here the flavor of the Althusserian materialism of the encounter. In these types of processes there's neither origin nor end; they are therefore «without consciousness», and because—Althusser continues—«it is common to ascribe consciousness to a subject capable of saying "I"» we shall call this type of processual entities «process[es] without subject» (Althusser 2017: 52).

No matter how whimsical and slippery these moving entities may be, they are not *un*-real; they do exercise pressures, constraints and causations. It is possible to ascribe them to what Tristan Garcia calls vectorial objects. A thing exists "vectorially" when it is considered to be a more or less contingent concretion or compound, a «secondary effect», «construction» or «illusion» which arises «at the intersection of several events or vectors of being» (Garcia 2014: 10).

Garcia rightfully puts Nietzsche, Bergson and evolutionary theory in this traditional line, to which we shall also add Althusser and, to some extent, Lacan.

However, here the contemporary realist of objects or of speculation is coherently pushed to pinpoint that there must be *things* which are neither vectorial nor non-vectorial; that is, things which *are* by their own means, which are real in a way that is independent from the vortexes of the swarming and from the point of view of a knowing subject. Thus, it seems that psychoanalysis fails to grasp the real *qua* material and *qua* subject-less reality. Psychoanalysis is a form of idealism, a label which recently took the name of «correlationism» (in Meillassoux' parlance). From the point of view of the contemporary realist, for the subject of psychoanalysis things *exists* only insofar as they are *manifested*. That is, their existence «continues to depend upon the conditions of manifestation» (Brassier 2007: 60).

Moreover, the type of readings suggested by realists such as Ray Brassier often ends up ascribing psychoanalysis to an idealism which portrays the «real» as merely «impossible» (ibid.: 137).

A very old critique, one must say. And also a misconception of psychoanalysis both as a theory and as a practice.

Luckily, not everything labeled as realism or materialism stands in contrast with psychoanalysis. One key contemporary example is the one of Adrian Johnston's transcendental materialism. In his incursions into neurobiology, Johnston suggests—in a fashion similar to our molecule-to-market argument—that material (and real) events occurring at the swarming level are nonetheless clues to understand the (Nietzschean) *real illusions* of self, morality, etc. As Gratton underlines in his survey of contemporary speculative realism, Johnston views the insights of neurobiology as demonstrating—in a positive way—the «transcendental or necessary illusion of much of what we take for granted at the folk psychological level being 'real'» (quoted in Gratton 2014: 165).

That's where the realism of the speculative philosopher seems to reveal a folk-ontological attitude, whilst psychoanalysis is first and foremost what furnishes us a theoretical dispositive to achieve the partition between the real-idealism of the swarming and the *reality* of the unconscious as a realm in which real *symbolic events* do occur.

In the Lucretian flows of the material swarming everything happens as an outcome of the dance of contingency and necessity. Statements and speech are also embedded within this mœbian flow of *eventa* and *coniuncta*. That is, the apparently two-fold nature of the swarming (things and languages) is in reality *one-sided*: «the world of things and the world of statements about things remain correspondent, parallel, symmetrical; and they lean in, collapse, fall, decline into one another» (Lezra 2018: 40). *There's no metalanguage*, as Lacan puts it. Signifiers are (as we will show) just like atoms and commodities, a theme surely belonging to the Marxian tradition. As Lezra puts it, everything is *paths* and *flows*, laws of spatiality, *Gesetz*, a continuous «unfolding of what is set out as potentiality for the atom-in-motion» (ibid.: 42–43).

Psychoanalysis is not, on its part, a form of idealism; it is—quite on the opposite—the quintessential aspect of realism: it acknowledges the material effects and contingencies of the Ego, the "I" grammatical token, historical grammars, deeply rooted repetitions, etc. all as belonging to the materiality of the swarming. Small Is' and paltry egoes—to borrow again from Lezra—are *false* (in Johnston's sense of folk-psychological illusions), but they are nonetheless *real* (at least in their effects). This latest point is what allows Lacanianism to break loose from the accusations of idealism: the distinction between the line of truth-values—*true/false*—and the line of the *real/ideal*. If we paid enough attention to these distinctions, this is also—and should be—one of the epistemological prerequisite of Speculative Realism itself. The *truthfulness* of arche-fossils (true enunciates representing ancestral reality) should be in no way confused with the *real* as what escapes the swarming, which is precisely made—we can now add—of imaginary, material and delusional bricks.

The truths and falsities of enunciates—given that they are subdetermined by the swarming—are in no way to be confused with the *truth qua reality* of unconscious materials. Lapsuses and dreams are such *real*—although often paradoxical—productions upon which the logico-representational grid of the *true/false* distinction would make little or no sense. *Truth* is the cause of the subject; a conception Lacan often underlined against truth as the mere true-false binarism or as *adaequatio rei et intellectus*. That is, for psychoanalysis "intellectus" and "rei" (things) are *never* "adequated". And indeed, modern science is—from a Lacanian point of view—what precisely got rid of the subject *via* the mathematization of Nature. The subject of psychoanalysis starts with a cut of the world; that is to say, neither with correlational idealism nor with folk-psychological illusions.

However, it is not surprising that psychoanalysts often dismisses history-as-swarming as irrelevant to the vicissitudes of human subjectivity. It is often as if the neurobiological aspects of human life (for instance) are excluded from 'what we are' broadly speaking. Indeed, there's plenty of reason to separate the level of the swarming, with its discorsive-material entanglements, from the level of the discourse of the unconscious. However, we're not suggesting a conciliatory view regarding these two levels, for this is precisely what psychoanalysis is all about: acknowledging the doubling of the human world into subject-less vectorial objects and unconscious desires.

Rather than conciliation, these two levels invite us to work on the *edge* where they show their mutual short-circuits. This edge is the locus in which the 'knowledge' of Nature and the structures of the unconscious bestow to Nature itself (in a broad sense) its lack. It is an edge in which the knowledge is lacking «at the point of sexuation» (Zupančič 2017: 15). As Miller puts it, the fact that the symptom varies individually for each one of us, tells us that «at the level of the species [humankind], there's a knowledge which is not inscribed into the real» (Miller 2003: 23). That is, at the level of humanity taken as a natural species there's no instinct guiding us towards the partner. Each subjective position looks for its «conjunct partner»—Miller further remarks—which is a multifaceted entity exercising attraction in always creative, singular and colorful ways. Thus the hysteric position has the conjunct partner of a fatherly figure, the obsessional has 'thought', the paranoid has the sayings and gazes of the others, etc. The point of subjectivity, when taken from the side of psychoanalysis, is: *with whom does he/she plays his/her match?* (ibid.: 31).

At the point of sexuation there's something missing in the biological real; this missing point is what sidesteps fitness and reproductive success. The subject is attracted to its conjunct partner, a figure which is already embedded in its own subjectivity as a counter-position of its singular symptoms and fantasies. *To each one according to his own subjective position.*

We thus suggest that reductionisms both on the side of subjectivity *qua* unconscious desire and on the side of the neurobiological swarming are to be rejected. Instead, it is precisely the task of philosophy to enlighten what happens in the vibratile and critical locus of their (impossible) interlacing(s).

However these two lines may seem to carry out a form of double reductionism, the explanations belonging to one or the other of these two lines are unable to give a comprehensive account of the vicissitudes of the human. Let's take another hormonal example, that of oxytocin.

According to recent findings in neurobiology and endocrinology, hormones such as oxytocin play a crucial role in social bonds' formation, parental care, group cohesion, etc. This little molecule seems to be responsible for a lot of diverse phenomena. It helps the human females during childbirth, it is linked to maternal stances toward cubs also in non-human mammals, it carries out "empathic" behavior, reduces stress and amygdala-driven types of response (such as immediate aggression and hyper-defensive behavior). The workings of oxytocin also shed some light into couple formation and long-duration partner choice.

According to neurobiology enthusiasts, such as Patricia Churchland, «[...]there's a *biofeedback* loop between oxytocin, parental care and social skills in young non-humans, and the same can be noticed in human beings» (Churchland 2012: 70). To cut short, the ultimate aim of such approaches would be to naturalize everything from morality to sociality, involving anything in the spectrum which lies between those. Churchland herself seems to lighten the heuristic power of neurobiology by acknowledging, for example, that when it comes to humans, they seem to be «flexible in couple formation» (ibid.: 75). That is, although oxytocin seems to explain a lot of phenomena, there seem to be still room for a cultural arbitrariness which locally modifies—via *institutions* such as marriage—the workings of such molecules. Some countries allow for polygamous marriages, some others don't. But nonetheless, the temptation of pushing everything down to the Procrustean bed of *naturalizing* the un-naturalizable is always behind the corner.

Such is the theory of the group, for example, advocated by Churchland herself, who claims that the crucial step «which pushes one from having care *just* of him/her-self» to having *care of the others* (like in mammals) depends on the «neural-and-bodily mechanisms which "maternalize" the brain of females» (ibid.: 46), an operation which is ultimately fulfilled by the neuropeptides *oxytocin* and *arginine*.

Here we come face-to-face with one of those *impossible interlacing* we already mentioned, for if it is true that oxytocin may be the natural (i.e. neurobiological) *paraphrase* of "love", it is—unfortunately—blatant to notice how maternal cares are replaced or alternated with aggression towards the object of care, or with hate, affective ambivalence and behavioral contradiction. Sadly, mothers (and fathers) sometimes end up killing or injuring their children. Partners as well end up hating and killing each other in the most gruesome ways. How are all this events accounted for by the deep history of a hormone such as oxytocin? And, moreover, what's the biological fitness of killing one's own children, children which are (as Richard Dawkins would certainly say) the main bearers and transmitters of one's genetical code? Or, how is it that a human male starts to have a genuine desire of adopting an infant? An infant which is not even in concrete and actual danger in front of his eyes? An infant which is not even present yet but inside the father's head?

We are all virtually (and quite ordinarily) also victims of the *acting-outs* of the (O)thers'. On the other hand, we are also and everyday *pushed to* repeat psychic 'automatism' in all sorts of domains: from workplace to family, from friendships to partners, etc. The truth of the biological real is thus, to repeat Miller's formula, *holed* with the space which hosts symbolic materials and fantasies. We're not just the containers of genetical and phylogenetic materials, but also the result of symbolic materials and familial complexes which in the end seems to exercise a key role in every domain of our everyday life. On one side we inherit something which is deeply rooted in our animal existence, on the other side we are tamed—so to speak—by what Lacan calls *nomination*. That is, even the name we're given by the (familial) Other already puts us into the domain of the symbolic order and, hence, of structure. Both these types of transmission lines allow for a certain degree of freedom and a certain type of constraints. The main task is, however, to think how these two lines do point—in fact—towards a possible *unified* 'secular-materialism'.

Clinically, evidence on the bodily effects of symbolic events and short-circuits are everywhere: from bodyweight changes correlatively to rancor and hatred to health decays caused by mourning, from worldview-changing insights to identifications leading to concrete everyday intentions, etc.

However, here again we encounter the problem of psychoanalytical resistances to claims regarding the transmission of phylogenic materials *into* ontogenic manifestations, a problem approached differently if one considers Freud's own (rejected) metapsychological attempts or Lacan's radical jettisoning of the phylo-onto-genic continuity.

Whilst Freud showed an «ambivalence *vis-à-vis* phylogeny» (Johnston 2014b: 64). Throughout his theoretical life, Lacan resolutely seems to reject—at a first glance—any attempt to endorse Haeckel's idea of recapitulation; that is, the idea according to which the ontogenic development *repeats* the phylogenetic one. However, as noted by Johnston, even in the Lacanian corpus there's plenty of material to «dialectically interpenetrate» psychoanalysis and life sciences toward a materialist and secularized framework (ibid.: 66). Indeed, this would be also our goal throughout our arguments: Smail's idea of 'deep history', along our idea of the material swarming, fruitfully resonates with the Lacanian idea that «history» is driven both by «failures to enjoy» and by «techniques and technologies of pleasure» (ibid.: 78) (and displeasure). Lacan, for his part, doesn't seem to strictly discourage any phylo-onto-genic approach. Rather, he warns us to «strictly» distinguish between the subject which is «carried by a signifier in its relation to another signifier» (discourse) on one side, and the «biological individual» on the other (Lacan 2002: 880). Here is also the place, however, where psychoanalysis acts as a corrective of the dreams of speculation (Meillassoux, Brassier, etc.). Both in theory as in the clinical practice the subject is somehow forced to notice that (*a*) *thought* doesn't belong to him as a capacity at its own disposal, and (*b*) *thinking* as such is first and foremost an *enjoyable* activity. Regarding this last point, it was Aristotle himself who portrayed the figure of a God which infinitely enjoys a timeless thought-activity. The God of the philosopher is something which self-referentially enjoys Thought *qua* Thought. Psychoanalysis both recognizes that *language* falls upon the subject as a parasitic 'exaptation' and that it creates a space in which the subject enjoys (and suffers) *linguistically*.

We are somehow forced to rap the speculative philosopher over the hand, and to remember him that 'thinking' as such is not an out-of-world activity; which is equivalent to say that it is a way of enjoyment, maybe our *peculiar* way of enjoyment. The subject doesn't simply satisfy a desire by matching its thought with a given material reality, it rather «enjoys to desire» (Lacan 2004: 323), as Lacan said; which is tantamount to say "it enjoys linguistically" and, as a corollary, that it will never find any thought-to-world adaptation as an ultimate satisfaction of desire. It's this reversal of the orders of enjoyment and desire which must be kept under scrutiny.

3 Descartes, Koyré and the Subject Without Qualities

Now, how does Lacanian psychoanalysis counterbalance the swarming account of history? It does so by introducing a non-gradualist account of history. History is not just the continuous flow of material and immaterial entities. That is, Lacan's idea of history is to suggest that this fantasy of the whole is in reality shaped by cuts. Lacan borrows this idea from Kojève and Koyré, and it is deeply linked to his own view on modern science. Both Kojève and Koyré, in fact, «held the view that history was punctuated by major cuts» (Glynos 2002: 53). One of the cuts that breaks with the gradualist idea is the one carried by figures such as Galileo and Descartes. That is, the mathematization of science and the coeval birth of modern science gave rise to modern subjectivity, the key precondition of psychoanalytical thought.

Lacan's non-gradualist account is precisely to get rid of the (sexual) fantasy of the whole held by Antiquity's thinkers. For example, as noted by Bruce Fink, Plato's *Symposium* fantasy is that «once we were all spherical beings lacking in nothing, but Zeus split us in two, and now we are all in search of our other half» (Fink 2002: 170). Every historical account that takes human and non-human entities to constitute a *whole* is nothing but a «fantasy of copulation» (ibid.: 169). Fink rightly points out that Lacan is generally suspicious of fantasies of the whole. If we take Antiquity's view of the world we find the idea of a «pre-existing harmony between *nous* and the world» (Fink 2002: 168). Fantasies of the whole, in sum, end up with the idea of a sexualized whole in which, for example, «form penetrates or inseminates matter; form is active and matter passive» (Ivi), etc.

While maintaining that humans are caught in the agency of material entities, Lacan individuates nonetheless a key evental cut in history which breaks with this fantasy of the whole: the birth of modern science and modern subjectivity. These two events are deeply connected. In fact, for Lacan, modern science is built upon a new and specific account of subjectivity and, in turn, psychoanalysis could not be born without the subject of science.

What is the evental cut that Koyré isolates and that Lacan borrows? It is a cut between Antiquity and Modern science. According to Koyré, the cut between antiquity and modernity lies in the mathematization of nature. Galileo is, for him, an authentic event. It is not, however, that antiquity didn't know any mathematics or their application to real problems. Koyré doesn't deny that the ancients had their own technique; that is, that they applied mathematics as to intervene in the real world. Rather, he pinpoints that, although antiquity has its own Aristotle, his idea of physics is radically different from that of modern times. To do 'physics' «in *our* meaning [...], means applying rigid, exact and precise ideas of mathematics to the real» (Koyré 2000: 90). That is, while the domain of «everyday life» is «not mathematical» nor «mathematizable» (Ivi), science is what creates the possibility of precision. Even if Pythagoras claimed that «the number is the essence of things», or even if the Bible «taught that God built the world upon "number, weight and measure"», only Galilean science really took seriously the idea of the mathematization of nature (ibid.: 97).

There's one key aspect in Koyré that Lacan maintains, namely the existence of authentic discorsive events occurring in the flow of history. According to Koyré's sociopsychological account, non-material entities such as ideas have their own role in explaining such events as Galilean science. As he clearly pinpoints: «[...] it is not the insufficiency of technique»—materialist thesis—«but the absence of the idea which gives us the explanation» (ibid.: 100).

What's the bond between Koyré's conception of modern science and Lacan's? And, further, between Lacan's view of modern science and the subject of psychoanalysis?

Jean-Claude Milner has systematized the key aspects of both thinkers in a way which may be helpful here. In particular, he has proposed some theorems to summarize the positions of these authors. Koyré's position holds that: (1) there's a cut between ancient *episteme* and modern science; (2) modern science is Galilean science, that is, mathematized physics; (3) having mathematized its object, Galilean science purifies it from its sensible qualities (Milner 1995: 38). Amongst the Lacanian lemmas outlined by Milner, one is worth mentioning: «everything modern is synchronic to Galilean science and there's no modern which isn't synchronic to Galilean science» (Ivi).

It is important to underline that Lacan is not only borrowing from Koyré the non-gradualist thesis, but also (see Koyré's theorem number three) a specific idea of the subject which is compatible (and necessary) to it: the idea of a *subject without qualities*. Modernity has the mathematization of nature as its *scientific* starting point; and it has the Cartesian subject as its *philosophical* starting point. As such, Descartes can be considered as the philosophical or epistemological counterpart of the evental cut of Galilean science. The fact that psychoanalysis and science are interconnected is thus based upon two characteristics. The first is based on homonymous «historical operators» which are «succession and cut» (ibid.: 37), which is tantamount to the the anti-whole fantasy of history which Lacan borrows from Koyré. The second is that science, like psychoanalysis, aims at a subjectivity devoid of sensible or secondary qualities which are, in the end, non-mathematizable.

Let's now focus on the second characteristic. When Lacan links the subject of psychoanalysis to the subject of science he isolates the Cartesian *cogito* as the philosophical counterpart of the modernization of science. According to Lacan's *Science and truth*, at the basis of psychoanalysis lies a «*modification in our position as subjects*» (Lacan 2002: 860); and this modification is «inaugural» and continuously reinforced by science itself (ibid.). This historical cut begins with Descartes and its name is the *cogito*.

In his *Method*, a text which is at the same time methodological and autobiographical, it's Descartes himself who warns us of the perils of false beliefs regarding ourselves. He is aware that we are inclined to deceive ourselves (*«nous sommes sujets à nous méprendre»*) (Descartes 2010: 15). Therefore, we are in need of a method to avoid our own self-deceptive nature. Regarding this precise task, it is striking to notice how it was Descartes himself who opened the path for the figure of the psychoanalyst. In a passage of the *Method*, he explicitly tells us that there seems to be «more truths in the arguments [*raisonnements*] made by each one» in respect to the things which are more dear to him/her, than in any scientific theory. He also evaluates the findings of the individual to be more reliable than the findings of the scholar in his individual intellectual pursuit, a pure psychoanalytical type of attitude, we might suggest. An attitude which seems to seek the *truth* of the *subject*. The philosopher seems to push this logic to the extreme conclusion that we shouldn't be so hasty in trusting what persuades us through «examples or customs» (ibid.: 29).

Surely a pure and authentic psychoanalytical stance. Nothing is granted, neither the *savoirs* of academics nor what I seem to know about myself. However, where do the paths of Descartes and those of Freud (or Lacan) diverge?

The difference lies in the reliability which Descartes ascribes to the fact that the subject *thinks*: «there's nothing entirely in our power, but our own *thoughts*» (ibid.: 64–65). This will, in turn, end up in the famous Cartesian *logion* of the "I think, therefore I am", "cogito ergo sum" (*je pense, donc je suis*).

Why should this precise consideration be elevated to the status of certitude? Isn't it just an enunciate among the others? What tells us that this exact enunciate holds a "special place" among other enunciates?

The Lacanian answer is: *Nothing. nothing guarantees us the certitude of this uttering.* What one can say regarding this supposedly special enunciate is that there's the presence of the grammatical «I» («I think»). But to derive from this the *fact* that *my thoughts* belong—strictly speaking—to *me* is a non-sequitur. Such is the methodological remark made by Lacan, whose comment about the Cartesian certitude explicitly underlines the fact that «I think» (*Je pense*) «is not a thought» (Lacan, Session of November 15th 1961).

What the psychoanalyst concede to the philosopher is that this very formulation of the "I think, therefore I am" is the result of a long process of thinking: Descartes *has to* think in order to land to the safe island of the "thought=certitude" conclusion. But again, what Lacan contends to Descartes is precisely the idea according to which this same "thought" is a "thought of a thinker" (*pensée de pensuer*) (ibid.). In short, "Thought" doesn't need *us* to think of it as thought. Or, to put it in a Saussurian fashion: *structure thinks for us*.

Arguably, thought is taught to us. Psychoanalysis teaches us that "thought" means being baptized into the realm of the Other. The Other which starts to categorize our body-events very early on by giving to it names and linguistic tokens. As Alenka Zupančič incisively remarks: «The unconscious comes to us from the outside» (Zupančič 2017: 11). The Other is the world-bearer, the *port-parole*, to use a term proposed by the psychoanalyst Piera Aulagnier. To put it in more vivid terms: the unconscious «enters our horizon as the unconscious of the Other» (ibid.).

This Other even teaches us to say «I» and, moreover, to say «I think», «I am», and so on. Our unconscious *is* the interpretation of the Other. This operation implies, as Aulagnier herself remarks, a certain degree of violence: *interpretation* is a kind of "necessary" violence ascribed inevitably to anthropogenesis, the second birth of the human into civilization.

The Other is thus not a simple subject, like *another* subject standing here and now in front of the human infant; rather, borrowing from Lacan himself, the Other is «a place» (*un lieu*) (Lacan, Session of November 15th 1961). It's a place made of "thin air" from which we will endlessly borrow our "traces of humanization".

In place of the Cartesian *logion*, we should coherently put "[the] I *thinks*, therefore it *is*". *It* is something, but what is it exactly?

Whilst the God of Aristotle is an enjoyment of Thought of Thought, Descartes re-proposes the God of the philosopher by ascribing to it the moral virtue of truthfulness and reliability. God becomes the ultimate Other who guarantees that, whatever the content of my thinking might be, it is nonetheless the only safe place from which to borrow certitude of knowledge. As Lacan argued, the Cartesian (big) Other is an Other *supposed to know*: God becomes tantamount to a placing of a «supposition of knowledge» (*supposition de savoir*). A supposition which ultimately fulfills a function similar to the endlessly thinking God but that saves the subject's always potential doubt by allowing the claiming of its existence. Everything could be delusional, everything *but* my thinking of it being delusional or not.

However, this Other is itself already *incomplete*. Moreover—as we will show in the case of symbolic objects (see Chapter 2)—one shouldn't be too quick in trusting the place of the Other, the treasure of language. And it is due to formal and logic constraints which are *already* embedded in the nature of language and structure as such. The Other itself is *holed* and *incomplete*; hence the attempt to find our own ultimate ontological constitution in the place of the Other is *logically* doomed to fail.

In sum, what's the difference between the level of the swarming, as I called it, and the level of the Symbolic, the Lacanian Other? I suggest that while at the level of the history-as-swarming we find neurobiological and material constraints, at the level of the speaking subject (*parlêtre*) we find *logical constraints*. Anything thus happens in between. While materialism (in a broad sense) is the knowledge of material and neurobiological constraints, psychoanalysis taught us to acknowledge the existence of logical constraints. One key example of such constraints is the logical (and Gödelian) incompleteness of the Other as a treasure of signifiers, what Lacan formalized by writing 'S(Ⱥ)' (a feature of the symbolic we will explain later on in this chapter).

Moreover, one might think that there's no space, *properly* speaking, for freedom: how can we imagine freedom for a being which is irremediably caught into a double-constraint, both material and logical?

The space of possibilities for subjectivity is the positivity which emerges *from* and *thanks to* the double constraints. To borrow from mathematics, where two negativities ("*minus* multiplied for a *minus*…") result in a positivity ("…equal *plus*"), we can say that "two constraints create a positivity".

The singularity of the subject emerges by being "squeezed out" of the material and logical constraints. *Two negations result in a vibratile positivity.* That is, human subjectivity floats in the space in between the neurobiological reduction and the symbolic reduction. It is a possibility which is due to the incomplete nature of their mutual translatability. They both work under the regime of constraints, economy principles and repetition; but nonetheless they are never completely superimposable.

While Lacan follows Descartes in his doubt, the philosopher seems to find an safe place which the psychoanalyst can't fully trust: the big Other (God) as ultimate guarantor of true knowledge. The merit of Descartes is that he «clearly formulates, for the first time in history [...] how the process of systematic doubting generates a purely punctual and fleeting subjective pulsation» (Glynos 2002: 56). But while Descartes' solution «involves evoking God, a non deceiving agency who guarantees the truth of our knowledge» (ibid.: 57), Lacan's solution is that there's no non-deceiving Other; and, moreover, much like Meillassoux' plea for a supercaos made of absolute contingency, nothing assures the subject its ultimate ontological constitution. But this is, in turn, due to the very essence of the split itself. The Cartesian subject is split between *knowledge* and *truth*. Lacan's emphasis is on the fact that the mathematization typical of modern science is a failed and continuous attempt to *forclose* (or 'suturate') the subject. Modern science starts as an attempt to get rid of the subject. That's why Gödel's theorems of 1931 are a proof of the logical incompleteness of the symbolic Other. The big Other works as a place into which the subject locates itself but, at the same time, this big Other is unable to really fulfill the subject's demand.

Being divided between *knowledge* and *truth* is a deeply structuralist theme. This division implies that *knowledge* is dispossessed from the subject and, to some extent, independent from it. Knowledge is not considered as an intimate skill possessed by the mind, but rather as a dispositive (made up of *formulae* and differences) traversing subjectivity from part to part.

This conception implies that there's no *outside* point of view from which to establish the completeness of a given knowledge. This absence of a metalanguage is what Lacan represented by using the Möbius strip, a topological one-sided figure in which it is possible to travel from side to side without any jump (Lacan 2002: 860).

As such, the 'knowledge' side of the split is often portrayed by Lacan as a *machine*. Thus, the traveling signifiers seem to stick to the human host as a machine which works and functions by its own rules. The «machine is the structure», Lacan remarks, but it is «detached from the activity of the subject. The symbolic world is the world of the machine» (Lacan 2006a: 56).

A subject, in this view, is like what Harman calls a «black box» (Harman 2009: 33). A black box is something we can isolate as a relatively autonomous entity of which we take «its interior for granted» (Ivi). We know that something *goes in*—language—and that something *goes out* (desire, identification, etc.); but ultimately, its interior workings are at first glance irrelevant. To rephrase this in Lacanian terms, we could say that such a (modern) subject without qualities is a de-psychologized subject.

In that, Meillassoux is quite helpful and in accordance with this idea of subjectivity. One of the task of its speculative materialism is to reestablish the distinction between primary and secondary qualities. An object's secondary qualities are qualities such as color, taste, etc.; that is anything dependent upon a perceiving and incarnated human subject. On the other hand, its primary qualities will be its *mathematizable* qualities such as volume, weight, etc.

The prominence Meillassoux' ascribes to primary qualities is a direct consequence of his plea for a philosophy which is capable of saying something about the absolute; and, indirectly, of a science which is capable of saying something about ancestrality.

As if that wasn't enough, Meillassoux also rejects Descartes' *weak* certitude based on the reliability of God. He explicitly criticizes the *cogito* and endorses the issue of modernity in a way similar to Lacan. For the speculative philosopher «the end of ptolemaic cosmology» means not so much a mortification of humanity, but rather a «mathematization of nature» which implies «the loss of any privileged point of view» (Meillassoux 2008: 143), even quoting Koyré himself.

But what about the 'truth' side of split? Here's is where Meillassoux' *ancestrality* diverges from Lacan's. Let's see why. While endorsing the object-oriented idea of the black box, that is, the idea according to which thought is not a privilege of consciousness but of the structure (and hence of the unconscious) (Milner 1995: 41), Lacan's nonetheless has a very specific account of *truth* which counterbalance this supposedly constructivist (or post-modern) thesis.

'Truth is the *cause* of the subject' means that the machine-structure in the blackbox we call a subject is far from being a 'well oiled' machine. The best way to explain this Lacanian ancestrality is to mention Plato's *Meno.* Lacan refers to the tale in which Socrates asks Meno to find the solution of a geometrical problem. The task is simple. Given a square, Meno has to find the exact way to construct a square which is double in size.

Without entering into the details of Plato's arguments, it is important to underline the specific way by which Meno fulfills the task. He firstly proposes to build a square which has the side doubled. Noting that this would end up in having not a square which is double in size, but rather quadruple, he proposes to have a square which has a side a little bit smaller. Still, this result proves wrong. Socrates guides the slave to the geometrical conclusion that a square which is double the size of the original square must be constructed using the diagonal of the original square.

The importance of this tale is not so much in the geometrical proves per se, but rather in the fact that, this way, Socrates/Plato proves his idea of knowledge *qua* recollection. The fact that the 'slave' is able to attain the right solution to the problem through the suggestions of the master (Socrate) is proof of Plato's theory of anamnesis: knowledge is soul's recollection.

Lacan propose to think of the position of the analyst as that of Socrates in *Meno*'s tale. Socrates is a precursor of the analyst. And this is for a formal and clinical reason that has to do with the general structure of the exchanges between Socrates and Meno. A structure I'd like to schematize this way:

$$S_a \rightarrow S_b$$

$$S_a \rightarrow \ldots \rightarrow S_b$$

$$S_a \rightarrow S^* \rightarrow S_b$$

The progressive solutions gave by Meno to the geometrical problem, despite being wrong, may be thought as a succession of signifiers (S_a, S_b). However, at each step a new missing position arises in the middle ('…'); a position which is then filled with the *missing* position (S*), which is finally the correct solution of the problem.

I propose to imagine Plato's tale as a model to reshape the supposedly black-box ontology of Lacan. We know what goes in and what comes out; we know, however, that something must happen 'in the inside' as to have a particular outcome. We may refer (along Freud and Lacan) to the *truth* of the blackbox as what is *repressed*. As in the case of Meno, the subject is moved by an ancestrality of repressed signifiers; these, in turn, hold the *truth* of the black box as internal cause.

This element further clarifies the image of the Möbius strip. That is, contemporary to the activity by which a subject is traveling its surface, a manifestation of truth arises through errors.

In his *Book of dreams* Borges recalls a dream of Bertrand Russell which is an elegant and simple display of such dynamics. Bertrand Russell once dreamed of a piece of paper in which it was written: «That which is written on the other side it's not true». Once he turned the piece of paper the other way around he also found: «That which is written on the other side it's not true».

The activity of the self-working machine/structure acts on the subject in a similar way: the subject may find *truth* by paradoxically following the succession of falsities.

Such is, I argue, one aspect of subjectivity which may link Meillassoux' plea for speculation with Lacan's conception of subjectivity. The split (knowledge/truth) is already a *mise en abyme* of Meillassoux' plea for a distinction between primary and secondary qualities. Both Lacan and Meillassoux rejects the Cartesian safe place of a God (Other) *supposed to know*. But while Lacan *accelerates* the Cartesian doubt by *hyperbolizing* it (Allouch 2001: 182), Meillassoux takes this as an opportunity to defeat correlationism. However, in the process of doing so, Meillassoux seems to leave subjectivity behind *tout court*. It should be clear now that *ancestrality* means also what is ancenstral to *myself*.

This partial result is what we will now use as to construct another argument which links Lacan to speculative realism (or realism in general). For until now, the argument regarding the split subject was to counterbalance the fantasy of the whole portrayed by the de-subjectivized materialism of the 'swarming'. What I will propose now is to endorse the issue of a Real *an sich*, a Being qua Absolute and detached from the activity of the knowing subject.

4 The Real Beyond Fantasy: Lacan with Meillassoux

One key accusation a philosopher could move to Lacan's notion of the Real is that, all things considered, the Real in the psychoanalytical framework is always a Real *for* a human subjectivity. It's not a Real *per se* nor a de-humanized Real.

On the one hand, this kind of statements are generally true, especially if we consider Lacan's peculiar view on scientific enquiry. More specifically, it is hard to find, in the Lacanian corpus, statements *a propos* Realism in the Speculative sense. On the other hand, Lacan's own realism seems to add a more refined conception of subjectivity and of the relation about subjectivity and science itself. Regarding this point, Alenka Zupančič has underlined that «it is […] rather astonishing how littile time Meillassoux devotes to the discussion of modern science» (Zupančič 2017: 77). As we already noted, the whole of psychoanalysis is unthinkable if taken out of the modern scientific inaugural gesture (the 'konwledge/truth' distinction).

And indeed, Lacan himself has spent some words for those attacking his conception of modern subjectivity. Against Lacan/Koyré, and in contrapposition to to this idea of the coeval birth of modern science and modern subjectivity, there lies «the realist argument» (Lacan 2006b: 33).

Lacan laments the «irresistible» objection by which «nature is always *out there*» (ibid., our italics). The realist claims that science is an instrument at our disposal and doesn't acknowledge the fact that we «are determined by it» (ibid.).

However, the point is still that of conceiving of a Real which is independent of a mind-to-world relation. Now, there is a rich gamut of meanings of the Real in the Lacanian teachings. However, for our purpose, it is sufficient to look at what is that Lacan conceives as an *absolute*.

Regarding the supposedly reality of objects, Lacan clearly embraces a correlation thesis: «every object [...] is included in a relation» (Lacan 2007: 117). That's why the structure/machinery in which the subject is immersed works with objects conceived as differential values. They are not, however, related through an *absolute* difference, but only as a constitutive (i.e. correlational) difference. Just as in the case of the signifiers 'Man' and 'Woman'; nothing catches here their essences, but they rather co-determine themselves thanks to the relation between them.

Next to those objects having an intrinsic relation there's Lacan well-known *object small a*, which Lacan—in a seemingly speculative move—calls «an absolute» (ibid.).

As I said, there's plenty of meanings of the Real in the Lacanian corpus. However, *object small a* helps us isolating a particular schemata which resonates with the theme of the 'knowledge/machinery' idea. This schemata is made of the symbolic machinery (knowledge, differentiality, etc.) on one side and their absolute remainder on the other side (*object small a*); or, to put it differently, the games of structure and the Real escaping them.

This schemata, however, is understandable only from the starting point of another Lacanian object, that of *Das Ding,* The Thing. It is an object which is irreparably lost by the subject. It is an unknown Arche-fossil, which must be postulated as a the precondition for generating the possibility of *objects* tout court. It is notably described as the Mother and what it means is the struggle by the subject to regain a former pre-condition of unity with what is lost once it enters the realm of language and the machinery-generated desire. As such, *Das Thing* is not a real nor material object, it is the loss itself, which generates the proliferation of the series of *object small a*(s). Object small *a*(s) are the correlated Real of the subject; that is, the objects which are (to some extent) *concretely* attainable after the loss itself and as an attempt to fill the empty place created by it.

Given this, even the *absoluteness* of objects small *a* is an absoluteness only in relation to a (given) subject. Nonetheless, object small *a* helps us understanding a key aspect of the conundrum between psychoanalysis and realism. In particular, object small *a* sets the coordinates to undermine a strict opposition to correlationism.

In fact, this object is what positivizes reality itself. From the premises of a basic insufficiency and biological lack of instincts in the human, the positivization of reality pursued by object small *a* is what compensates what we can call a *representational deficiency* of the bare human. What I mean by this is that, for psychoanalysis, the formation of objects to counterbalance the former *loss* (Das Ding) is strictly linked to the difference between *neurosis* and *psychosys*.

One of the key insights of Lacan was indeed to reverse the neurosis-psychosis notions. And this very reversal of the two is deeply rooted in his invention of the object small *a* (Miller 2000: 90–94).

If we follow his conception of *fantasy*, that is, the very structure which relates a subject to its object small *a* (cause of desire), we are forced to notice that one of Lacan's novelty—at least for the common reader—is that the order and genetic hierarchies between neuroses and psychoses is reversed. Following the psychoanalyst, neurosis and psychosis are fundamentally reversed in their clinical "hierarchy". It is *not* the case that psychosis is a "worsening" of neurosis but, on the contrary, neurosis is a case of *failed* psychosis. It is—as Miller pinpoints—a failure of the extraction of the object *a*, and hence the failed constitution of a "field of reality" by the complementary constituion of a visual frame (or point of view). This failure ends up in a uniform totality from which the subject is not able to detach herself, as it is clearly shown in cases of schizophrenia in which the voice *of* the subject becomes *a voice* amongst the others.

It is for this reason that the clinical set is able to unleash a dormant psychosis as a *failure of neurosis*. Following the schemata we proposed, then, the operation by which a subject enters structure is necessary but not sufficient. It is an ingredient of the neurotization of the subject into civilization but not the only one. The other one is that of the extraction of a positive entity—object *a*, the absolute—which is then reutilized as a framing positivity upon the otherwise empty and *paranoid* representation of the outside reality. The subject must pursue this extraction of something which is more (*en plus*) than reality. Something which is the Real of the Real. For this reason, neurosis is the continuation of psychosis by other means.

It is not a case here that I'm using 'paranoia' as the name for the failure of this extractive operation. Just recall our argument about modern science as an enterprise willing to *forclose* the subject; that is, to get rid of it despite having it as its precondition. As Glynos underlines (Glynos 2002: 65), the fact that for Lacan «modern scientific practice resembles paranoia» is directly linked to the fact that «paranoia is characterized by the forclosure of the Name-of-the-Father and the production of highly elaborate, though rigorously logical, delusional systems».

Modern scientists' activity is also a «subjective drama» (ibid.), a subjective drama—Glynos continues—«which is not infrequently accompanied by suffering, often resulting in admissions to mental institutions» (ibid.).

In this, Meillassoux' plea for a Realism obtained trough speculation isn't dissimilar from the attempt to forclose the subject. If anything relatable to subjective knowledge (or subjective presence) is correlational, the goal seems to be that of a material reality devoid of human cognition.

In this, Meillassoux' own idea of scientific enquiry is not so much about a Real of which we can say *true* statements, but a Real which doesn't give room for the reality of subjective life.

Let's focus once more on the problem of paranoia and object small *a*. I've stated that psychosis, for Lacan, is the outcome of a failed neurosis, that is, of a failure of a proper placing of object small *a*. In his 3rd Seminar, dedicated to psychoses, Lacan describes the paranoid as someone who «symbolizes what happens in terms of signification. Very often, […] he doesn't know if things are favorable to or unfavorable to him, but he seeks what is indicated by a certain behavior of his fellows, by a certain trait observed in the world, in that world *which is never purely and simply inhuman because it's human-made*» (Lacan 2010: 25, our italics).

The paranoid suffers of a *totalizing view*. Lacan is here explicit: the world of the paranoid is *human-made*. By this Lacan means that it is a world which is full of signification; everything lies within the infinite set of the artificial, everything is *made*. Hence, anything lying in front of the paranoid belongs to the realm of signification. The failure of the extraction of object *a* and the failed phantasmatic positivization of the world give rise to a runaway representation. That's why Lacan underlies, *en passant*, that paranoia is strictly linked to political organicistic fantasies; that is, ideas ascribing to the nation the totalizing representation of a biological totality.

There's a passage from David Mean's novel *Hystopia* which exemplifies the nature of the totalizing ontology of the paranoid. In it, the two characters, Wendy and Singleton, happen to find a man lonely walking along the beach:

> That's how a rumor gets started, Singleton explained. It's absurd to think that an old man who happens to be walking along the beach in a suit would be a spy of any kind, and yet the desire to fit him into a specific story is stronger than reason, and if you're going to fit him into something that is absurd, or at least partly absurd, it might as well be a vision President Kennedy happened to have during his recovery from the assassination attempt, with his poor sister as a focal point of his deep meditation. If you're going to find a story for that man, who maybe just happens to like to walk on the beach dressed to the nines, cold the way old people are always cold, then you're going to have to find a tool to force fit him into a conspiracy, or at least some complex social system, and that tool is going to be the idea that he's a spy. (Means 2016: 113)

The peculiar paranoid move leverages *not* the fact that the perceived thing must be strange or out of place; it rather leverages on the *human-made* character of sense and signification: the thing must fit into a system. Reality, devoid of its surplus object *a*, paradoxically becomes *too signifying*. This is the paradox linked to the Lacanian reversal of psychosis and neurosis. The paranoid gaze is usually described as a gaze constantly seeking for a trace in the world, a trace which contradicts the supposed regularity of it. Such a gaze is thought as 'having to find' the ticklish detail upon which the paranoid builds up his suspicion; as it was a single and localizable piece of the world which escapes meaning. Actually, it is rather the opposite, it is the *whole* of the represented outside reality which becomes isomorphic to the *whole* of the human-made, that is, to the symbolizable. The failed extraction of the ontological surplus makes reality an uncontrollable proliferation of signification.

The paranoid creates all the conditions for his paranoia to come true. It is as if he's always—by definition—*right*.

We find such a dynamic described in Seminar XI, where Lacan describes the painting competition amongst Parrhasius and Zeuxis. The two greek painters have to paint the most realistic picture. The winning of Parrhasius over Zeuxis is due to the peculiar deceptive nature of the veil painted by him. It is a *trompe-l'oeil* which is, Lacan underlines, related to object *a* (Lacan 2003: 110). In drawing a realistic *trompe-l'oeil* of a veil, he let us think that there's something *behind* it. That's why object *a* recalls—to some extent—the idea of the Kantian noumena. The realistic nature of Parrhasius' picture is not due the the abundance of details, as if the painter was aiming to a photographic realism. Rather, it is realistic because it is deceptive: it makes its observer think that there's something lying behind. This thing lying behind is the surplus of object *a*.

5 Ontological Surplus and Paranoia

Until now, we have just focused on the real obtained through the ontological surplus of the object *a*. For human subjects, objects are always experienced phantasmatically, the field of reality always contains something *more* than reality itself. Perception, in this sense, doesn't equate to a simple observer-to-picture scenario. In this, *fantasy* works like the concept of ideology. The two are similar in that they can be explained through the well-known philosophical argument of the pair of glasses.

Fantasy, just like ideology, implies that reality is not *mere* reality, it always has an added dimension of enjoyment ascribed to its representation.

Now, one of the problem, from a philosophical point of view, is whether this pair of glasses is necessary or not. Meillassoux refers to this problem as the one concerning the 'necessity of correlation'. As one may expect, for the realist, correlation is nowhere necessary.

Correlationist advocates may use—Meillassoux explains—the argument of the *performative contradiction* as to rout the realist position. According to this argument, even when the realist admits the possibility of thinking the non-necessity of the subject-to-world correlation, he's still *thinking* about the absence the correlation, without concretely getting rid of it and, hence, he's performatively (by thinking) contradicting himself. If we think of our relation to the world without the ontological surplus, and if we try to detach the from our cognitively finite and limited existence of perceiving subject, we are still entrapped into a subjective representation of these very realist attempts.

Is it possible for psychoanalysis to conceive a Real which is not just correlated to the human subject?

Here we can face the problem more closely. And here is also where the realist (philosophical) argument misses the target when compared to the Real(ism) of psychoanalysis (that is, of subjectivity).

When facing the problem of finding the way out of correlation, Meillassoux makes (quite often) the case of radiocarbon dating. Beside the already mentioned plea for a knowledge made of statements regarding primary qualities (i.e. objective and measurable), the philosopher adds the emblematic example of the technique thanks to which contemporary science is able to postulate the date of a piece of matter by positioning it within a range of time so ancient that there wasn't the slightest material condition for subjectivity to be born. Science tells us something about a Real which is prior to the very birth of any correlation (and to its preconditions).

Psychoanalysis, too, is the attempt to let the subject find its own Real; as Alenka Zupančič explicitly says: «[…]the common ground shared by psychoanalysis and science is nothing other than the Real in its absolute dimension, but they have different ways of pursuing this Real» (Zupančič 2017: 83). So what's the point where Meillassoux and Lacan seems to be incompatible in their efforts?

Meillassoux makes it explicit that «for a correlationist, *ancestrality* can't be a reality which precedes subjects, but only a reality assessed and thought by the subject as coming before the subject» (Meillassoux 2013: 17). This is why the case of carbon dating takes a special place in his philosophical plea for the absolute: arche-fossils break with this supposedly correlational Real.

The speculative philosopher's move has to be the one of somehow *autonomizing* the scientific dispositive as to portray it like a detached truth-values dispenser. Realism only works by paradoxically idealizing science. But even if this case, Meillassoux' supposed (up-to-date) materialism doesn't spend much time in developing any argument about the relationship between non-correlational thought (i.e. modern science/physics) and the reality described by it.

The problem is that this supposed automation of the truth-values 'dispenser' doesn't really allow for a purified or detached knowledge enterprise, but it rather hysterizes the philosopher's or the epistemologist relation to metaphysical claims.

Leaving the example of the carbon dating aside, just look at how far-fetched the ontological problems become when confronted with the problem of individuality and identity for quantum particles. On the one hand, modern physics works along the lines of what we previously mentioned as the type of realism ascribable to Adrian Johnston or Ray Brassier: *since our cognitive capacities*—of which evolutionary dynamics are responsible—*are limited, there's no need to think that the mathamtico-experimental dispositives of science furnishes us with results which are directly convertible into direct representative everyday experience.* And indeed, with its use of models, modern science doesn't strictly need the support of the perceiving or representational capacities of the human subject. As it is well put by Ladyman and Ross «[…] there's no reason to imagine that our habitual intuitions and inferential responses are well designed for science or for metaphysics» (Ladyman and Ross 2007: 2). There's no reason to think that our brain are modeled to have a supposedly direct representation of the outcomes of physics.

Ladyman and Ross further name this general attitude of making scientific claims translatable into 'mundane' representation the «metaphysics of domestication» (ibid.: 4). And, according to them, it «consist[s] of attempts to render pieces of contemporary science—and, at least as often, simplified, mythical interpretations of contemporary science—into terms that can be made sense of by reference to the containment metaphor», this metaphor consisting in an account of the world «as 'made of myriad little things' in roughly the way that (some) walls are made of bricks» (ibid.).

Despite their often rough scientist stance, the authors are here making an explicit Lacanian point, which Meillassoux never really seems to face: the problem of fantasies metaphysically assisting scientific pieces of knowledge. Much like the 'swarming fantasy' of object-oriented ontologies, Ladyman and Ross see this attempts as «attempt[s] to domesticate twenty-first-century science by reference to homely images of little particles that have much in common with seventeenth - and eighteenth-century mechanistic and materialist metaphysics», and proclaim this attempts as «forlorn», further claiming that for them «there are [...] no little things and no microbangings» (ibid.).

One of the latest philosophical attempts to domesticate science as to make it suitable for human representation was that of Kant. He envisaged the Newtonian system to be true because it basically relied on Euclidean geometry: a representation of time and space which allows for a cognitive representation of physics. *We perceive in a Euclidean way*; that is, the time-space is a container in which bodies, along with their masses and volumes, occupy specific portion of space. Modern physics seems to get rid of all of this, and Meillassoux undeniably sticks to this facet of the scientific enquiry.

The Real of physics doesn't have much to do with subjective experience and, as such, it is even more non-correlational than speculativism. Modern science doesn't need folk-psychology, just as psychoanalysis doesn't concede any direct nor transparent self-access to the workings of structure; nor—we must add—to the presumably reliability of description of affective states, thus rejecting Heidegger's distinction between *authenticity* and *inauthenticity*.

Nevertheless, there is always room for inscribing—within physics—the outcomes of the scientific enterprise into simpler ontological accommodations. But this problem, and all the possible ways to resolve it, always revolve around the problem of *reference*: how is it that the Symbolization has effects on the Real? Even in this case, one cannot but see the organizing power of fantasy over a putative uncritical harmony between the Symbolic and the Real. In their take on the problem of individuality for quantum particles, some authors have suggested—despite the ontological *vibratile* nature of identity for subatomic physics—that we should treat them «as individuals, just like classical particles, chairs, tables and people» (French and Krause 2006: 149).

Regarding this problem of the relationship between the Symbolic and the Real I should talk in the next paragraph. I suggest that further inquiring into this philosophical and psychoanalytical conundrum of the relation between *words* and *world* (or between symbolization and material reality) is what helps us pursuing two tasks: (1) to counterbalance the Realist position by allowing the Real of subjectivity to enter the whole scenario, and (2) to defend a conception of psychic life which is intrinsically realist.

6 Nature, Language, Temporality

Accordingly, what Meillassoux calls 'ancestrality' is still inscribed in time *qua* physical time; that is, it is a portion of time (far away) which belongs to the past-present-future triad. He nonetheless thinks about a time which is not conceived as a physical pre-human time, but as a kind of *pure* time as something belonging to the regime of intensity rather than extention.

In his plea for a reality of facticity he proposes, beside ancestrality, a conception of time as a "Platonised" «Begson's *durée*» (Austin 2015: 166). It is a time which holds together two apparently contradictory (and mutually exclusive) features of traditional conceptions of time. Because, on the one hand, it is a time which is out of the material developments of past-present-future, but it nonetheless eschews the Platonistic idea of eternal ideas. On the other hand, however, it is not really a "containing" pre-condition (as in Kant) of experience per se; it is rather an idea of an active time, a «pure time» which «contains nothing, no past and no future», and which is, then, «pure chaos and absolute illegality» (ibid.: 167). Meillassoux calls this time *time-itself*. It is to be conceived as a time charged of possibilities (*superchaos*) and, as I would like to suggest, with a violent (and constitutive) tare of *arbitrariness*. What this conception of time allows us is that we can find, thanks to it, the means to portray the subjective life described by psychoanalysis as based upon it.

Whether we endorse a conception of time or another is crucial to solve a philosophical problem: Meillassoux links the problem of time to that of Arche-fossils and, in a passage from *After Finitude*, he underlines an aspect of this problem which, I suggest, has important psychoanalytical resonance: «the problem of the arche-fossil», he claims, «is not limited to ancestral statements»; it is also about «every discorse the meaning of which includes a *temporal lag* of thought and being» (Meillassoux 2008: 139). Arche-fossils are then about not just events preceding human existence, but also about those events ensuing the disappearance of men. Science is what make it possible for a knowledge of diacronic statements which are true independently of material ontic existence(s). Meillassoux claims that «the truth or falsity of a physical law [...] is not found on our existence: that we exist or not, it is of no influence on the truth of the law» (ibid.: 141).

He makes nonetheless the case of the exception of certain laws of quantum physics, in which the presence of an observer is crucial in determining its outcomes; but even in this case, this property of the law itself which is independent from the observer's existence. He sees science as an open enterprise in which *contingency* is more relevant than *necessity*. He takes the example of non-Euclidean geometries, which, despite being an alternative to the supposedly transcendental objectivism of the Euclidean world, are nonetheless valid and self-coherent. Now, this openness of the field of science is deeply linked to two relevant postulates of Meillassoux' speculativism: on the one hand, the problem of how is it possible for a material and physical reality to host *knowing bodies*, that is, bodies which are equipped with a transcendental power such that science is possible in a material world (i.e. true knowledge). And, second, the fact that science may be the tool to revise our own habitual *prima facie* representations of causality. Indeed, Meillassoux makes a plea for a non-necessity of causality. When discussing Hume's theory of causality, Meillassoux rejects the necessity of the causal link in its Humean heritage. In sum, the problem is that of the reliability and stability of the laws: *is it possible to demonstrate that the same effects will—in the future—follows the same causes* ceteris paribus? (ibid.: 106). Is Nature uniform? How can we tell?

Hume's solution to the problem is that of a skeptic one: humans developed a naive notion of causality due to their limited and linear ideas of causation. If we saw A followed by B, say, a hundred times, we are somehow inclined to believe in a world made of linear A-to-B causations. The stability of the sun rising tomorrow is thus confined to a tottering and always renewable experience of the co-occurrence of two events, one following the other.

Now, the discovery of Freud and its further Lacanian elaboration, is that language plummets upon the human infant and, by ascribing the subject into the metonymic play of signifiers, it constitutes the body as a new entity. That is, language gives birth to subjectivity by inevitably deregulating the body as biological organism. Thus language is what in psychoanalysis is responsabile for a creation and for a loss, a plus and a minus. By ascribing the subject into structure, it co-creates the lack and the drives. While the (always failed) inscription within the big Other creates alienation, a configuration of the body and its objects proliferate as to create a constitutive asymmetry. The body is thus not a mere biological entity, nor it is forclosed by language games and compensatory identifications: the Freudian body is already a hybrid entity, something which lies in the middle of the nature/culture distinction. The name Freud gives to this hybrid entity is *Trieb*, drive.

Regarding this issue, scholars are often prone to conceive 'language', in the Lacanian framework, as having the only agency of alienating subjectivity in the Symbolic register, or as simply deregulating the a somehow merely *natural* and energetic aspect of libido. Actually, it is more the case of a co-creation of the two: the energetic aspect of subjectivity can be thought only as an entropic remainder of symbolization. Even in this case, however, one may imagine that while energy comes in the shape of a fluid and 'intensity-based', the power of structuration is what intervenes by superimposing an 'extensive' (i.e. discrete) partialization of this energy.

I argue that this image is true only to some extent. In order to prove that, I would like to propose the presence, especially in later formulations of Lacan on the symptom and the three registers, of a theory of a *double regime of language*. That is, one can find in Lacan not just the simple idea of language deregulating bodily experience, but rather the idea of a synchronic double regime of language upon the materiality of the body.

Lacan famously relies upon the distinction between the registers of the Symbolic, the Imaginary and the Real. The whole of subjectivity relies upon the well-made bond between these three registers; a function which is not fulfilled by these registers *alone*, but that it's already at work in the *sinthome*, which is a fourth element which has the function to bond with the other three. *Subject*, in a very broad sense, *is* exactly this: it is the way in which a speaking body had the capacity—in all its incommensurable idiosyncrasy—to fulfill a bonding of the three dimensions. Needless to say, already at the level of this type of formation all kinds of asymmetries and hierarchical disparities are made. Now, the Real, properly speaking, has a special position amongst the others; and surely it is special in all of Lacan's formulae.

The Real is not just an element put in parallel between the others, it is also what the Symbolic and the Imaginary cannot comprise. The Real is, as such, «a hem or a core», says Lacan, but then adding that «it is a core around which *thought weaves*» (Lacan 2006c: 119, our italics).

Thought is the attempt to say something around this Real which is so made that it «relates to nothing» (ibid.). It is a non-correlational and non-correlatable piece.

However, there's a specific reason for this constitutive asymmetry within the three registers. Indeed, Julien has pointed out at a performative contradiction inside the Lacan schemata. A contradiction which is, I must underline, recognized by Lacan himself. The fact *itself* that we can name the three registers as three different and discrete domains makes them *de facto* as belonging to the Symbolic. As he pinpoints: «[…] the *naming* which operates this distinction»—that between Symbolic, Imaginary and Real—«is *itslef* within the Symbolic as privileged fundament. To name with a proper noun each of the three dimensions means situating oneself within the symbolic, giving a privilege to it» (Julien 2008: 68).

And indeed, this performative contradiction gives Lacan the opportunity, in one of his latest seminars (Seminar XXIII) to draw two different representations of the relationship between the three registers. On the one hand, we have a version of the three registers as distinguishable and discrete entities, which is the Borromean knot (Fig. 1).

Fig. 1 The Borromean knot (Julien 2008)

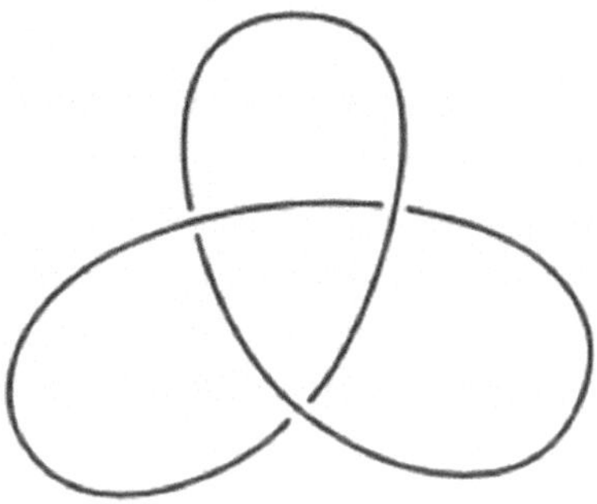

Fig. 2 The trefoil knot (Julien 2008)

It is a topological representation which, although maintaining the interdependence of the three registers, keeps them graphically distinguishable. However, Julien also recalls another representation which is analogous to the first, but in which the distinctions are not possible (Fig. 2).

As Lacan underlines, the trefoil knot «*comes from the Borromean knot*» (Lacan 2006c: 83). It has the shape of a continuous line. And, accordingly, it is a topological representation of object small *a*, the real cause of desire, before the over-codification pursued by the operation of the naming. Indeed, at this stage, object small *a* «is a *unique* and *same* object» (Lacan 2006c: 82, our italics). It is a a cause of desire *qua* Real enjoyment and hence not an enjoyment which is doomed to rest on the symbolic function. Arguably, Lacan links the operation of naming to the religious heritage of the Bible. Indeed, it is in the Adamitc tale where we can find the imperative to give names to all things. In the Lacanian jargon, this operation is fulfilled by the Name-of-the-Father, expressly echoing the Christian God.

That's also the agency of structure, which Lacan borrows it from Levi-Strauss. The Name-of-the-Father is a re-elaboration of Freud's myth of the horde. As such, the myth of the father of the horde—which has to be killed by the brothers in order to gain access to the women—«moves the paternal complex in its collective form and gives to the father, as dead, a social, religious and legislative function: the totem "block" the drive's urges which are always [...] of incestuous nature» (Lippi 2018: 35).

Broadly taken, analysis as a practice is an attempt to discover and enlighten the Name-of-the-Father in order to let the subject get rid of it. It is an operation of re-coding (the *sinthome* at the place of the symptom). An operation which is paradigmatically (for Lacan) fulfilled by artistic practices. Here, "artistic" doesn't simply mean drawing or sculpting, it must be conceived in the broad sense of *not getting caught* into the imperiousness of *naming*: the topological *versus* the structural thus means considering a Real which is not doomed to belong to the hierarchy of the three orders. A Real of enjoyment which plays in a plastic way rather then remaining a piece achieved *through* the workings of the other registers. Indeed, it is a Real as not-already overcoded or no-more overcoded by them. It plays a particular place in temporality because it is something which is "forgotten" through naming but that it may be achieved in a subtractive way and not in a linear and progressive fashion. It is at the same time what comes *before* and what comes *after*.

Duane Rousselle rightly calls for a distinction between a first order Real and a second order Real: «the decision to bracket external reality allowed Lacanian psychoanalysts to introduce the *object petit a* as that human part of the thing situated uniquely within the place of I refer to as the 'second order' real» (Rousselle 2018: 34). Thus, the presence of object small *a* in the Lacanian frameworks portrays the relation between subject and its enjoyment as belonging to a whimsical temporality.

Rousselle underlines that, in one case, «the subject, as $, is bracketed by the thing», while in another case, «the *objet petit a* is bracketed by the subject, $» (ibid.: 40). He then follows that because of this operation «we no longer have access to the thing, but instead only have paradoxical access to *objet petit a*» (ibid.). This is, in fact, a double dynamic.

If we maintain the Freudian element of the human body as not just an object amongst other objects, but as a hybrid entity, the Lacanian schemata of the *oneness* of object small *a versus* its Borromean structuration takes an even more important meaning.

As such, the subject is paradoxically caught into a double relation with desire and enjoyment. On the one hand, there's the line of desire achieving enjoyment. Due to the fact that demands are very early in the infant's life translated into desires, one temporality may be thought as aiming at gaining enjoyment through culturalized and social means. On the other hand, Lacan also pinpoints the fact that language as such is already a form of enjoyment. And, for this reason, it is not surprising to find a passage of his seminars in which he explicitly makes the case that «the subject doesn't simply satisfy a desire, *he enjoys to desire*» (Lacan 2004: 323, our italics).

There's a double line, or, as we may put it, a double *bracketing*. It's a play of disappearances: desire makes it that the thing disappears in the proliferation of object small *a*(s); enjoyment makes it that subject disappears within enjoyment. Hence we have the other line of double temporality: language is *already* enjoyment. It is, we might add, the way Lacan re-establish the significance of sublimation, which is not to be found in some remote activity of institutionalized practices (such as arts) but in language itself as a way *desire* at the same time postpones and re-acts enjoyment.

The human body is such a thing that delays the absolute (i.e. non-correlational) enjoyment by enjoying linguistically. The problem of the emergence, in a material reality, of the transcendental is not resolved by psychoanalysis by objectifying the categories (a possibility both Meillassoux and Lacan agree to reject); but rather by conceiving subjectivity as introducing a syncopated temporality in time itself. Given this,

I would like to venture a formula: *mind* is the name for the *deferment* of enjoyment.

Let's now return to the problem of the performative contradiction showed by the two knots. To rephrase now that problem as *not* being problematic in itself, but rather as a constitutive character of subjectivity, would imply considering *language* in two different ways. More precisely, although language is *one* as an activity, it has two different modalities, each ascribable to the two versions of the knot.

There's a tendency, for signifiers, to aim at universality. It is a constitutive ontological desire of signifiers themselves to escape their peculiar arbitrariness and rise to universalizable meanings. While in the vicissitudes of the subject there's a tension of his/her own idiolect to gain this level of untouchable meaningfulness, language *at the same time* plays a more sibylline operation of metonymically inscribing itself upon the bodily and drives-ridden life of the speaker. It is a double life of language, we may say. The reason behind Lacan's paradigmatic take on the work of James Joyce is understandable if viewed from this articulation. Joyce has somehow grasped this intrinsic universalistic vice of meaning and put it to work in his writings by deactivating the Name-of-the-Father.

This doubling of the effects of language upon the speaking human is what can be reframed as an always ongoing option between the *continuous* and the *discrete*, the *intensional* and the *extentional*. Upon this interpretational grid a contemporary philosophical battle is formed. For example, Deleuze and Guattari recognized the essence of this dynamic when they claimed that there's an unavoidable desire, for what they call desiring machines, to *forget their organization* (Deleuze and Guattari 2002: 13). The problem with these type of reading is that they seem to split the intrinsic doubled ontology of the (Freudian) body by ethically preferring the continuous over the discrete. The whole problem, according to these type of positions, is to get rid of the power that the *organizational* side exerts upon the supposedly continuous and constructive force of desire. Authors such as Benjamin Noys pinpoint that in such philosophical frameworks there's strict opposition between an intrinsic productivity of material assemblages—be them natural, artificial, or hybrid—against the 'bugbear' of negativity (Noys 2012: 55).

And, I argue, it is a problem that psychoanalysts (Lacan included) solved by ascribing to Nature the feature of being the realm of *plenitude* with no room for negativity at all. Arguably, it is often the case, even for Lacan, that the relationship between language and nature seems to be that of a structure-with-holes falling upon an otherwise non-holed (and full) ontological naturalism. Nature *doesn't know negation.*

This is a conundrum from which we can tackle the speculative problem of the knowing body (i.e. transcendalism) as an entity arising in a material and physical world. Notably, regarding the problem of negativity and the not-all of Nature, there's (at least) one exception amongst contemporary forms of materialism. I'm referring here to Adrian Johnston's materialist position. He opens the possibility for a conception in which it is possible to maintain a materialist up-to-date ontology but that it is capable of hosting negativity *via* the Lacanian subject.

On the side of the psychoanalyst (and not of the philosopher), the problem is the one of the *writing* of the unconscious. Both Freud and Lacan envisage the unconscious as something which is made of language. Lacan further radicalizes this linguistic nature of the unconscious as to make it *structured* like a language. Freud famously uses the image of the 'magical bloc-notes' (*Wunderblock*). The image is that of a double-stratum. There's an exposed surface, an exposed sheet in which a stylus creates forms. A wax-like underlying stratum is made so that the writing on the above sheet/surface leaves traces on it. The unconscious is the real impression of the underlying wax or, as put by psychoanalyst Pierre Fédida, the «Writing» (itself) is an «unconscious memory» (Fédida 1978: 34). The structuration happens as a writing of language on the living flesh of the human. As such, both the Freudian and the Lacanian body is conceivable—I suggest—as an entity which is sensible to inscriptions. This hybrid entity has, *a fortiori*, the capacity to function as an always potential 'reminder': what is forgotten, the body maintains and remembers in the form of traces in the wax. It returns in the shape of the repressed.

Still, if I mentioned Johnston's example of negative materialism, is because what is needed here is an idea to counterbalance the psychoanalytical idea by which negativity is *unknown* to nature. How is this writing (and structuration) of the unconscious consistent with the sort of

Hegelian (i.e. negative) portrayal of nature in which positivity is always put together with negativity?

The argumentation involves rephrasing *negativity* as *incompleteness*. I won't develop here a full and exhaustive argument regarding this type of position; I will draw on some findings that seem to be important if we want to understand what negativity *qua* incompleteness means.

7 The Real as Retrodetermination

Latest developments in biology and studies on the mind have underlined the importance of the emergentist position. Arguably, the mind as organizing and decoding dispositive is a 'late' achievement in the long story of matter or, to use Meillassoux' parlance, in physical time. Most of the times, however, emergenitsm is paired with only one side or aspect of it. Namely, the fact that new entities emerge as the result of the activity of other entities. As such, what we call 'mind' is an emergent property of the activity of neurotransmitters and the activities of the brain. Very simply taken, emergence is what allows us to ontologically dignify 'higher' and ontologically different types of entities by nonetheless avoiding hard biological or material reductionisms. Emergentism of the mind allows for an enrichment of ontology by pluralistically letting entities exist in a form that eschews equating Being with naive materiality.

One of the text-book example of such phenomena is that water, and I will draw on it just to clarify what I mean with negativity *qua* incompleteness. Water itself is an emergent phenomena. That is, the combining of oxygen and hydrogen makes it so that a new entity with *new* properties emerges out of them. Most of the times, classical portrayals of emergentism underlines the fact that the newly emerged entity has possibilities and characteristics which are radically new in comparison to its components in their initial non-combined state. For example, water, contrary to oxygen or hydrogen *per se*, has the property of functioning as a conductor for electricity, or to put out a fire. That is, emergentist positions often rest solely on a positive and stratified account of ontological reality in which subsequent entities are formed through an augmentation of the capacities of lower strata of being.

While this picture is—to some extent—true, it doesn't take another aspect of emergence seriously enough. Namely, the fact that any time there's emergence, there's also a *loss*. In the conventional example of water, while it is true that there's a gaining of new features, there's also a loss of former (lower strata) ones. In this case being, for example, the inflammability of oxygen. Emergence is not just an always potential formation of new positive entities out of simpler ones, it is rather a play in which entities are local vibrations between *loss* and *gain*. Emergence implies a loss of something.

This form of dynamic incompleteness is what links the two dynamics of the *continuous* and the *discrete* (or *organizational*) to (1) the incompleteness of the Lacanian Other and to (2) incompleteness of the human body *qua* biological entity.

I've already spent some words in underlying the fact the the ultimate horizon of meaningfulness of the symbolic Other is, for Lacan, holed; the functioning of the structure(s) revolves around this blind spot that makes objectification in the 'social' world always incomplete. On the other hand, there's an objective 'push', for the human mind, to achieve an ultimate ontological consistency by overcoming the original loss (*Das Ding*). What links the dynamic of the failed inscriptions into the big Other to the problem of ontological consistency is a very tenuous dispositive which Lacan calls the *phantasme* (fantasy). It is a compromise which tries to link the lack (*$*) to the achievable fragments of enjoyment (object small *a*). As such, this compromise dispositive of fantasy comes at a delusional price: object small *a*(s) retroactively gives the illusion of the guarantee of the Other (Lacan 2011: 31). The name by which psychoanalysis indicates the fact that subjectivity is an attempt to overcome all of this is repetition. Repetition of the 'evil' same scenario is due to this nature-culture hybridization itself.

Given all of this, and adding in the ingredient of 'negative' emergentism, the human body becomes not just a hybrid of nature/culture components, but this very hybridization is what makes the Real itself—conceived as an objectifiable whole—a Real which hosts the novelty of a non-ordinary temporality into physical time itself. As Johnston claims: «the brain and body of the human organism are shaped by and shot through with more-than-biological [...] mediating influences»

(Johnston 2014a: 61). As I put it until now, this 'more-than-biological' aspect of the body is what deranges temporality into syncopation. The Real of the subject is a Real of a disjointed and rhythmical time. Lacan, for his part, proposes a whole new version of modal logic, the type of logic which studies the functioning of enunciates when considered in their temporal validity. The Real *qua* impossible is what Lacan equates with what «doesn't stop not being written» (Lacan 2011: 88–89). Furthermore, what «stops not being written» is contingency, and what «doesn't stop being written» will be necessity (ibid., see also Lacan, Seminar XXI, February 19th 1974 session).

Impossibility, contingency and necessity are, for Lacanian psychoanalysis, a matter of *writing* and *temporality*. Confronted to the aims of speculative realism, Lacan seems to endorse an even more radical realism. In this «ultra-realism» (Johnston 2014a: 64), the subject is what makes a real difference in the Real itself. All these lacks and incompletenesses of the writing call for the exact opposite of a naive reification of the knowing body within the physical time. The problem of how and when physical reality could host a knowing body doesn't belong to the problem of the supposedly objectivity of the transcendental as a miracle of nature. But it's rather a matter of allowing oneself to reflect on the fact that being is not mere positive plenitude, it also what hosts all sorts of incompletenesses and 'failed' attempt at writing (in the above modal logical meaning). As Johnston underlines, this realism is a realism in which «the negatives of impossibilities unrepresentable but *nonetheless influential* within the representational economies of subjects both conscious and unconscious [...] are causally efficacious (non-)beings in addition to the positives of the experiential and ideational contents of minded life» (ibid.: 63, our italics).

The question now is: how does this modal time described by Lacan work with the concepts of impossibility and incompleteness? In order to explain this interactional play between the *writing* and the types of negativity I mentioned above, I would like to borrow from the concept of *attractor*. In particular, I borrow from the mathematics of fixed point attractors. I suggest that the idea behind this concept helps us in clarifying the functioning of the Real.

Let's take the mathematical function '$T(x) = x^2$'. This function works by 'generating' an outcome (x^2) when given a certain initial value (x).

If we have 'x' as having the value of '0.50', the outcome ('x^2') will be '0.25'. Now, let's just imagine to re-apply the same function to the obtained result.

The new 'x^2' will have the value of '0.0625'. We notice that the more we repeat (through *iteration*) this operation, the more we come close to '0', the attractor of the function. Of course, this holds true only if we consider what is called the *sensitivity to initial conditions*. That is, the fact that this function has '0' as an attractor only if the values we give to the initial 'x' are in between the range from '-1' to '1' (extremes excluded). We say, then, that '$-1 < x < 1$' is the *basin of attraction* of '0' for the function '$T(x) = x^2$'. Within this range, or this basin, the function—in its iterations—creates an orbit toward the '0'. In the study of such functions, those (fixed) points toward which a function tends are called attractors.

Not surprisingly, this field of study also describes another entity which functions in the opposite way: that of the *repulsor*. Just as the name suggests, it operates as a contrary of attraction. While an attractor gravitationally 'pulls' the iteration, the repulsor is what 'pushes' away the results of the iteration.

The idea—or the image—behind the concept of attractor (and repulsor) is what, I suggest, furnishes us an imaginary framework for the Real and its impossibility.

On the one hand, indeed, the Real is, for a subject, what endlessly escapes the attempts to fit it into the Imaginary and Symbolic registers. It is nonetheless what always finds its way. It is the uncanny remainder which always finds its way by re-presenting itself into subject's life in a often abrupt and non-codifiable way. What escapes symbolization returns in the form of the Real.

Indeed, this mathematical representation somehow assists the Lacanian *topos* of the 'hem' with the image of a Real which is made of *peaks* and *valleys*. The attractions and repulsions of the Real seem to suggest—given we accept this representation—an agonistic dynamic of subjectivity in which the impossibility of inscription and its necessity play in a sibylline way in the vicissitudes of one's life.

As such, this Real is not something that can be reached through a linear and intentional effort, it is more conceivable as what continuously reminds us of its powers. As such, the Real of Lacanian psychoanalysis is not like the reality of arche-fossils *tout court*, it is more like an underlying Real conditioning the whole of the subject's past-present-future triad as something always actively vibrating beneath. As Zupančič argues, «[t]he reality of arche-fossils or objects of ancestral statements is no different from the reality of objects contemporary with us—and this is because neither the former nor the latter are correlates of our thinking, but are instead *objective correlates of the emergence of a break in reality as a homogeneous continuum*» (Zupančič 2017: 83). The Real is what *fait trou*, creates a hole; and it is also what never ceases to reoccur.

Given this characterization, the syncopated time of the Real has to do more with retro-determination than it has to do with linear causation. We can reinterpret Freud's *Nachträglichkeit* by merging it into this picture.

The common view on the necessity of linear causation is that a given set of events has to occur if we want a particular outcome. If we take a given causal bond of, say, 'A causes B', to cause a B event would mean to put an initial A and wait for it as its outcome. I take the risk of being accused of eccessive speculative naïvety and propose that the time of the Real of subjectivity works in the opposite direction. Contrary to traditional 'human-scaled' views of time, I argue that the Lacanian Real works as if the *outcome* or *future state* is 'already' there and that it exercises a modeling scabrous power on what is contingent so that it can realize itself. Of course, I do not extend this schemata as to comprise regular (Euclidean/Newtonian) explanations of events. I nonetheless suggest that the particular coevality of the *ancient* and the *present* underlined by Zupančič makes it possible to rethink this particular temporality of subjectivity as made of retrodetermining elements. The idea behind the Real of attractors/repulsors as a landscape of tendencies and impossibilities calls—I suggest—for the idea of a Real which creates 'backward' its conditions to *reoccur* throughout the conscious life of the subject. To put it in a formula: *it will return, because it was already there*. Lacan's favored concept of what is *Nachträglich* was indeed that of 'après coup': the Trauma of the subject is not something to be placed in the linear physical time of subject's history; it is rather a resurfacing of a Real which non-linearly determines *ex post* the existence of this texture made of peaks and valleys. The Real of a subject is what escapes correlation through symbolization exactly because it works by showing its hard 'shape' in this backward manifestation. The paradox of the Real is that rather than being given in a possible face-to-face speculation, it functions more as if through the subject's own *historiole* (Lacan's saying for the mere bio-graphical) something like a texture of attractions and repulsions (*repetitions* and their *imposibilities*) emerges or is retroactively suggested.

Hence, the theme of a Real with such powers is linked to the one of repetition. However, Freud's *Widerholung* is split by Lacan as belonging to the registers of the symbolic and of the real. During the 11th Seminar, Lacan proposes two names for such repetition(s): *automaton* and *tyche*.

Repetition *qua* automaton, since it belongs to the symbolic, inherits all the characteristics of the symbolic *qua* linguistic. That is, the game on which *automaton* is played is that of speech its potentially indefinite power of displacement (Lacan 2016: 119–120). Broadly speaking, 'speech' is here intended as the automation of *syntax*; that is, the fact that—as Chomsky would suggest—the possibility of forming new linguistic compounds through *iteration*. At this level, indeed, signifiers distributes themselves in a «circular way» [*d'une façon circulaire*] (Lacan 2006b: 330).

This embodied capacity to repeat the automation of syntax or—as I put it above—of iteration is then counterbalanced by a repetition which is, this time, placed as belonging to the register of the Real: the *tyche*, the encounter (Lacan 2003: 52). Repetition *qua* encounter with the Real is what re-surfaces within subject's life in a non-circular way: it is the intrinsic asymmetry of the time and space of the 'attractor model'. The doubling of temporality is due to this double articulation in which two kinds of incompleteness merge and manifest themselves in turn as having to do, once, with the incompleteness of the Other (negative of the structure) and, second, with the impossibilities (repulsors) of the Real.

Given that, I would like to suggest that the clinical side of psychoanalysis is then not so much an effort to put the subject in a position of immunity in respect to the Real; a goal which subtends a homeostatic view of a subject reconciled with cultural demands; rather, it is an attempt to let the subject 'stick' to his/her own constitutive asymmetry. A constitutive asymmetry which then, to re-evoke our argument on the materiality of the psychoanalytical idea of the body, directly touches the problem of the relationship between language and matter. Indeed, one of the stakes of this 'materialization' of Lacanian psychoanalysis is precisely that of comprising the idea of repetition (which is linguistically founded) and that of the drive. And indeed, as Johnston pinpoints, there's always an ambiguous trend amongst both philosophers and psychoanalysts when facing the this problem. That is, Meillassoux' appropriate questioning of the arising of the transcendental in a material world seems to call for a re-adaptation of the cultural/artificial (or nature/nurture) dyad into an ontology which is consistent with the Freudian/Lacanian framework. The concept of repetition and the consequent recurrence of drive-pressure call for a kind of up-to-date non-adaptationist ontology which is able to host all these instances. But it is at this intersection where both philosophers and psychoanalysts seem to split: the question of *metapsychology* ends up revolving around a tendency toward a «desomatization» (Johnston 2005: 273) of the drive factor. The problem is twofold: on the one hand—as I mentioned above—the overall tendency of Lacanianism is to detect incompleteness and structural inconsistencies *only* in the machination of the cultural, hence leaving the 'natural' as a mythical field of positive or self-balancing games of stimuli and material synergies. Indeed, Lacan is often keen to borrow from Von Uexküll notions of environment (Umwelt), hence reproducing Heidegger's schema of animals as entities which are one with their biological field of stimuli and interections. On the other hand, psychoanalysis starts off from the premises of a basic helplessness and ontogenic insufficiency of the human newborn (Freud's *Hilflosigkeit*).

8 The Real and the Materialization of the Transcendental

In order to assess the problem of a material (and non-correlational) account of the Real, I will outline a brief detour on the relationship between Lacan and the biological problem. It is indeed often the case that Lacan seems to be at odds with phylogenetic (and Darwinian) approaches to human evolution. However, if seen more closely, the relationship between the biological and the cultural are more apt to merge into a unified view based on asymmetries and 'unorthodox' evolutionism(s). For this reason, I tend to suggest a view which, by resurrecting Lacan's/Koyré's discontinuous account of history, re-interpret the nature/nurture bond as "punctuated equilibrium" (see Johnston 2014a: 155).

According to the Lacan of the first Seminar (May 12, 1954), to take an example, Darwin's myth of the *struggle for life* is nothing but a political myth determined more by the racist and industrial milieu of Darwin's time. Lacan is therefore keen to reject the idea of the «survival of the strongest species» (Lacan 2014: 210). Moving from his well attuned Hegelism of the slave-master dialectics, the psychoanalyst seems to reject—at first—any Darwinian account of aggressiveness as not sufficient in explaining how human desire is to be accounted for. Due to the fact that desire is always *desire of the Other*, to push everything down to the Procrustean bed of selection by aggression would seem way too reductive. Exiguous quotations of Darwin are then found later on in Lacan's seminar, although always with a critical tone.

There's another key point where Lacan's bias on Darwinism manifests itself. During his seminar dedicated to the function of the *I* in the Freudian theory, he underlines the fact that the psychoanalytical discovery of «repetition» is «explicitly opposed to the idea that in life there's something aiming at *progress*», an element he ascribes to the «traditional optimism of evolutionism» (Lacan 2006a: 30, our italics). Moreover, he discredits evolutionism for its lack of explanations regarding sense of reality and adaptation itself.

Let alone the reason why Lacan envisaged adaptation as incompatible with the discoveries of psychoanalysis, the arguments concerning the non-adaptive nature of subjectivity are not in contrast with evolutionary theory. The caregiver-child relation is thus just a piece of the whole picture. It is a space in which basic features of human life are formed: identity, thought capacities, sense of reality, meaningfulness, desire, and so on.

In no way, then, should the two paradigms or the two lines of reasoning be in contrast to one another.

Freud discovered that subjects, such as in the example of dreams, tend to perpetuate painful and pernicious scenarios. That is, the general law according to which the organism seeks the least amount of displeasure doesn't seem to hold for human beings (not always, at least). There are two points worth noticing here. On the one hand, Lacan seems once again to portray evolution as a teleological theory of *progress* towards a pre-determined goal, which is—strictly speaking—not the case of Darwinian theory. On the other hand, however, a few pages after this critique he puts forward one of his crucial teachings, that of the «autonomy of the symbolic» (Lacan 2006a: 45). There are traces in the whole of the Lacanian corpus pointing to this autonomy of the symbolic. And it is striking to notice the affinities between this feature of the symbolic (language) and that of a evolutionary theory.

The only issue concerning this parallel, we argue, is the one concerning the modalities of propagation of the line of discourses and the line of selection. The only way to differentiate these two lines would be to distinguish between «inheritance» (Darwin) and «transmission» (Lacan).

While the line of evolutionary phenomena works under the possibility of the individual to inherit the traits of its precursors, the birth of the subject works under the *transmission* of the *said* and the *un-said* of the caregivers.

Jacques-Alain Miller draws an analogy between the biological concept of the «germ» and the psychoanalytical concept of the «letter». In repetition what is at work is a «reproduction of the letter», a reproduction which supposes «the exteriority of a knowledge [...] regarding the body» (Miller 2000: 29).

Thus, repetition must be understood in two different—but specular—meanings. On the one hand there's a repetition which "transcends", so to speak, the individual: that's the repetition of discourses cross-generationally. On the other hand, there's an "immanent" repetition by which these materials "survive" throughout the life of the individual *per se*.

These resistant materials are the out-of-sense of the subject. By saying that «the signifier represents the subject for another signifier», Lacan is able to put the discourse of the Other outside the realm of sense. Of course, psychoanalysis as a practice is the attempt to construct a knowledge of this very non-sense. What he also emphasizes, however, is that the clueless mortifications and *non-sequiturs* of subject's un-said discorsive materials *were always already there*; they do shape the self and its overall sense of being in the world by being always silently active.

Pushing the Lacanian analogy between the letter and the germ a little bit further, we could very well say that language acts upon the body of the newborn as a parasite. Psychoanalysis, especially in its clinical practice, looks for repressed signifiers which will help in constructing the un-said of the said. That is, it puts the subject face to face with its parasite.

The elements constituting discorsive materials are blind «replicators» (Dennett 2012: 197) and, therefore, in no way should they suggest any idea of teleology. There's no pre-given adaptive goal. As Daniel Dennett says: «Nothing had a purpose, nothing had something vaguely resembling a function; the world was devoid of teleology» (ibid.).

In the same fashion, nothing is adaptive in unconscious desire, it is not there for the sake of fitness to a given social milieu. The subject, in psychoanalytical terms, just wants to keep *being*. But as long as it confuses being with the discorsive materials engulfing him/her, repetition will be the only recurrent pattern of his/her life.

Of course, however, signifying materials are not "inherited", as we already underlined, but "transmitted". And the main difference between these two operations is that transmission always involves an unavoidable noise: transmitted materials modify themselves from passage to passage. The shapes they take vary each time, although maintaining an inner "truth".

That's why Lacan effortlessly disjointed the issue of "sense" from the issue of "truth". The truth speaks through my sayings, despite the logical and semantical short-circuits they may show at first. It is possible to endorse this exteriority of knowledge (the linguistic structure of the unconscious) and to make the radical claim that language has to do with an epiphenomenality and with its exaptation. We borrow the notion of 'exaptation' from the works of biologist Stephen Jay Gould. In sum, Gould (and Lewontin) «challenged the idea according to which every trait, even the behavioral ones, were adaptive» (Smail 2017: 141). Smail proposes an example which fits perfectly with the Lacanian's idea of an external knowledge: «human beings use their brain for a lot of things which are not explainable as products of natural selection. *Language* can be adaptive, but surely the cognitive abilities allowing us to compose music, play chess or to take up theoretic physics are the *by-product* of some other natural process which made the brain grow so much and in such a complex way» (Smail 2017: 142, our italics). These types of behavior are *exaptations*. This notion stands for any trait which evolved for *one* function but that subsequently became available for *other* uses; uses which are different from the original ones. One example is—according to Smail—human sexuality which, along with bonobos' sexuality (for instance), is "exapted" as a tie-forming instrument and as a source of fun (or *jouissance*). It is, so to speak, not merely reproductive. If we radicalize this idea, it is possible to grasp a schematic similarity between the general biological account of human traits and the idea of the unconscious structured like a language.

That is, one has to consider signifiers as having this peculiar iterative (and reproductive) capacity. Here, 'by-product' can be rephrased as 'epiphenomenal'. By this I mean that the agencies of language broadly speaking—computational, communicative, etc.—are *not* the direct explanation of it, but that they rather comes as secondary after an operation of 'mentalization' has occur. 'Mind' and 'mentalization' meaning here what I above called a *deferment* of enjoyment. In other words, after the voice is exapted so that structure (in the Levi-Strauss' sense) is formed. Just like a 'germ' (to use Miller's parlance) or as a *parasite* (to use Serres'), signifiers comes upon the biological body already entangled to one another and performing a deferment operation.

And indeed, this operation is not meant as to emerge progressively in a given community of not-yet-speaking humans. Such a view would imply falling into mythology, an operation Lacan (as most linguists) would reject. This mythology of a tool or an instrument progressively emerging amongst pre-linguistic groups implies a fantasy best described by Benveniste: «We are always naively inclined to imagine an original time in which a complete man would discover one of his fellows, complete as well, and between them, step by step, language would be elaborated. It's pure fantasy. We can never conceive man separated from language and we never catch him in the act of creating it» (Benveniste 2010: 311). All we can say is just that 'mentalization' and the deferment of enjoyment are one and the same thing and that, in ascribing this structure/desire-forming capacity to the effect of an expation of an otherwise by-product we are already *out* of the nature/nurture controversy. As the psychoanalyst John Gedo underlines in a passage of his *The Biology of Clinical Encounters*: «[…]The nature/nurture controversy begins to sound absurd, for every adaptive challenge draws on our biological resources, as amplified by our training, in a given human (and social) context. Our biological equipment is continuously changing, for better or for worse, and the direction and extent of these changes is to a very large degree determined by environmental input. Even at the somatic level […], human encounters are just as significant in determining such changes as are encounters with microorganisms, toxins, or pharmacological agents» (Gedo 1991: 20). The emphasis must be put here on the examples given by the author: microorganisms, toxins, etc. In subject's life, signifiers are just as iterative (i.e. self-reproducing) as a parasite. That's why it is more the case that *language* speaks through *us* and not the contrary.

I suggest this position as one consistent with the "blurring" of the boundaries between psychosis and neurosis (see above), for the phenomenological apperception of the Voice is genetically posthumous to the neurotization carried out by the signifying chain. Here, 'hearing voices' must be configured as one of the primary effects of the *foreign*—but "internal"—object *a*. "My voice", however intimate and personal it may be perceived, is truly the first alien object to "cope" with. The voice is always and already a detached object. For it to be recognized as "My voice" a dialectical dynamic must be put to work. The (hard) affirmation by which *language is an exapted epiphenomenon* implies that no matter how much the "blabla" is a non-functional parasite, it is nonetheless subjected to an exaptation by the very existence of *demands*. This is why any question concerning the *origin* of language is doomed to be answered in incomplete ways. The very central question should become: *How is it possible that the subject "keeps" on talking?*

«Epiphenomenon» means that it isn't—prima facie—in any aspect *useful* or *evolutionary advantageous.* It would be superfluous here to enumerate all the empirical examples of species carrying out the genetic transmission of biological codes without any *need* of language.

«Exaptation» means, on the other hand, that for reasons that belongs to the pure contingent material assemblages shaping the lives of human beings, the utterances of the speakers become *objectifiable*. That is, what I say is first and foremost a "something" which I *deliver* to the Other. This strange type of *deliverance* involved in the speaking situation finds its very *condicio sine qua non* in the "objectifying packaging" of *what* I have to say. The Lacanian emphasis on the matter in question comes to rescue us, for the key two elements that the psychoanalyst isolates in the speaking activity are the *What* and the *To Whom* ('A', the big Other). It is worth to underline that when we speak about "exaptation", we mean it in a very broad aspect. More specifically, we don't want to portray the image of a language activity becoming *useful*—later on in ontogenesis—for communicatory tasks. What we mean by *exapted* (- epiphenomenon) has less to do with a *gained function* than it has to an *always ongoing* "exercise of neurosis" carried out upon (and against) the basic pre-individuation realm of psychosis. It is, to draw again from a Chosmkyan concept, more a matter of *competence* than it is of *performance*. Hence, the language of madness is nothing but the very kernel of civilization. And, moreover, the basic category to be underlined when giving any account of human subjectivity has to be the one of the *alien*. Subjectification comes at a price of Objectification. An objectification which must not be confused with *realization*. Alienation into the big Other is «far from indicating a pathological case»; it is, rather, «the very measure of normality, that is, of the normativity inscribed into language» (Zizek 2018: 30). And this alienation constitutes the necessity to create real objectifications. That is, to create a place (the big Other) that constitutes a horizon of meaning.

Language is nothing but the *continuation of sexuality by other means*, to paraphrase a famous aphorism. It is an exaptation (in our weak sense) due to the fact that it takes the *alien thing* (the voice, the gaze, etc.) to be folded into a horizon of objectivity. However, there's no room here for a pacificatory ontology of adaptation, for the accommodating folding of this *alien thing* just repeats the *alien thing* into a (second) new alienation. This is what gives rise to the Lacanian insistence on the *non-accountability* of the object small *a*. Its always ongoing escaping attitude is the product of two alienations: the first comes as *perturbing foreignness*, the second comes as *perturbing possession.* It's a strange dynamic, we might say, by which alienation of the alienation is not equal to ordinary «Being-in-the-World» or "Being-at-Ease-with-It", but rather, it is equal to the double facet of the cause of desire: contemporary (1) *possessed* («It is my desire to…») and (2) *dispossessed* («It's stronger than me…»). Hence the double alienation has the basic result of a "fear" of *possessing*, and conversely a "fear" of *dispossessing*. The closeness of the object small *a* is anxiety; the remoteness of it is vulnerability.

References

Alliez, É., & Lazzarato, M. (2016). *Guerres et Capital.* Paris: Éditions Amsterdam.

Allouch, J. (2001). *Le Sexe du maître: L'érotisme d'après Lacan.* Paris: Exils.

Althusser, L. (2017). *Essere marxisti in filosofia.* Bari: Dedalo.

Austin, M. (2015). Time. In P. Gratton & P. J. Ennis (Eds.), *The Meillassoux Dictionary* (pp. 165–167). Edinburgh: Edinburgh University Press.

Benveniste, É. (2010). *Problemi di linguistica generale.* Milano: Il Saggiatore.

Brassier, R. (2007). *Nihil Unbound: Enlightenment and Extinction.* New York: Palgrave Macmillan.

Braudel, F. (2006). *Civiltà materiale, economia e capitalismo: Le strutture del quotidiano (secoli XV–XVIII).* Torino: Einaudi.

Bryant, L. (2014). *Onto-Cartography: An Ontology of Machines and Media.* Edinburgh: Edinburgh University Press.

Bryant, L. (2015). Correlationism. In P. Gratton & P. J. Ennis (Eds.), *The Meillassoux Dictionary* (pp. 46–48). Edinburgh: Edinburgh University Press.

Churchland, P. (2012). *Neurobiologia della morale.* Milan: Raffaello Cortina.

Coates, J. M., Gurnell, M., & Sarnyai, Z. (2014). From Molecule to Market: Steroid Hormones and Financial Risk-Taking. In R. Mackay (Ed.), *Collapse: Philosophical Research and Development* (Vol. VIII, pp. 417–461). Falmouth: Urbanomic.

Deleuze, G., & Guattari, F. (2002). *L'anti-Edipo: Capitalismo e Schizofrenia.* Torino: Einaudi.

Dennett, D. C. (2012). *Coscienza.* Laterza: Che cosa è.

Descartes, R. (2010). *Discorso del metodo.* Milano: BUR.

Fedida, P. (1978). *L'absence.* Paris: Gallimard.

Fink, B. (2002). Knowledge and Science: Fantasies of the Whole. In J. Glynos & Y. Stavrakakis (Eds.), *Lacan & Science* (pp. 167–178). London: Karnac.
French, S., & Krause, D. (2006). *Identity in Physics: A Historical, Philosophical, and Formal Analysis*. Oxford: Oxford University Press.
Garcia, T. (2014). *Form and Object: A Treatise on Things*. Edinburgh: Edinburgh University Press.
Gedo, J. E. (1991). *The Biology of Clinical Encounters: Psychoanalysis as a Science of Mind*. Hillsdale: The Analytic Press.
Glynos, J. (2002). Psychoanalysis Operates Upon the Subject of Science: Lacan Between Science and Ethics. In J. Glynos & Y. Stavrakakis (Eds.), *Lacan & Science* (pp. 51–88). London: Karnac.
Gramsci, A. (2014). *Quaderni del Carcere*. Torino: Einaudi.
Gratton, P. (2014). *Speculative Realism: Problems and Prospects*. London and New York: Bloomsbury.
Harman, G. (2009). *Prince of Networks: Bruno Latour and Metaphysics*. Melbourne: re.press.
Johnston, A. (2005). *Time Driven: Metapsychology and the Splitting of the Drive*. Evanston: Northwestern University Press.
Johnston, A. (2014a). *Adventures in Trascendental Materialism: Dialogues with Contemporary Thinkers*. Edinburgh: Edinburgh University Press.
Johnston, A. (2014b). On Deep History and Lacan. In L. Chiesa (Ed.), *Lacan and Philosophy: The New Generation* (pp. 63–83). Melbourne: re.press.
Julien, P. (2008). Du Nom-du-Père au Père-du-Nom comme sinthome. In P. Julien (Eds.), *Psychose, Perversion, névrose: La lecture de Jacques Lacan* (pp. 67–77). Toulouse: ERES.
Kiarina Kordela, A. (2017). *Essere, Tempo, Bios: Capitalismo e ontologia*. Verona: ombre corte.
Koyré, A. (2000). *Del mondo del pressappoco all'universo della precisione*. Torino: Einaudi.
Lacan, J. (2002). *Scritti*. Torino: Einaudi.
Lacan, J. (2003). *Il Seminario Libro XI: I quattro concetti fondamentali della psicoanalisi (1964)*. Torino: Einaudi.
Lacan, J. (2004). *Il Seminario Libro V: Le formazioni dell'inconscio (1957–1958)*. Torino: Einaudi.
Lacan, J. (2006a). *Il Seminario Libro II: L'io nella teoria di Freud e nella tecnica della psicoanalisi (1954–1955)*. Torino: Einaudi.
Lacan, J. (2006b). *Le Séminaire Livre XVI: D'un Autre à l'autre (1968–1969)*. Paris: Seuil.

Lacan, J. (2006c). *Il Seminario Libro XXIII: Il Sinthomo (1975–1976).* Roma: Astrolabio.

Lacan, J. (2007). *Il Seminario Libro X: L'angoscia (1962–1963).* Torino: Einaudi.

Lacan, J. (2010). *Il Seminario Libro III: Le psicosi (1955–1956).* Torino: Einaudi.

Lacan, J. (2011). *Il Seminario Libro XX: Ancora (1972–1973).* Torino: Einaudi.

Lacan, J. (2014). *Il Seminario Libro I: Gli scritti tecnici di Freud (1953–1954).* Torino: Einaudi.

Lacan, J. (2016). *Il Seminario Libro VI: Il desiderio e la sua interpretazione (1958–1959).* Torino: Einaudi.

Ladyman, J., & Ross, D. (2007). *Every Thing Must Go: Metaphysics Naturalized.* Oxford: Oxford University Press.

Lezra, J. (2018). *On the Nature of Marx's Things: Translation as Necrophilology.* New York: Fordham University Press.

Lippi, S. (2018). *Sigmund Freud.* Milano: Feltrinelli.

Means, D. (2016). *Hystopia: A Novel.* New York: Macmillan.

Meillassoux, Q. (2008). *After Finitude: An Essay on the Necessity of Contingency.* London and New York: Continuum.

Meillassoux, Q. (2013). *Tempo senza divenire.* Milano and Udine: Mimesis.

Miller, J. A. (2000). Biologia lacaniana ed eventi di corpo *e* L'esperienza del reale nella cura analitica. *La Psicoanalisi, 28*, 14–100. Roma: Astrolabio.

Miller, J. A. (2003). La teoria del partner. *La Psicoanalisi, 34*, 22–83. Roma: Atrolabio.

Milner, J.-C. (1995). *L'Œuvre claire: Lacan, la science, la philosophie.* Paris: Le Seuil.

Noys, B. (2012). *The Persistence of the Negative: A Critique of Contemporary Continental Theory.* Edinburgh: Edinburgh University Press.

Rousselle, D. (2018). *Lacanian Realism.* London: Bloosmbury.

Shaviro, S. (2014). *The Universe of Things: On Speculative Realism.* Minneapolis and London: University of Minnesota Press.

Smail, D. (2017). *Storia profonda.* Torino: Bollati Boringhieri.

Žižek, S. (2018). Marx Reads Object-Oriented-Ontology. In *Reading Marx.* Cambridge: Polity Press.

Zupančič, A. (2017). *What Is Sex?* Cambridge and London: MIT Press.

2

Openings of the Object: Values, Gestures, Events

While the first chapter focused more on the Real as a non-correlational absolute, in this chapter I will focus more on the 'object-oriented' side of psychoanalysis. Some authors (see Bryant 2014: 216) have suggested that it is possible to describe objects by borrowing from the late Lacanian schemata of the Borromean knot (Symbolic, Imaginary and Real). The 'Borromean' moment, in Lacan's teachings, is set to show a key moment in his development concerning the relationships between the three registers. Indeed, while these often display a kind of overcoding hierarchy, in the latest period the three registers are «treated as being on equal footing» (ibid.). That is, it is a moment in which a 'flat-ontological' Lacan situates the three registers as each having their own ontological dignity. This is possible, however, by maintaining that while they are *theoretically* autonomous (the way we access them), they still can't be thought as separate when looking at their interplay in subjectivity. While this overall argument is true, I also put forward what can be called the *collapse hypothesis*. This hypothesis was first proposed by Alfred Sohn-Rethel, resurfaced in studies about Freudo-Marxists' conception of fetishism, and lately is being readopted by the critical readings of philosophers such as Kiarina-Kordela. In sum, it is the idea

Y. Di Liberto, *Being and Contemporary Psychoanalysis*,
The Palgrave Lacan Series, https://doi.org/10.1007/978-3-030-18476-6_2

according to which ontology *is isomorphic* to capital. Notably, Alexander Galloway impugns the validity of contemporary realist object-oriented philosophies due to their unspoken coincidence with late post-fordist capitalism (Galloway 2013: 347). What the collapse hypothesis suggests, however, is not that we should seize all of this as a basic counterargument against object-oriented ontologies, but rather embrace this isomorphic collapse of thought and reality as a de facto transformation pursued by what Lacan called *capitalist discourse*.

By this, I mean the fact that if we look more closely to this late Lacan and his engagement in matters concerning language and subjectivation in capitalist discourse, we can grasp the scope of an epochal turn in civilization. Moreover, Lacan's reactualization of Freud has its roots in the economical and historical transformation pursued by the Weltanschauung of capital. Desire (and its objects) undergoes a transformation which makes it isomorphic to the type of functioning normally ascribed to *value* in the economical sense. Hence, this holds true for subjectification itself.

In any case, I leave open the idea for a reconceptualization of the object which counterbalances the object-oriented scenario. It is an idea of the object *qua* the 'speculative'. In doing that, we come close to a Real of subjectivity itself rather than a Real of the object.

1 Value Is Structure: Symbolic Objects and Differentiation

In order to trace an immanent genealogy of subjectivity we have to look for the basic operations fulfilled by the caregiver, the first incarnation of the Other. In its function of *word-bearer*, the Other is responsible for subject formation and—at the same time—for what we might call a *naive ontology*.

That is, the initial locus of the subject-object distinction is to be found in the activity of *baby talk*. In every caregiver-to-infant relation there is at work a mutual exchange of verbal and corporeal events alongside their interpretations carried out by the caregiver itself.

Approximately when they're two months old, in the form of a wail or a cry, «newborns start to say "mama"» (Falk 2015: 155). This initial form of uttering is in turn *interpreted* (ibid.) by the parents as meaning "mother" and consequently retransmitted to the infants. What starts as a cry or a wail is metabolized by the Other and symbolically "regurgitated" on the infant as a signifier charged with meaning. By the time they are six months old, the infants understand that «"mama" refers *exclusively* to *their* mother» and not to any mother.

This initial game of bodily and verbal events, along with their coming back in the form of signifying materials, sets the roots for the distinction between ordinary objects and the "special" object of the mother (or caregiver). By building their minimal vocabulary, infants are taught to differentiate between objects.

As Sasso underlines from a neuro-psychoanalytic standpoint, what appear to us as «material objects», «perceptively stable» entities, are initially mixed with the material body (Sasso 1999: 163).

The co-transmission—*back and forth*—between verbal-corporeal events by the infant and their concomitant interpretation by the caregiver carries out a split of the first anatomical fantasy, namely that of a continuity between the body of the mother and that of the infant. The body, initially one, becomes split into two and, moreover, this very split is what allows for the possibility of *counting* oneself as a "one" separated in the "two" of the relation. An environment which is initially «undifferentiated» and made purely of stimuli (acoustic, visual, tactile, etc.) trains the newborn, by hosting *interpretation*, in understanding the difference between the object-mother and the other objects. Moreover, Sasso remarks, at this stage the infant also gets a first glimpse of a distinction between «animate and inanimate objects» (ibid.), a function which is far from being obvious, as the cases of schizophrenia seem to show; cases, indeed, in which there's an ongoing out-of-the-ordinary confusion between animate and inanimate entities. These initial events, belonging to the caregiving of the other, set what we may refer to as *naive ontology*. What is initially *prima facie* 'bodily' is "digested" into civilized material. In sum, *I* am the cogito of the caregiver. This first supply of cares is consubstantial to a transmission of a first trivial ontology. The mother tames the infant to the being of things. By the time this game of cuts is set in motion the infant learns how to distinguish between objects, in particular between the "special" object of the caregiver and the series of "ordinary" objects. The reason behind Lacan's equation between 'Being' and 'Language' finds here its *raison d'être*. Subjectivity starts as an onto-linguistical grid of valuable objects.

A theoretical digression is here worth taking. In his answers to the students of philosophy (Lacan 2013: 208), Lacan explicitly endorses the question of language in the Marxist tradition. By stating that his own theory of language is *Marxist* (ibid.)—and hence, *materialist*—, he quickly recalls the debate generated amongst soviet intellectuals on the issue of language. Simply put, the debate developed around the following question: *Does language belong to 'structure' or 'superstructure'?*

Without going too deep into the vicissitudes of Russian Intelligentsia, the important aspects to notice are the two possible answers to that main question. For, if one considers language as belonging to the *structure* (economic relations), then what follows is the characterization of *intellectual theories* as intrinsically ideological, due to the fact that they belong to the *superstructure*. If one, on the other hand, takes language to be just another *secondary* product of economic forces, hence putting it into the *superstructure*, then language becomes structurally synonymous with *ideology*. It is worth remembering that some Russian theorists effectively took the road of the second hypothesis. For this reason, they started to propose a *new* language, explicitly made for a communist society, which would take the place of ordinary language; surprisingly enough, this new language was supposed to be taken from the Orwellian *Newspeak*.

From a Lacanian point of view, however, the hypothesis of language belonging to the superstructural domain makes little sense. Lacan takes here a more nuanced position. Since it is not 'language' (a reified essence) which makes social bonds, but rather *discourse*, any effort put into creating a purified and non-ideological version of historical languages is nothing but a dream. If there's no *metalanguage* there can't be any non-locally-determined language either. Hence, language is *ideological* in its very essence. There's no realm in which it can be purified. Discourses are ideological (in this 'weak' sense) due to their engulfing and bonding dynamics. The primary/secondary dilemma concerning the supposed ideological nature of language itself belongs to discourse and, a fortiori, to *ideology*. We thus suggest it is by no means useful nor important to deconstruct specific languages as ideological, for doing so would be—at best—impossible or—at worst—just the beginning of a new and refined ideological language.

Hence, the Lacanian thesis of the non-existence of metalanguage means, to use the Marxist jargon, that language is not to be positioned in the superstructure. Some authors have suggested, for this matter, to speak about a «substructure» (Arribas and Rouse 2011: 221–222). Balmès, commenting on this aspect, underlines the fact that the syntagma "structured like a language" in the *logion* "the unconscious is structured like a language" is a kind of pleonasm. In the late formulations, for Lacan structure *is* language (Balmès 2011: 25). That is, any time we meet with differentiation, structure and oppositions of elements, we are situated at the level of the onto-linguistic grid of the symbolic.

In order to understand the way in which this dimension functions, we have to emphasize two key points where Lacan implicitly (and often explicitly) uses Marx as an advantageous point of view to pinpoint his own linguistics. It is worth underlining that, although borrowing from Marx, Lacan's 'Marxism' is *methodological* rather than *ontological*. More specifically, this methodological Marxism is condensed into two general attitudes towards language and subjectivity. First, Lacan links the categories of 'Being' and 'Value' by ascribing them to the realm of differentiality. This way, Lacan is able to put his (post)Saussurian take on language alongside the lines of Marx's theory of commodities: meaning is what emerges through the relationships between adjacent signifiers, semantic value is *differentiality* itself. One can never think about 'value'—be it semantic or about commodities—in an isolated or essentialistic way. Value is always a product of a matrix or grid of polarized entities. At this level of analysis, the level of the Symbolic, objects are isomorphic to values.

Second, Lacan is also explicitly Marxist in that he acknowledges his theoretical debt to Marx in anticipating the discovery of object small *a*. Moreover, Lacan envisages Marx's theory of *plus-value* as «homologous» to object small *a* as a remainder of the work of signifiers.

The first aspect (value as differentiality) is what allows Lacan to translate his Saussurian point of departure into a kind of Marxist linguistics and hence to acknowledge structure (of the unconscious) in an "externalist" way. The second aspect (object small *a* as the surplus of work) is what builds the bridge between the workings of signifiers and their entropic—and Real—remainder.

We have to linger over these two interrelated subjects in order to understand the key features of the human being as she enters "civilization" and starts to "desire". In order to theoretically isolate the idea of symbolic objects, we will focus now on the first of these aspects.

When it comes to objects, Lacan states that «every object» (object *a* excluded) «is in relation» (Lacan 2007: 37). He further specifies that, since there's language, «relations are expressed through epithets» and that these epithets induce the schemata of the «*yes-or-not*» (ibid.).

This yes-or-not grid has to do with the fact that relations between (symbolic) objects are to be conceived as relations in which different objects have a relation of proximity due to their difference.

It is a grid which shapes objects into relations which maintain closeness through negation. One could easily grasp here a structuralist flavor in its Levi-Straussian classical framework. Hence, the value of 'Man' holds only if taken in the broader yes-or-not ensemble of 'Man = not-Woman'. Levi-Strauss' anthropological study on tastes even goes further in the analysis of alimentary traditions by putting elements of local food cultures into such semiotic grids: e.g.,'dry = not-wet'. One can indeed extend this logic so that every thinkable symbolic object always seems to recall its proximal negativity: 'Old = not-Young', 'Poor = not-Rich', etc.

Semantic values, just like signifiers in the subject's psychic economy, are to understood not as having an intrinsic (and hence magical) value; just as values are broadly conceivable as having to do with proximity and negation (within a given set of adjacent values), signifiers work by showing the inherent mechanical workings of particular subjective idiolects. I would like to recall now once again that when speaking about the symbolic, Lacan equates machine with a detached activity: «the symbolic world is the world of the machine» (Lacan 2006a: 56).

Furthermore, the myth of meaning as a one-to-one relation between a word and its entry in the dictionary mimes the myth of what Marx called an intrinsic exchange value. In one passage from the first book of *Capital*, Marx states that «exchange value seems to be therefore casual and purely relative; an intrinsic exchange value, immanent to the commodity (*valeur intrinsèque*), would be a *contradictio in adjecto* [contradiction in terms]» (Marx 2013: 109).

The complete arbitrariness of signifiers in the subject's life is immanent to the schemata of exchange value (*Tauschwert*). The modality of signifiers—*doesn't stop being written*—gives a hint about the fact that «political economy and subjective economy have the same structure which their common schematism puts to value» (Lew 2013: 150).

Marx himself talks about an *arbitrariness* of the value (*etwas Zufälliges*, something random), an arbitrariness which is «purely relative to the exchange value which doesn't contain this function intrinsically, but only as given by another exchange value» (ibid.: 135).

Just like «[…] no value stays by its own», no signifier stays by its own, but only «by the adjacent signifying» (ibid.: 136).

It is in this intersection where Lacan makes an explicit Marxist move. His critique of the Hegelian Nation-state as an entity which gathers «natural needs» (see Tomšič 2015: 124) in a Totality is what pushes Lacan to propose the schemata of the *capitalist discourse* (Fig. 1).

The meaning of this graph is that the subject (*$*) and its enjoyment (*a*) are directly connected without the intermediating function of signifiers (S_1 and S_2), a possibility originally forbidden by the master discourse, the graph from which this one is obtained. The epochal change is that subjectivity lives the illusion of a final liberation from the symbolic register and its unavoidable castration (which gives access to enjoyment). Against the Hegelian scenario of the master as having the function of deferment on the slave, and hence constituting desire (on the side of the slave) as an outcome, the schemata of the capitalist

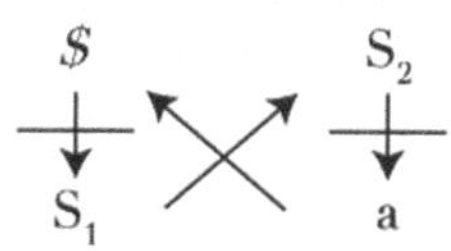

Fig. 1 The capitalist discourse

discourse functions as a kind of perpetual crisis in which the access to the absolute ('once and for all') enjoyment of the thing is paired with a machinic detachment of the symbolic register. This is why the introduction of the capitalist discourse and the idea of the structure-as-machine must be understood reciprocally. The in-depth analysis of Lacan's 'Marxist moment' has less to do with a mere analogy than it has to do with the attempt by Lacan to re-place psychoanalysis within the capitalist moment.

This reformulation of the relation (and its constitutive crisis) between subject and object paves the way to a reactualization of the object in the mother-infant scenario. The possibility of differentiating the 'Ur-object' (or Object with capital 'O') from the objects in their seriality is here substituted with a dynamic which flattens the magic and ancestral character of the former to be replicated in the series of the others. The automation of the symbolic register implies a constitutive moment which can be defined as a kind of 'dark' Spinozism. In the capitalist discourse, the rejection of the castration on the side of the subject reemerges on the side of the object. It is a flattening of the world in which the world is subjected «to the signifier and the economic value» (Kiarina Kordela 2007: 46).

Once the object has entered the game of exchanges «it is not its materiality itself which counts, but the quantitative rapport in play which regulates the exchange in question and that it integrates in its own side of the exchange. […] *commodity has the same structure of the signifier*» (Lew 2013: 135, our italics).

Commodities, just like automized signifiers, become «"supersensibles" like human "language", because both exchange values and signifiers are determined in a purely differential way within their respective synchronic systems, in which there isn't any "grain of matter"» (Kiarina Kordela 2017: 41). Given that commodities are, just like their semiotic counterparts, taken into their synchronic systems of differential values, they obey the same laws. It is a 'dark' Spinozism which Lacan more emphatically names the *universalization of the signifier*.

It is possible, given these premises, to isolate three particular features of such entities. Symbolic objects—semantic/economic values—follow the same laws which are: (1) the law of *vicarious positivity*, (2) the law of *evocation of the synchronic context* and (3) the law of *untranslatability*. These properties or laws of symbolic objects are related to one another.

One key aspect which recurs in our reading is that of the synchronic state of the system. Indeed, the concept of 'synchronic state' is paired with that of desire as linguistically structured. In the Seminar devoted to 'Desire and its interpretation' (6th Seminar), Lacan emphasizes the fact that desire must pass through the 'code' of a given language (its grammar). The notion of 'synchrony' jumps to the fore when he states that «the code is the set of taxemes of a language, language in its synchronicity» (Lacan 2016: 32). Now, the concept of 'taxeme' can actually be interpreted in a syntactic and a semantic way. I would like to take the 'semantic' route, however, because of the deep affinities between it and the basic facets of symbolic objects *qua* differential values.

A given taxeme is a set of minimal elements in a given language. Linguist François Rastier makes the example of the class of cutlery. The class of cutlery may be made of «"knife", "spoon", and "fork"» (Rastier 2003: 429). The concept of taxeme (or class/set of semantic values in a given language) doesn't work as a Porfirius-type of eternal ideas or essences, but is rather a tool to isolate synchronic pieces of language in which some elements are related to each other through a relation of proximity. As such, it isolates a portion of synchronic semantic values.

The fact that Lacan emphasizes the synchronic state of a language as having to do with desire can be interpreted as the fact that when one desires a given object, he/she is structurally *evoking* the synchronic context (the class of proximal elements) in which this object is found. To put it in a banal way, in the case of the class of cutlery, the choice of the "fork" evokes the 'yes-or-not' grid we saw above: it would be "fork = not-spoon,not-knife". Thus one element evokes the others in a negative way. Symbolic objects come always in clusters, the synchronicity of which is always historically mutable.

Symbolic objects are thus complex constructs in which there's an «identity of determination and negation» (Lezra 2018: 63). It is, one might argue, a problem which is directly linked to the semantic one. Lezra, indeed, emphatically asks «how do we go about *naming* a thing? Do "we" derive or borrow an identity, for instance a professional or class identity, from the names "we" give things? From our *naming*?» (ibid.: 64).

And, of course, the answer would be negative: we don't give things a name as in the fantastic scenario of the Adamitic tale; things are already pre-sorted in the machine, in the structure.

Culture is the name we give to the partition of objects. They do dispose themselves along the blurred edge of values and what is invaluable; culture works therefore as an edge, a cut between the exchangeable and the sacred. Symbolic objects are thus caught into what I may call a *vicarious positivity*: they are not single one-to-one 'intentioned' objects, rather they are clusters (or pieces of language) with an inner differential economy. Thus, the *vicarious positivity* of symbolic objects intrinsically rejects the classical conception of identity according to which, for example, «a *potato* is, after all, a potato, and a *table* is a table, over time and to all effects» (ibid.: 65). Symbolic objects are «determined inside their own synchronic system through [their] differences from all the other elements […] of the system, and in themselves, without differentiation, they would be nothing» (Kiarina Kordela 2017: 37).

The implication for the individual economy of desire is that at the unconscious level objects hold each other in a way which makes them explorable through a particular one-person perspective. When wanting, say, 'X', the proximal context in which this 'X' is found makes up its overall meaning ('I desire X because of it being not-Y or not-Z'). Symbolic objects evoke their adjacent negations in a way which is unconscious.

There's moment in George Orwell's 1936 novel *Keep the Aspidistra Flying* in which the protagonist, Gordon, finds himself stuck in a neurotic position in which the commitment to a mundane professional cause is undermined by his disregardful attitude towards matters of business. He finds himself reading a tale about a starving carpenter who pawns everything *but* his aspidistra. The Aspidistra becomes, for Gordon, the flower of England, emphasizing that it should be put on the country's blazon, at the place of the lion and the unicorn. He then adds that there will never be revolutions in England till there will be Aspidistras.

Here, it is the position given to the Aspidistra in the general psychic economy of Gordon that counts. It not an object per se. It rather stands in a relation of proximity to 'not-revolution', 'not-lion' and 'not-unicorn'. It is the *whole* of the thing which is evoked. In the general economy of values objects are intrinsically plural. Their proliferation is what allows psychoanalysis as a practice to evoke and then disentangle this always moving map of synchronic pieces, objects in which it is possible to find both contingency and necessity in the forms of local crystallizations of meaning.

I shall call this feature the *evocation of the synchronic context*, a feature which is directly linked to another feature of symbolic objects, that of *untranslatability*. Here, *untranslatability* is understandable as a synonym of *incommensurability*. Symbolic objects are radically pluralistic, but because of the idiosyncratic arbitrariness of their adjacent values, a given object doesn't maintain the same meaning from subject to subject. The 'X' of a subject could be apparently identical to the 'X' as expressed by another subject. This likeness is, however, only a surface phenomenon. The 'X' of one subject doesn't have the same meaning (i.e. adjacent values) of the other.

The property of *untranslatability* simply states that desire is incommensurable from subject to subject and that, *a fortiori*, there can be no collective desire, which must be placed rather in the Imaginary register. Of course, I'm not here denying the fact that there are, already at the level of discourses, dispositives which work as 'aligning machines', but these are already operations fulfilled at the level of language itself. I will return to this later when I discuss a special case of symbolic objects, that of personal pronouns.

For now, I would like to pinpoint a consequence of the three laws (or principles) I outlined. The Other is far from being a complete entity. This feature of the Other as a *not-whole* fits within the schemata of symbolic objects by introducing a *logical* negativity. Pierre Skriabine formalizes this aspect of the non-wholeness of the Other (Ⱥ) by having recourse to a logical property of sets, a property which is valid for symbolic objects. Skriabine asks if, given a set of elements 'a, b, c, d', it's possible to have a cohesive and unified representation of the set itself as a whole.

Given, however, the differentiality of its elements, he underlines that it is logically impossible to do so. Indeed, we can define each of the set's components through the strategy of the 'yes-or-not': if we take 'a', we are able to define it by saying 'a≠b, a≠c, a≠d'. We thus obtain the subset 'b, c, d'. Of course, we can repeat the same operation for each element of the set, thus always obtaining an incomplete representation. By repeating this operation «we will be able to define a whole, a set, on condition that each time, one will not be there, that there will be an exception» (Skriabine 2004: 81).

In order to have a possible set as a whole, one should have recourse to an operator which is not that of difference but instead that of identity: $\forall x, x=x$. However, the completeness of the set as something 'self-founded' comes at the price of *tautology* ($x=x$). The result of this is that while we aim, through language, at meaning (the correspondence of '$x=x$'), the logic of the signifier suggests difference. One cannot obtain the one without sacrificing the other. Completeness of a given set comes at the price of a tautology. Conversely, the possibility of co-defining the elements through differentiality pays the price of incompleteness. It is for this reason that two particular Lacanian *logions* are interconnected: (1) there's no other of the other and (2) there's no metalanguage. The incompleteness of the Other (1) is due to the fact that there's no outside privileged point of view from which we can grasp its supposed totality (2).

2 A Special Case of Symbolic Object: Lacan and Deleuze Against Hume's Law

If we follow the rules on how to identify symbolic objects, a particular case comes to the fore, namely that of personal pronouns. More specifically, the personal pronouns 'I' and 'You'. I suggest that they are a *special case* of symbolic objects. That is, they are symbolic objects which, by maintaining the basic feature of differentiality, exercise a specific role in intersubjective activities and in subject-formation.

The point of view which allows for an analysis of the activities of these special grammatical tokens is that of seeing them as traveling (and transmittable) entities which are used as tools, by subjects, to take positions in discourse and in their relations to the Other.

Just like normal symbolic objects, the 'I' and 'You' pronouns must be understood as constituting an immanent couple in which they co-define themselves. As Benveniste underlines in his reflections on pronouns: «It's 'ego' which *says* 'ego'. In this we find the fundament of 'subjectivity', which is determined by the linguistic *status* of the 'person'. Self-consciousness is thus possible only in contrast. I don't use *I* but if I have to address someone else, who in my allocution will be a *you*» (Benveniste 2010: 312).

The 'I/You' is a symbolic object which shows how pronouns are traveling negativities with persona-forming capacities. Indeed, all the disjunctions perceived by the subject as separations between 'me' and the 'others' *or* 'me' and 'society' are rather to be placed in the imaginary. As Benveniste underlines, all these «antinomies of the 'I' and the 'other' fall down, along with 'individual' and 'society'» (ibid.: 313); or, to recall a Hegelian reflection on the matter, language is the place of universality. All these types of dualities can't be reduced to a putative original role of the *I*: the *I* token can't be understood in isolation, it takes its value according to a *You*, which is the *you* of the Other. That is, when using the 'I' we already entered the Other in its detached and supra-individual dimension.

Of course, if we are to take a materialist account of such entities, we must first and foremost underline the fact that pronouns also, just like every other symbolic object, are transmitted. We're tamed by them as much as we perceive them as instruments at our disposal.

Pronouns work as parasites: they are transmitted and reproductive tokens. Michel Serres, in his essay on the functioning of parasites, proposed some reflections which are worth noting. In particular, when speaking about pronouns, he treats them as 'quasi-objects'. Just like in Latour's formulation, these quasi-objects are «marker[s] of the subject» in the construction of «intersubjectivity» (Serres 2007: 227). Serres asks «"We": what does that mean? We are precisely the fluctuating moving back and forth of "I". The "I" in the game is a *token exchanged*» (ibid., our italics).

Here, 'quasi-objects' (and quasi-subjects) means that the boundaries between subject and object are not fixed at the very beginning, but instead go through all sorts of exchange games. Pronouns are transmitted tokens which are then used to take position in front of the Other.

Intersubjectivity is then to be conceived as primordial. One may here criticize this idea by saying that in speech we find real bodies and not mere detached grammar tokens. We find *real* subjects with their own *wills* and *intentions*. On a closer look, however, Lacan's reflections on the matter in question suggests a more refined account of the intersubjective play. It is a game which involves all of the three registers, the symbolic, the imaginary and the real.

In a given language exchange, a subject draws the other speaker's attention by relying on the symbolic object of the 'I/You'. Communication is then possible as a mutual exchange in the use of the I/You which is rebounded between the speakers. The whole of the activity itself must be understood as made up of different strata. Lacan distinguishes between the symbolic 'I' and the imaginary 'I', the latter occupying the psychoanalytical category of the Ego properly. Indeed, the use of the 'You' to draw someone's attention works by capturing only a certain aspect of the listener in its *here and now*. As La Mantia suggests, the 'You' catches the Other by *hooking* him/her (La Mantia 2017: 96–103). The symbolic stratum is evoked by the subject as something which helps him/her grapple the other with a grammatical 'hook'. This operation comes at the inevitable price of leaving the other (in its bodily wholeness) with a fundamental residuum. The 'You' hooks onto something which leaves the Real of the other (object *a*) as a remainder.

In this game in which speaker and co-speaker exchange the 'I/You' position by taking mutually alternative positions, a real remainder is always falling out of the grammatical grid. Indeed, the 'I' is what oscillates between the mere symbolic stratum and imaginary one as an attempt to resolve this basic non-wholeness of the intersubjective play. In its essence, the I is «an imaginary function» (Lacan 2006a: 44).

The imaginary stratum works as a dynamical place in which the subject recreates the constitution originally lost in the symbolic and real strata. Accordingly, Lacan acknowledges this dynamic by stating that the I must be considered both as a function and as a symbol (ibid.: 47). It is at this level, he further explains, «that operates the ambiguity. The I, imaginary function, doesn't intervene in psychic life but as symbol» (ibid.).

In this intersubjective play, our human experience is to be placed within the imaginary order (ibid.: 44). This kind of dynamic by which the speaker tries to regain consistency (in the face of the real remainder) is pecisely what distinguishes us from the realm of nature: «We find the imaginary function in nature», Lacan underlines, but only as «Gestaltic captations related to the parade, so essential for the maintaining of sexual attraction in the species». Lacan is here equating the imaginary with the aesthetic function of sexual selection through the evaluation of specific traits. However, «the function of the I presents, in the human, different characteristics. This is the big discovery of analysis [...]», that in the human «there's a deep perturbation of vital regulation» (ibid.: 45).

It is a perturbation which is due to the involvement of all three registers in intersubjectivity. Lacan acknowledges that the I is a whimsical entity. On the one hand he underlines the (gradualist) link between the imaginary of the humans and that of non-humans; that is, he acknowledges that, in non-humans, there's a germ of *I* (or 'proto-I') in the form of Gestaltism. However, this all sums up to an idea of an aesthetic whole. On the other side, the I is first and foremost, for speaking animals, a symbol.

The symbolic has this power to 'tokenize' and to make the 'I' not just a mere imaginary function, but also a modality by which the subject accesses structure.

As Lew remarks «Each interlocutor is situated on a side of this Möbian exchange in which they speak [*prise de parole*]» (Lew 2013: 143). From this perspective, intersubjectivity must not be confused with the 'We' of conversation. 'We', as Serres remarks, is a mythical subject:

> [Will] is an automorphism, and by that word I mean the projection or the reproduction of what was thought to happen within me in this new mythical subject, the "we". It is a retranslated egology. Who can assure that the "we" has the same attributes and the same faculties as the ego? A thought, an intelligence, a will. Why not desires, appetites, or sexuality? We have made the same error about the collective as about God; we made it in the image of the ego. (Serres 2007: 124)

There's a basic asymmetry between the 'I' of the 'I/You' and the 'We'. When the subject says 'We', it is not as if an equivalence of the I and the You is created, a mere grouping of them into one single unity. It is rather the case of a *junction* between 'I' and 'non-I' (Marrou 2016: 21–22).

Now, the problem is here to find a proper *order* or *hierarchy* between the different strata involved in the intersubjective situation. One can here follow two different paths to solve the problem. Deleuze and Guattari, by recognizing the importance of grammar—Lacan's *code* (Lacan 2011a: 86)—and by acknowledging the importance of Benveniste's reflections on the 'I/You', portray a scenario which, nonetheless, turns the linguist's schema upside down.

On the one hand, indeed, Benveniste acknowledges the fact that subjectivity creates, in language, the «category of person» (Benveniste 2010: 316). He also underlines that «*I* can't be identified but by the discursive situation which contains it, and just by it»; more emphatically, «*I* counts only in the situation in which it is produced» (ibid.).

However, it is precisely in defining this *situation* that we prefer to take a path which is suggested by Deleuze and Guattari. In their reflections on linguistics, they examine Benveniste's account of performative speech acts.

According to Benveniste, instances of this type of speech act, like 'I appoint you X' or 'I baptize you in the name…', do not «refer to acts, but to the property of *self-referential* terms (the true personal pronouns I, YOU…, defined as *shifters*): so that a structure of subjectivity, of a preliminary intersubjectivity in language, allows to comprise acts of speech, instead of presupposing them» (Deleuze and Guattari 2017: 131). The problem, according to them, is that of the proper *place* in which to situate the 'I/You'. They lament the fact that, according to the "classical" account of Benveniste, the pronouns are to be taken as what allows subject-formation in the panoplia of human and social practices.

To make a long story short, this «subjectivation» or «intersubjectivity» (ibid.) is what is needed *at first* to explain *all the rest*, that is, everything which follows from it: the performatives. According to this view, I can commit myself to saying 'I appoint you leader of…' because there already exists, preliminarily, the couple of pronouns 'I/You'. Or, as Deleuze and Guattari say, «the phenomenon of self-reference» enables the possibility of the «performative» (ibid.).

According to this view, it is because there's a *grammatical* subjectivity (I, you, …) that it is possible to construct proper social objects such as promises or baptisms. But it is exactly this argument which Deleuze and Guattari try to overcome.

They propose to see the use of deictics such as 'I' and 'You' as explainable from the standpoint of concrete historic and social acts and practices which are culturally transmitted. In the examples we borrowed, it will be the existence of practices of 'baptism' and 'designation' which explain self-reference, and not the other way around.

This view implies that language as code is subordinated to the concrete practices of subjectivation: it is the concrete pragmatic consequences (such as when we say 'I love you' to someone else) which explain the power of deictics. The performative power of such acts is based upon specific «juridical acts» or «equivalents of juridical acts, which distribute processes of subjectivation and assignations of subjects in the language» (ibid.).

Self-reference is not original. This pragmatic linguistics is much more radical: *subjectivity* is possible only because there's *civilization* (juridical aspects, institutional practices, schools, etc.).

A grammatical rule is, then, «a mark of power, before being a grammatical mark» (ibid.: 128). Deleuze pushes this logic of argumentation so far as to conclude that «personal pronouns, far from being in relationship with the proper noun, they are the cancellation of it in a function of *capitalist exchange*» (Deleuze 2010: 61).

It is the practices which *need* pronouns, and not the other way around. What one may view as the most intimate and authentic process of self-reference and individuation, the 'I', is a token which shifts in a differential grid of exchanges. Lacan's portrayal of subjective life as something made of a constitutive 'dispossession' is due, then, to the fact that «the core [*der Kern*] of our being doesn't coincide with the I» (Lacan 2006a: 52). Deleuze puts this in a more radical, but still Lacanian, way: «Do you know what to do to prevent someone from speaking in first person? Let him say "I"» (Deleuze 2010: 61).

«I» is conceived by Benveniste as a «mobile sign» (Benveniste 2010: 305), just like—we may now add—a parasite: it is able to survive only by moving from partner to partner, it lasts as long as the game goes on. But it is a game made of entities which shatter the famous Humean distinction between the *ought* and the *is*. In the game of the code, the moral is *already* included in the ontological.

Deleuze and Guattari propose the concept of the *password*. This notion doesn't isolate a particular new specific entity amongst the ones of the performative, the illocutionary, etc. They call *passwords*:

> «[…] the relationship of any word or of any enunciate with implicit presuppositions, that is, with speech acts which are fulfilled in the enunciates and that can be fulfilled only in it. Passwords do not refer only to commands, but to all the acts which are bounded to enunciates by «social obligation»». (Deleuze and Guattari 2017: 132)

By password we mean the relationship between every word or enunciate and its implicit presuppositions. And what is implicit in every enunciate is, they add, a «moral obligation». They make the example of the enunciate: «You're a child no more…». This enunciate must be taken as including an *incorporeal transformation* (i.e. symbolic). It forces the receiver into an almost infinite set of expectations: 'You should get married' or 'It's better for you that you find a job', etc.

The *ought to be* is already in the *is*. Deleuze and Guattari elaborate on this example by specifying that «bodies have an age, a maturation, an aging», but things like «retirement pension» are incorporeal transformations which are (suddenly) attributed to bodies, in this or that society (ibid.: 135).

By putting Hume's guillotine upside down, the principle according to which we can't borrow normative principles from bare facts, Deleuze and Guattari suggest that, quite on the contrary, every time the speaker is involved in speech (such as in the case of 'You're a child no more'), she is, de facto, proscribing and forbidding something. In speech, we are already ascribing obligations and expectations to bodies, beyond their peculiar and concrete physical characteristics.

Here Deleuze and Guattari make a very Lacanian claim when they say that language «isn't established between the seen (or perceived) and the said, but it always goes *from a saying to another saying*» (ibid.: 129). *There's no metalanguage*, to use the Lacanian logion.

So, if we take the example of 'You're a child no more…', we can construct a chain of possible enunciates such as '…you should get married', '…it's time for you to have a family', etc. Against Hume, then, we can suggest that every speech act is, to some extent, rich with prescriptions. Language *says* what we ought to be. There's no subjectivity (or self-reference) without it being already captured in the discourse of the Other.

Hume's famous distinction between the normative and the factual is to be abandoned. For the speaking animal, enunciates are not isolated entities; they always come in *packs* of virtual enunciates which proliferate invisibly by introducing the normative into the apparently factual.

The body is already a spoken entity: «what happens before […], and what happens next, […], are actions-passions which modify bodies (body of property, body of the victim, body of the sentenced, body of the prison)» (Deleuze and Guattari 2017: 135). There are no identical bodies, because they are already hosting normativity.

One point, however, must be clarified. This parallel is possible only under the necessary precaution of avoiding a constructivist or identity-based discourse, for the attention must be focused not on the supposedly creative powers of the normative upon the 'natural' broadly taken, but rather on the fact that *any* appeal to the symbolic machinery has no favourite zero level. That is, one could think of this baptism of the human body into the symbolic as something from which the subject is supposed to free himself later on in his life. To a great extent, this is the possibility foreshadowed by Deleuze and Guattari themselves. But when it comes to Lacan, the psychoanalyst suggests another more elaborate possibility. Indeed, in Lacan's works it is rather hard to trace the possibility of a liberation from the normative via a detachment from the workings of the symbolic horizon. As I will show later on in this chapter, this possibility is rather substituted in Lacan with a more nuanced and intricate dynamic, based more on a dialectical play of appropriation and misappropriation of the Name-of-the-Father rather than on a one-sided liberation from the symbolic.

Still, it is possible to link some of the hints regarding the concept of the *password* to the Lacanian framework. The exchanges between the I and the You and their mœbian bond call for a materialist account of such processes of exchange. One of the novelties of Lacan regarding this matter is that of avoiding an instrumental-like account of pronouns; and he does so by introducing a constitutive asymmetry in the play of such entities.

For this, it is possible to maintain a general materialist thesis—symbolic materials are transmitted in their *use*—but we can also add that this materialism of the (transmission of) signifiers hosts an intrinsic imbalance.

Everything that exists *here and now* must have had some means to be *here and now.* Repetition is the name psychoanalysis gives to the insistence of re-producing signifiers. But signifiers themselves are not mere surfacing linguistic entities, they are embodied in a subject's life. More radically, as long as psychoanalysis starts from the fact that the subject-world relation has both knowledge-contents *and* desire-contents, such intimate materials as signifiers, fantasy and structures, they do all exercise a key role in how *Homo sapiens* gives "meaning" and "sense" to his own actions (and missing actions alike). Plus, mundane clinical experiences show how these ancestral materials do exercise the role of feedback story-telling effect on the subject himself. The subject justifies the meaning and sense of both his own fortunes and misfortunes by revolving around recurrent signifiers.

We're nothing but the hosts for what Lacan calls «the Other's desire». Up to a certain point—and at a certain level—we're made of alterity.

That's why it is not only the case that the subject is «supposed» (*supposé*), but also that the «I» doesn't really know what «I» *wants.*

«I» is as such a grammatical token co-evolved with the Ego as function. That is, like any other signifier in a differential grid of opposite values, the «I» couldn't be there if it wasn't for the «you», a point Lacan doesn't refrain from exploring. Indeed, in one of his passages on the matter, the psychoanalyst takes the example of an abrupt 'You!':

> To this *Toi* [You] which I called taming, which tames nothing, *You* of vain rapture, of vain bond, corresponds what could happen to us when a certain order comes to us from a nowhere [...]. It is what we answer when something is blamed on us or will be charged in our account: *I*! What is this *I*? *I* alone, by his own, what is it, if not an *I* of defense, an *I* of rejection, an *I* of *I don't, it isn't my thing*? (Lacan 2008: 66)

Here, the point to be underlined is that in no way should one detach the material dynamic of propagation from the active role these entities

(I, You) exercise in the asymmetry of specific speech acts. In the 'I' of the example already lies rejection, defense, etc. To cut short, one can't take the *function* and the logic of *transmission* as two separate domains, for the one is dependent on the other.

The 'You' in Lacan's example has already a specific facet.

The human trains the newborn in the use of "I". The function or grammatical token of «I» is also, then, cooperative regarding moral contents. Indeed, the «I/You» comprises the whole of the moral dimension. The very possibility of grammatically tokenizing the Ego is necessary when it comes to the only moral value worth exploring from this standpoint: complicity. That is, when I say «I», I'm already complicit with the other standing in front of me in that this little token helps "us" individuate *this* speaking body. This moral dimension already inscribed in the grammatical possibility of the «I/You» couple manifests itself quite ordinarily. For example, when we feel guilty for something we committed, we often ask ourselves: «What have I done?». And this happens even if no one is physically there to listen. There would be no sense of guilt or concern if it wasn't for these reproducing-repeating signifiers. Moreover, what psychoanalysis says, especially through the mirror stage dynamic, is that the event of symbolic identification became somehow necessary through time. The moral dimension of this Ur-complicity of the «I/You» is what repeated itself to the point of becoming a necessary requisite of the sense of reality itself. The me/non-me distinction is thus triggered, so to speak, by the caregiver at the time of every new birth. As a matter of fact, this me/non-me distinction is already elicited in the chitchats between caregivers and the fetus in the womb. The novelty for linguistic animals, however, is that the calling and individuation powers of the I/You couple are already entangled with the genesis of morality itself.

I argue, then, that the only moral power exercised by linguistic animals is complicity and that, conversely, all the other types of contents morality can comprise are derivative.

We say «I» so that we «are» in front of the Other. This Other is, however, a discourse made flesh, our own desire. Guilt, anxiety and inhibitions are a few of the manifestations exercised by this inner alterity.

One of the key consequences of placing the I/You complicity deep in the core of morality itself is that the *friend-or-foe* political category of Carl Schmitt is in no way necessary, but rather a matter of a reproducing contingency *made* necessary through the means of complicity. Conscience and complicity (morality) are two sides of the same coin.

That's why the I/You is to be placed *within* the borders of selection and adaptivity. Conversely, then, it is no surprise that the unconscious is considered to be the only «real». It is the "saying" which escapes selection and adaptivity due to its non-normative (i.e. out-of-complicity) character.

Nonetheless, we can't but speak through the I/You framework: the view from a *first-person* perspective is so deeply embedded in our inheritance as human beings that everything emanating from the real core of the unconscious is often perceived as frightening. Indeed, the unconscious manifests itself in meshed up, contradictory and monstrous ways. It works, as a matter of fact, under a logic which is not that of the strict I/You structure. It is the non-adapted living core of subjectivity.

It is not an "I" or a "You", although the subject unfolds the text of dreams from a first-person perspective. The unconscious is an «*it*» (*ça parle*, «it speaks»).

But before getting close to this vibrant—and real—core, one has to abolish the hierarchical order which places the *I* at the top of subjectivity. Against the Kantian idea of an I exerting the function of a *synthesis*, a "dotting" of reality into the experience of "a reality from this standpoint" (*me*) or against the Cartesian *Ego* as the locus of the certitude of thought, we argue that the I—which is always differentially caught into the I/You couple—is a functional social illusion. It's a token which is capable of performing *culpability*: in its key evolutionary function, it allows given groups (i.e. civilization) to consider a given event as attributable to *this* body *hic et nunc*, be it with praise or with judgement. Linguistic parasites—to use Serres' parlance—are molded by our everyday activities but, at the same time, mold us as a necessary outcome of our entering into human groups.

Accordingly, this theme is what sets the possibility of a materialist account of psychoanalysis. This trope of subjectivity as the price of civilization surely comprises the Nietzschean account of consciousness.

It is what Nietzsche calls genealogy, one of the most prolific attempts to ground consciousness on materialist and evolutionary grounds. Moreover, Nietzsche could here be taken as a theorist of symbolic castration and as a herald of psychoanalysis tout court. In the *Genealogy*, thus, morality is directly linked to the linguistic capacity of making promises: the «long history of responsibility» is tantamount, according to Nietzsche, to «taming an animal which is capable of making promises…» (Nietzsche 2018: 46).

The I/You is directly linked to culpability and debt and Nietzsche stigmatizes them as «fixed ideas» straight away. According to the evolutionary account the 'I', in its symbolic-imaginary function evolved as a special type of fixed idea, is obtained at the price of an intrinsic systemic violence (institutional, religious and political); or, as Nietzsche himself says, these fixed ideas have served us in «primitive demands of social coexistence» (ibid.: 49). That's why, «guilt» is what has taken the place of the material notion of «debt» (ibid.: 51).

3 Motor Cognition and Umwelt: Imaginary Objects and Simulation

If symbolic objects can be grasped as values, imaginary ones can be thought of as gestures, which I will define as being close to the idea of a simulated action. So far, I began this chapter by reestablishing the object-oriented assumption that the three Lacanian registers of the real, the symbolic and the imaginary, could be treated as indicating three different types of things. Levi Bryant proposes indeed a philosophical translation of those which resembles what we're doing here. In his ontology of machines (or Machine-oriented ontology), he treats the symbolic, the real and the imaginary as standing respectively for: the semiotic, the material and the phenomenological.

Here, semiotic means the normative or 'sorting' power of machines, such as in the case of our exempla of differential couples: 'man' as 'non-woman', 'black' as 'not-white', etc.

The material comprises the concrete pieces or compounds of machines. And the phenomenological stands for the ways in which a machine (or, simply, an object) perceives another machine.

Our characterization of the three registers resembles Bryant's but it nonetheless deviates from the latter by maintaining that the object-oriented plea for a *flat* account of the three registers is possible only through a forced operation of *maquillage* on the late Lacan. That is, I argue that the same asymmetry we've seen (see Chapter 1) between nomination (the symbolic) and the three registers is repeated in the latest of Lacan's works by—this time—placing the real as a 'special' realm above the three registers taken together.

However, despite this difference in the outcome of a supposed 'Borromean ontology', there's much information in hand to follow Bryant in stating that—for example—the imaginary could be treated as something having to do with phenomenology.

The best way to tackle this point is to underline the notion of space. Accordingly, Bryant's phenomenological characterization of the imaginary is based on Lacan's often quoted Jacob Von Uexküll. This path is what leads us to consider space as an ontological *plenum*. It is a space, that of interacting machines, which doesn't have to be considered as a mere blank space. If a space of an object/machine is such a 'full' space, it is because it is constituted by densities, resistances, viscosities, etc., given by other objects/machines. This is the line of thinking which makes object-oriented ontologies as belonging to the theoretical phylum that goes from Bryant to Gibson, from Uexküll to Deleuze, and lastly to the more recent enactivist perspectives (such as Evan Thompson's).

Indeed, in Gibson's perceptual ecologism we find theorized an ineluctable action-information circle due to which *action* is a function (and a result) of *information*. That is, action is guided by information but it nonetheless allows information to be extracted from the environment. Bryant thus considers the space as being dense, a significative space, an ontological plenitude without action at a distance. As Bryant underlines, when it comes to living objects:

> Space is not an empty field, but is rather a field populated by machines of all sorts. As these machines encounter one another, they encounter resistances, torsions, densities, and so on. A machine will generally follow the

> path of least resistance, before coming to a state of rest because its movement is impeded by another machine. Spaces are composed of paths and flows. Paths are not something other than machines that flow along them, but rather are themselves densities and fluid vectors produced by other machines. (Bryant 2014: 143)

The importance of such a kind of space, as a space made through the interactive needs of the living body with its environment, is due to the way in which Lacan himself sets the differences and the similarities between the human and the animal. In the whole of the Lacanian corpus, this question often raises a lot of controversies regarding the way Lacan treats the human/non-human distinction. It is a matter of setting the boundaries and/or the continuities between the two domains. For my part, I argue that there are plenty of reasons to consider Lacan as theorizing a non-linear continuity between the merely biological and the human. Indeed, nowhere is Lacan denying the biological in favor of the merely cultural, a possibility which would consequently justify a supposed logocentrism (or even intellectualism) of psychoanalysis. The importance of language is not tantamount to a qualitative superiority of the human over the animal, but rather quite the opposite: it is a matter of how language deranges enjoyment in an animal (the human) which is lacking in its *instincts*.

In order to envisage the similarities and differences between humans and non-human animals in the register of the imaginary, Lacan often borrows from the categories of Jacob Von Uexküll. Accordingly, there are a lot of reasons to take this path, for the precious insights regarding the subject-environment relation shed a light on the register of the imaginary when it's taken as the realm of the phenomenological. For this reason, it is useful to pave the way for language by starting off from the premises of the imaginary as the locus of motor cognitive elements.

By the time Lacan formulated his category of the imaginary, much of the contemporary evidence on the functioning of action representations was yet to come. However, the theorization of the "imaginary bubble" of the animal via the works of Von Uexküll constitutes—I argue—the missing link upon which it is possible to build a bridge between the imaginary and what Marc Jeannerod calls motor cognition (Jeannerod 2006).

Von Uexküll's account of space is that it is always limited:

> The space surrounding us is always limited. Maybe one can mentally imagine an unlimited space, but our sensory instruments can't know it at all. They rather teach us that we are constantly surrounded with a soap bubble, maybe fragile, but nonetheless unreachable and impenetrable. Each one of us carries this soap bubble like a stable shell throughout the entire life. Between us and the bubble there's a mutual constraint. (Von Uexküll 2013: 41–42)

The environment (*Umwelt*) is constituted by perceptive world and operative world (ibid.). The aspect that must be emphasized is that these two worlds *always come together*: «[…] every animal subject confronts its object with the tips of its pliers, one perceptive and the other operative» (Von Uexküll 2010: 47).

Lacan's own appropriation of such arguments is that the entering of the human into language creates a basic mismatch in which the intrinsic unmediated (or 'weakly' mediated) subject-to-object interaction of the animal is put out of sync. Lacan's animality is tantamount to the fact that the animal doesn't *question* its 'knowing': the object of need is already out there and it is achievable through the Umwelt (perception and operation). The distinction between knowing and not-knowing what one wants is thus unavailable to the animal as such. The facticity of language shapes the interactions between the human and its environment because the latter is already a 'signified' or 'linguisticized' entity.

Here lies the conundrum of spatiality and action for a human and a non-human animal: the imaginary/phenomenological bubble is such a space that it is not characterizable through the image of the empty box. It is not a three-dimensional space with objects occupying portions with their volumes and masses. It is a space which suspends Newtonianism and Euclidean geometry. A rich space made of imbalances, paths and resistances. And, due to these peculiar features, Lacan is able to replace knowledge along the lines of a non-Kantian framework. That is, while Lacan is able to bridge the gap between human and non-human through the arguments of Von Uexküll (later resurfacing in Heidegger), he rethinks the position of knowledge by placing it on the side of the unconscious.

During his public appearance *Television*, when asked «What can I know?» (the Kantian question *par excellence*), Lacan answers back by stating that his discourse «doesn't allow» for such a question because it starts from the premise of the subject of the unconscious (Lacan 2013: 529). While it is maintained that the imaginary dimension does, in fact, have a role in human and non-human animals, knowledge is not a question of its conditions of possibility. The unconscious is such a not-known knowledge, a kind of knowledge 'I already knew', or that 'I always knew'. I will elaborate later on the unavoidable conclusions which can be borrowed from such a displacement of knowledge.

For now, however, I will maintain that imaginary objects, as long as they're conceivable as having to do with Umwelt or Gibsonian space, can be thought of as simulated gestures.

Lacan often ascribes to the imaginary a kind of vicarious function: it serves as a support to resolve the intrinsic mismatch between the symbolic and the real or, so to speak, between words and matter. In any case, the fact that the imaginary is conceivable—in its Borromean economy—as a support for the other registers doesn't preclude the possibility of its characterization (that is, *iuxta propria principia*).

Here, the results of Jeannerod are to be put as belonging to that theoretical lineage which goes from (at least) Von Uexküll to Lacan himself.

The space of the imaginary can be defined as a space of imagined actions, or as a space of representations of actions «in the absence of execution» (Jeannerod 2006: 23). The crucial aspect to be underlined is that experimental findings, as shown by these studies, point toward the idea that represented (or simulated) actions do share the same constraints as their material and actual counterparts. I won't display the whole of the experiments proposed by Jeannerod, but I will underline their theoretical outcome.

To put it in simple terms, when asked to carry out a specific mental action, subjects do show the same constraints and possibilities of executing it materially. That is, representing an action, such as moving a glass on a plane, or executing it are «functionally equivalent» (ibid.: 41). The times and the efforts of the execution are the same when the action is mentally simulated or concretely carried out. But there's more: this idea gives room to the hypotheses that (1) there's a bodily encoding of space and time *qua* representation of actions independently of their material equivalents and that consequently (2) *consciousness* of an action is postponed or delayed in regard to the actual *will* of a subject executing it.

Moreover, the nervous system anticipates the effects of self-produced actions. Space and time are conceivable as a non-Newtonian field of embodied simulations.

> […] visuomotor representations share properties with both perceptual representations and action representations. First, because they encode visual properties of objects, they resemble perceptual representations, or at least that part of perceptual representations that has no conceptual content (the visual percept). Secondly, because they anticipate the state of the visual world that will take place when the action is executed, they resemble action representations: the function of visuomotor representations is not to acquire explicit knowledge about the visual world, it is to feed in intentions for acting on the visual world. Finally, because they have no conceptual content, they can operate rapidly and automatically […] (ibid.: 5)

Here we find the idea of a space-time as a niche of possible gestures allowed by the body. The results suggested by these studies show that, even when a subject is tricked with a play of mirrors, the appraisal of the action remains coherent if the image displayed through the trickery is coherent with the body image.

While on the part of symbolic objects the Other was portrayed as a treasure or place of signifiers (despite its being a 'holed' space), at the level of imaginary objects qua gestures, the Other is conceivable as the embodied specular receiver of a simulated action. We're not talking here about the Other which stays in front of me, but rather of the Other as an internalized double which is an internalized exteriority. This somewhat 'unconventional' internalized Other is what resurfaces when Lacan explains his mirror stage. Indeed, when developing his notorious dispositive of subjectification, he makes a clear remark on the imaginary moment—that of the specular image—as having to do with sexual libido and aesthetics simultaneously (Lacan 2014: 145).

It is one of the cases in which Lacan doesn't refrain from plunging into ethology and the non-human counterparts of human subjectification.

The Other as an internalized entity stands, at this level, for the plethora of gestural, and hence libidinal, gratification pursued by simulated actions. Thus, Jeannerod himself underlines that the self-other distinction is impaired in cases of schizophrenia, cases where there's a «defective simulation mechanism» (Jeannerod 2006: 97).

What is important here is that imaginary objects as gestures, if so portrayed, do enact at the same time the self-formation of subjects (mirror stage) and the coeval libido-laden possibility of taking pleasure from simulated actions. The Freudian and Lacanian insights on the blurred edge between the human and the animal, despite their shortage, point to the fact that this 'self-aesthetic' of the body (of the subject's own body) is *already* made of sexuality, a trope which is coherent with Lacan's idea of sublimation, as I will show.

The human is as such characterized by this possibility of obtaining pleasure by carrying out simulated actions. It is no surprise that this intrinsic 'onward' directionality of subjectivity is made up of anticipated pleasures carried out by an internalized body image.

Anticipated pleasure and displeasure, given the basic derangement pursued by language, are not to be taken as a kind of Pavlovian reflex of stimuli and effects: the bodily encoding of subjectivity is already what places gratification in the form of activity as such. At this level Lacan would rather speak of the Aristotelian *soul* rather than the *subject* of psychoanalysis. While this idea of a pleasure in the activity for the sake of the activity is a deep Aristotelian trope, Lacan's subjectivity is rather to be placed in the realm of a symbolic lack, thus setting already the difference between pleasure in its philosophical version (*virtue*) and in its psychoanalytical sense (*sublimation*).

4 Object *a*, Sexuality and the Peafowl's Tail

Psychoanalysis introduces a libidinal element in the scenario of the imaginary. That is, the framework of the self-body relationship (via internalized simulations) is retranslated by Freud (especially in the idea of narcissism) and Lacan (in the mirror stage) by introducing the issue of pleasure in the otherwise merely cognitive plateau.

The issue of the continuity/discontinuity between the animal and the human realm is better clarified if we look to the genealogy of the sense of beauty itself. If, at this level of imaginary objects, relationships are to be understood as asymmetrical exchanges in which individual *loci* of self are formed through embodied simulations, the way in which these relationships are forged could shed some light on the way sexuality is already inscribed in such dynamics.

In his study on the genealogy of the sense of beauty, Winfried Menninghaus tries, indeed, to construct a comprehensive evolutionary approach to the issue. The underlying focus of his work is to acknowledge the basic fact that in nature itself we find the roots for the aesthetic function. A function, I want to recall, Lacan inscribes in the mirror stage itself.

Menninghaus draws attention to the case of the Peafowl. Notably, the peafowl's tail is an ornament which is the result of female selection. That is, the showy character of the peafowl's tail is due to the fact that an endless selection of this trait was pursued by the female members of the species. As such, Menninghaus points out the fact that nature is full of examples of choices made on the basis of aesthetic appreciations. The interrogative that led Darwin into formulating his idea of *sexual selection* (*vs. natural selection*) was indeed that of explaining how such a monstrous thing like the peafowl's tail could be accounted for. The problem, for the peafowl, is that its beauty comes at the price of being more susceptible to predators; it is a beautiful trait which comes at the price of a kind of *handicap*: that of being more vulnerable to possible aggressors. That is, if selection aims at the maximization of *fitness*, how is it possible then that such a risky trait could have emerged at all?

There's a clear-cut answer for such a question, a possibility that Menninghaus holds as valid only to some extent. The idea is that of an intergenerational feedback loop between the choices on the part of the females and the amount of changes in the tail's characterization. According to this view, while we can't disregard sexual selection *tout court*, we have to posit the limit of an outside source of danger (the easiness of being killed) as a negative and opposing feedback. Once the machinery between the aesthetic choice of the females and the developmental possibilities of the tail reaches its peak, an external form—a negative feedback in the form of predators—has to be posited as putting sexual selection itself in a state of equilibrium.

In the place of this model (Menninghaus 2013: 127), the author suggests a more refined view which comes close to the Lacanian trope of the imaginary qua aesthetic function (and qua embodied self). The fact of beauty is not conceivable as a mere contingent result of repeated feedback loops, but instead shows the presence, already in nature, of a sense of '*wonder*': a prototypical idea of aesthetics as the possibility, experienced by the sight of both mates and potential predators, to be *amazed* or *astonished* by the brightness of a colour or by the unique monstrosity of a shape.

Indeed, the same dynamic unfolded in the case of the peafowl's sexual selection holds true in complementary cases in which a predator avoids aggression because of this sense of petrifying (or monstrous) wonder in front of prey. The two events are due to this intrinsic (i.e. already natural) possibility of a gaze to encounter an untouchable object.

In a quick remark on the function of the *imago*, Menninghaus quotes Lacan's mirror stage as showing how «fictional moments of expectations and desires» are already embedded imaginarily in the «construction of the self» (ibid.: 227).

Regarding the gaze of the Other as what constitutes the germ of the I, Lacan indeed envisages this very gaze as at the same time carrying «fascination» and «terror» (Lacan 2006a: 60).

The Peafowl's tail is nothing but one paradigmatic example of how *beauty* and *vulnerability* are conjoined. Moreover, this 'non-standard' evolutionary approach to sexual attractiveness adds to the line of thought according to which the *gaze* of the Other is a desirable object per se, because it is implicitly embedded in our evolutionary heritage. From the Lacanian point of view, it is quite curious to notice that despite his repeated critiques of (standard) Darwinism, Lacan's conceptual toolbox already comprises all the ingredients to make the theoretical "jump" from non-human to human aesthetics.

The *agency* of sexual selection is not then to be taken as an adversary of the *agency* of natural selection, but instead its prolongation (Menninghaus 2013: 71).

Lacan acknowledges the intrinsic bond between death and the signs of the body and introduces the role of the object small *a* as cause of desire in the underlying logic of attraction (through the gaze).

He makes the distinction between *love* per se (French '*amour*') and love qua *amur*, a neologism created through the crasis of French words 'a' (*on the*) 'mur' (*wall*). Lacan's conceptual integration on the issue of love is due to the fact that psychoanalysis should allow for a knowledge of love which doesn't fall into the fantasy of the whole of the sexes. That's the reason for the 'wall' in the neologism *amur* ('on the wall'): it depicts the theoretical presupposition of the discourse on sex (and on *sexes*) as being a matter of barrier or difference rather than a mythical pre-given harmony.

In one passage, Lacan links *amur* with «what appears in the bizarre signs of the body» (Lacan 2011a: 6). These bizarre signs are those «sexual traits coming from the afterlife, from that place we believed we could observe with through the microscope in the form of the *germen*» (ibid.). Here's where the reader could grasp already a hint of the *discontinuous*: Lacan acknowledges the *germen* as the genetic locus of the eccentricity of the trait, but he nonetheless portrays it as insufficient for defining life. Indeed, he further emphasizes that the transmission of the trait/germen «brings also death, the death of the body, in its reproduction» (ibid.). It is the theme of the peafowl dying because of its hereditary sexual traits.

On the one hand, then, we have this material-imaginary dynamic of the *amur*; on the other hand, Lacan's theorization of love is structured so that the *real* lack of sexual relation laps over its putative direct reproductive goal.

But even in this second case, love is explained through an optical metaphor. In his XXth Seminar, dedicated to the problem of love and sexual difference, he relates the problem of the enjoyment of the Other's body to the functioning of object *a*. He states that «everything that has to do with love» functions as if the *suit always makes the man.* He reverses the ordinary saying—*the suit doesn't make the man*—by reestablishing the prevalence of pretense/appearance: «the suit loves the man [...]. In other words, what lies beneath the suit and which we call the body maybe is no different from that remainder which I call object *a.*» (Lacan 2011b: 7). Here reemerges the idea I've been talking about (see Chapter 1) concerning the Lacanian emphasis on the dialectic of appearances *vs.* essences.

The image, Lacan proceeds, holds only because of the remainder; the whole of representation (or representation *as a whole*) holds only because of a surplus (such as in the *trompe-l'oeil*): analysis is what shows that love is fundamentally narcissistic. This element doesn't need to be interpreted as a solipsistic deviation of the psychoanalytical discourse; it is rather to emphasize that in love, the other is *charged* with an ontological surplus; this is what psychoanalysis (since Freud) calls narcissistic love.

We can summarize this dialectic of appearance and essence this way: Lacan rejects the idea according to which the essence lies *behind* the appearance, hence his rephrasing of the saying in 'the suit always makes the man'. What is at stake, for him, is thus not really the essence/appearance couple per se, but rather the fact that the *image* of the Other qua *total image* is due to the fact that the Other becomes the support for object small *a* (the cause of desire). It's not, then, a matter of essence *over* appearance, of noumenon *over* phenomenon or of truth *over* falsity; it is rather a matter of how the gaze is involved in the operation of totalizing the Other's image in its magnificence by ascribing a remainder (object *a*) beneath this totalized image as its cause. It is, we might say, a matter of a dialectic between *whole* and *part*.

For that matter, it's not hard to see a non-Kantian twist in the workings of Lacan. Georges Didi-Huberman underlines a crucial passage in the history of the image in which the psychoanalytical discourse destabilizes the Kantian edifice on the image. According to him, reflections on the image have historically revolved around the theme of a possible 'intellectualized' closure of the image; he frames this closure as a «*closure* of the visible on the readable», and of these «on intelligible knowledge» (Didi-Huberman 2016: 29). Ranging from Kant himself to post-Kantianism (as in the case of Panofsky), the theoretical tradition on the image revolved around the overlapping of the interpretational grid *upon* the image.

The image, conceived merely on representational grounds, becomes the field in which the representational powers of the subject take place.

To this idea, Didi-Huberman opposes the fact that interpretation itself, after Freud, becomes not a locus of closure or point-to-point representation, but rather an open activity; an activity pursued through an imbalanced economy between the totalizing image itself (what he calls the «visible») and what escapes the representation itself (which is what helps the author in defining the «visual»).

It is the opening of subjectivity pursued by psychoanalysis which is, for him, responsible for such a paradigmatic shift: it is because of the opening of the «question of the *subject* - now conceived as cut [*déchirure*] and not as closure», and hence a subject which doesn't coincide with «synthesis», that Freud «reopens the question of knowledge» (ibid.: 32).

And it is for this impossibility of subjectivity qua synthesis that psychoanalysis could reopen the question of the object *tout court*. The prominence of Freud in Didi-Huberman's work is due to the fact that the deformity and imperfection of the image are taken as being constitutive of the image itself. The ethico-methodological novelty of Freudianism, compared to his predecessors, is that for the first time the image—one could say, the *dream*—is not put under *judgement* but rather under *interpretation*.

Furthermore, the difference between the former and the latter is isomorphic to the difference between Kant and Freud/Lacan: psychoanalysis has had the «role of a critical instrument within 'humanities' in general - in the guise of their symptom, […] as their return of the repressed» (ibid.: 208). To know something about the symptom «doesn't require more knowledge, a more sophisticated knowledge: because it is not *relevant* as such, but needs, more radically, the modification - after Kant required us to do so - of the *position of the subject of knowledge*» (ibid., see also Lacan 2002: 686–687). This psychoanalytical move beyond Kantianism is meant to acknowledge what I above called the dialectic of *part* and *whole* and the libidinal economy underlying the gaze in its relation to the Other.

If we were to sketch out the fundamental Lacanian reversal of the Kantian dispositive, we could portray it as a displacement of synthesis and division; the point made by Lacan in *Television* (see above) regarding the possibility of knowledge is thus to be conceived as the positing of the object itself as something exercising a *splitting* agency over the subject ($). Didi-Huberman makes this point clear when he criticizes the idea of the subject as a mere describing dispositive.

This critique is built upon the idea of the *hem* as opposed to that of the *detail*: he opposes them on the base that the former escapes figurability qua representation because it indicates always a 'not yet' of the interpretation. The *detail*, instead, is precisely the element which betrays the representation-centric appraisal of the image. That is, the piece *en plus* (+1 or *a*) is instantaneously reabsorbed into the representational grid as a mere detail (or vagary) of the image itself in its totality. The idea of the *hem*, instead, is something which lies in the middle, as a token which links the image already in the hybrid space between representation and fantasy.

The object of the hem «is not the object of the detail. The object of the detail is an object of the representation of the visible world; despite revealed in the plane of the symbol, it presupposes, at the end, an *object of reality*, of which it tries to draw the contours and stabilize its legibility» (Didi-Huberman 2016: 335). And, to this idea of the detail, he opposes the «object of the hem» as «intrusion - presence - of the pictorial in the representational system of the drawing»; and hence as a «*real object of painting*, in that it poses the 'real object' of the gaze as a pulsatile function [...]» (ibid.).

The *hem* as such is the imaginary counterpart of object small *a* because it slips out of the image itself. The reality of the image is always an *augmented reality*, a feature which psychoanalysis ascribes to the function of fantasy: reality is already an augmented reality, there's more in the image than the image itself. As underlined by Le Gaufey, it is a matter of acknowledging the fact that there's something excessive which doesn't pass through the senses (Le Gaufey 2012: 45).

As such, the hem (object *a*) works more as a holy relic: it is a piece invested with the power of linking the mundane to the transcendental. The subject is *dissolved* in the presence of object *a* (Lacan 2016: 117). Or, as I tried to explain, it is the *object* which divides the subject, and not the other way around.

The image as *total* is possible under this condition of putting the surplus as the cause of the totality itself; and it is in true love that the other becomes magnified in its totality (*despite*—and *thanks to*—its objective defects or incongruences). Accordingly, when speaking about the relationship between men and women, or the way a man configures his relation to the woman, Lacan often speaks about the perils of confusing love with perversion. In the latter case, the relation to the other revolves around mere organ pleasure, or—more precisely—*piece pleasure*; the relation is based on the detaching of specific pieces/portions of the body as loci of gratification.

This libidinal augmentation of the image is what justifies the emphasis Lacan puts on the naivety of courtly love (see Lacan 2011b: 65). As an historical manifestation, courtly love is the preferred place where this basic psychoanalytical machinery (that of fantasy and object small *a*) is put as a problem; in courtly love there's an attempt to overcome the «lack of sexual relation» by assuming «it is us who obstruct it» (ibid.). Again, the representational (and Kantian) machinery of the synthesis is restaged here in that in courtly love there's a tireless effort to stick to the idea of the harmony of sexes, of their mythical bond. The split (*$*), also in this view, is not of the subject, but in the thing itself and it is up to *us* to solve it. The existence of love is based on the absence of sexual relation.

5 Sublimation and Anti-Philosophy

The question regarding the aesthetic function has pushed us into portray a quick comparison between representation and fantasy; or, to put it in equivalent terms, between Kant and the subject-to-world relation as portrayed by the psychoanalytical discourse. The departing point for what I've been calling 'imaginary objects' (objects with both self-awareness and an aesthetic aspect) is that of the introduction, in the philosophical discourse of representation, of the libidinal/sexual ingredient.

It comes as natural that the *augmentation* of reality pursued by fantasy raises the more general question of how to place Lacan in the philosophical discourse. While, on the one hand, the Kantian heritage of Lacan is surely undeniable, on the other hand the psychoanalytical discourse poses a series of problems to the overall pursuit of philosophy, especially when it comes to metaphysics.

The argument about the image and the centrality of fantasy may suggest that psychoanalysis is *also* a way to re-enchant the world, the world of the subject. One may here—for sure—take these types of arguments as pointing towards an even more idealistic appraisal of the subject-to-world relation. However, psychoanalysis is the attempt to radicalize these 'enchantments' of subjective life into a comprehensive materialist framework. It is only in a second moment of speculation or second-order conceptualization that the idealism/realism conundrum arises. In other words, it is the particular way in which the subject relates to his own fantasy that unfolds the two tropes of *idealism* or *realism*. Two tropes, or *moments*, characterized by the way the subject poses itself in respect to the object; here 'object' means *the* object, this hybrid and evasive entity I explained via the notion of object small *a*. In this regard, Lacan himself often portrays key paradigmatic subjective positions as figures of the positions between *$* and *a*. That is, the whole of the Lacanian corpus is disseminated with paradigmatic *extremes*: the Saint, Socrates, the pervert, etc. In sum, his own theory could be also interpreted as a combinatorial dispositive which functions by generating specific paradigmatic (and historical) figures from the plethora of positions the subject can take when facing object small *a*.

This kind of materialism (if we may call it so) raises the overall question of how it is possible to conceive philosophy itself from the standpoint of psychoanalysis. If the aim is to propose an "up-to-date" materialism consistent with psychoanalysis, then one is forced to choose between two options: getting rid of philosophy and ontology *altogether*, or accepting the possibility of a non-philosophical ontology. For example, some authors have suggested that Lacan oscillates between a 'mocking stance' in which he simply portrays ontology as a matter foreign to psychoanalysis, and another possible reading which suggests the idea of a specific psychoanalytical ontology (see Soler 2016: 86). If we look closely to Lacan's own remarks on this problem, we notice that the second theoretical strategy seems to be the most viable option. This is because, despite the caustic remarks toward ontology, Lacan seems to take a critical stance toward it only when it's paired with *philosophy* tout court. Indeed, it comes as no surprise that the psychoanalyst admits to having (at least) an «implicit ontology» (sic.).

The question then is: What does Lacan say about Being? Is it the case, for Lacanian psychoanalysis, of an incorrigible anti-philosophical and anti-ontological standpoint? It is worth underlining some key oscillations in Lacan himself concerning the issue of ontology, for his acclaimed anti-ontology becomes more and more "blurred" if one reads some of his explicit statements on the issue.

At the beginning of a session of the XIX Seminar (Lacan 2003: 30), Lacan is confronted by Jacques-Alain Miller on whether the psychoanalytical conception of the unconscious gives room to an ontological discourse. Concerning this matter, Lacan characterizes the unconscious as something which «doesn't give access to ontology» (ibid.), mainly due to the assumption that the unconscious is nothing *substantial* (i.e. it is structured like a language). On the other hand, despite the fact that the unconscious is to be conceived beyond the «being»/«non-being» distinction, Lacan claims to find this question concerning ontology «not inappropriate», for the *fault* of the unconscious is an «ontological function» (ibid.). During the same seminar he firmly claims, therefore, to have an «implicit ontology».

It is already crucial to notice that a few sessions later, Lacan complains firmly against the accusation of *idealism*. In short, psychoanalysis is not an «ontology of [primitive] tendencies» (ibid.: 52), which are allegedly conceived as *already there* inside the subject. This critique of the "idealism of the tendencies" finds its roots in the very beginning of psychoanalysis. Idealism of the tendencies stands, briefly, for the idea that the determination of the aims and objects which shape the vicissitudes of the subject is already predetermined by the internalization of the first objects encountered in the life of the infant. Hence the very old critique arises: *according to psychoanalysis every investment of the subject is nothing but a dreamy hallucination of the first object*. Lives and choices are predetermined in that objects (with small 'o') are nothing but spurious repetitions of the *Objects* (with capital 'O').

It is striking to notice how Lacan rejects the idealism of the tendencies by stating that the subject's life is not «a dream». Hence, he underlines that the praxis of analysis is oriented towards «the core of the real» (ibid.). It is this *real* which is not, strictly speaking, synonymous with philosophical realism. In short: *neither idealism nor realism*.

While giving room for a kind of 'nuanced' ontology—or «functional ontology»—Lacan famously also criticizes it in its broader aspects when it is automatically paired with philosophy *tout court*.

Amongst the huge number of disseminated claims about the philosophy-psychoanalysis relation it is possible to isolate—in Lacan's corpus—three 'criteria' or 'principles' of anti-philosophy.

We can summarize these three symptomatic criteria this way: (a) Every theory which gives no room for an ungraspable *remainder* [*écart*], that is, a philosophical system aiming at an ideal of completeness, is to be rejected (see Seminar XII, Session of December the 2nd, 1964); (b) a close reading of Lacan's «individual myth of the neurotic» shows a clear second criterion, for the neurotic move par excellence has to be conceived as a projection of the division ($) upon the outside Object; (c) the third and even more convincing factor lies in a passage from Seminar VI, where Lacan states that «the subject-object relation, which is thought, so to speak, immanent to the pure *dimension of knowledge*, will give us more complicated problems *when it's a matter of desire*» (Lacan 2016: 116).

All three of these principle are present in the theorization of the image: (a) the totality of the image holds because of the non-representable excess (object small *a*), (b) the tendency is—both historically as in courtly love and subjectively—to ascribe the split to the outside, and (c) both in the oneiric world and in the image, the directionality of the subject-to-object relation is left *open* (such as in the case of interpretation).

If we were to be loyal to these three principles, Kant would test positive for all of them. Hence the conundrum of the relation between philosophy and psychoanalysis becomes more important the more we can imagine how it is that psychoanalysis is grateful to the Kantian position while maintaining a critical difference notwithstanding.

Kant famously argued that the only firm foundation for metaphysics and—hence—science, is through a progressive *synthesis* of judgements coming from a priori reason, thus the true question the metaphysician should first and foremost ask is: «How is synthetic a priori knowledge possible?» (Kant 2006: 55).

That is, if the only true and reliable knowledge is the one that has as its background a stable and un-empirical a priori Erkenntnis, how are we to explore fantasy, the cognitive-enjoyment core of subjectivity? If fantasy is a phrasal crystallization such as "a child is being beaten", where can we place it amongst Kant's analytic-synthetic and a priori-a posteriori grids?

On the one hand, the phrasal crystal of fantasy—such as in the Freudian example of 'a child is being beaten'—furnishes the subject with specific trajectories which are both "pleasure-seeking" trajectories and "sense of reality-building" trajectories. If Lacan's third criterion for anti-philosophy holds true (the 'desire-over-knowledge principle') then the Erkenntnis carried out by phantasmal structures shakes the Kantian edifice from bottom to top. On the one hand, in fact, fantasy seems to be empirical (i.e. a posteriori) in that it is not self-evident in subject's life; that is, it is a posteriori knowledge in that it must be "discovered", to put it roughly. It is not a matter, then, of something reachable through reason alone; something must happen in order to give some clues on the phantasmal structure itself. As Lacan puts it, fantasy shows off in the discourse of the analyst as this furnishes fantasy its proper spacetime.

On the other hand, fantasy seems also to be a priori in that if it is already—always—there, it gives to the subject the very conditions for his further volitional acts, whether they end up being pleasant, unpleasant or both at the same time (which is actually the case). The a priori nature of fantasy thus displays its modeling powers as *prior* to any acknowledgement of it. The subject, strictly speaking, doesn't need any empirical validation for his ideas of what is desirable and what isn't, for his split (the '*$*' side of Lacan's fundamental fantasy) doesn't simply look for a fulness (the '*a*' side of the fundamental fantasy). Fantasy as a priori knowledge is rather portrayable as what lies beyond the subject's knowledge, but which nonetheless determines the very means by which the subject is capable of saying anything whatsoever about himself and about objects themselves. It is a phrasal crystal embedded with causative properties, remaining nonetheless outside conceptual grasp (if we consider, of course, clinical practice *not* as a conceptual endeavor).

This is the crucial reason why Lacan's theory of truth was neither *correspondence* nor *unveiling*, but rather *causative*. The psychoanalyst often laments the fact that philosophers didn't think about truth as the "cause" of the subject. A given fantasy is not truer than any other, but instead it has its own "truth" for the subject who 'hosts' it. If fantasy is also a priori, then, it is not because of a missing *need* of empiric evidence, but because the very distinction between empirical and logical facts doesn't hold in the realm of desire. For this reason, the principle of 'desire-over-knowledge' finds its ally in the (second) 'primacy-of-the-split' principle.

As long as fantasy in its fundamental form (Lacan's matheme) decrees the remoteness of the real cause of desire (object *a*) from the self-knowledge of the subject («What do I really want?»), the neurotic (following the philosopher) will be more inclined to project his own split upon the outside world tout court. Thus it will not be the subject who recognizes his own symbolic insufficiency, but instead the object which will become lacking and always insufficient (or split into phenomenon and noumenon). Lacan links this crucial aspect of the myth of the neurotic to the affect of melancholia. What is the gaze of the melancholic under the moon if not the pure embodiment of this projection of the split upon the (outside) object?

Whenever the subject tries to overcome the primacy-of-the-split principle it ends up ascribing incompleteness and secretiveness to the object itself, portraying the world as something foreign and, by the same token, as something "hiding" the secret of subject's own existence, its sense, its meaning.

Desire comprises then a phrastically-ridden dimension and is, therefore, neither a priori nor a posteriori. Although, we must add, it inherits aspects of both a priori and a posteriori knowledge. At best, one could say that fantasy is "unknown knowledge".

Here we face another crucial problem, for judgements in a Kantian sense are only conceivable through the subject-predicate structure. If we take the example of "a child is being beaten", it's quite easy to classify the enunciate as a synthetical one, due to the information the predicate adds to the subject "a child". Thus "a child" could be "beaten" or not and, in this precise sense, "being beaten" is not an essential analytical feature of "being a child" tout court (there can be "non-beaten" children).

The problem arises, however, if we underline the fact that phantasmal/phrasal crystals are given before the subject even recognizes them to be either analytical or synthetical. The importance stressed on this point is a mandatory condition for assessing the whimsical nature of fantasy. Due to the fact that fantasy determines bodily attunement with the world in both aesthetic and reality-forming ways, it makes little sense to speak about the *extension* of the phrasal crystal conceived as a judgement. If fantasies were analytical, it would mean that nothing in their predicate side adds new information on the subject side, hence displaying the extensions of the two sides of the Kantian predicate to be the same. If fantasies were synthetical, it would mean—conversely—that one of the sides of the phrasal crystal effectively adds new information in respect to the object.

I will advance here a third possible type for enunciates (next to the analytical and the synthetical) for fantasy, a possibility I will now mention *en passant* and that I will fully develop in the next chapter.

This third type of judgement which stands next to the synthetic and the analytic ones, is what I define as the diagrammatic. As I will show later on (see Chapter 3), diagrams are the particular *shapes* that enjoyment takes in particular subjects; they are the result of the action of language upon the body. Judgements are then to be thought as analytic, synthetic or diagrammatic. In the latter case, a judgement gets beyond the margins of analytic/synthetic classifications, and it is neither informatively-additive nor a definition: it *works* as a constantly re-adapting description which fulfills repetition. In Freud, for instance, it is a compromise function which, in its particular structuration (which involves *personagges*, scenarios, pieces of the body, etc.) helps the subject in overcoming its relation to its own enjoyment. Hence, following our reading of Lacanianism as an "accelerated Kantianism", we can enrich Kant's theory of predicates this way:

Analytic–Synthetic–Diagrammatic

Kant envisaged pure reason as the only trustworthy point of departure for any inquiry, be it metaphysics or (subsequently) scientific research. Yet this trust put in the subject's reason is what reveals the basic bias of the philosopher tout court: his subject of knowledge is always an idealized entity. That is, the reasoning and/or perceiving subject is taken to be "healthy" in its default starting position. Although the Kantian scholar could here reply by saying that Kant's first *Critique* was nothing but an attempt to overcome this precise unreliability of reason, the philosopher's hygienistic fantasy is to find the route for the de-fantasized universal subject of (true) knowledge.

It comes as no surprise, then, that Kant fiercely rejects the skeptical position, a position which states "there's no safe knowledge" (Kant 2006: 17). But the opposite of the subject of potentially universalizable knowledge is not plain skepticism, a position I am far from ascribing to the general context of psychoanalysis, but rather a subject who's able to acknowledge how and in which ways his fantasy is diagrammatized. In other words, there's a position lying in the middle of the *pure-or-skeptical* dichotomy. That's the position held by a subject whose fantasy (in its cognitive-aesthetic aspects) is recognized, acknowledged and put—to some extent—into question. This is far from anti-Kantian, for if Lacanian fantasy is what conjointly affects the subject's knowledge potential and his pleasure-seeking trajectories as well, then digging into our very jungle of phrasal crystallizations would be the only way out of the misery of disillusion (knowledge level) and unnecessary suffering (pleasure).

The representationalist position on the mind-world relation, inaugurated in philosophy as a counterpart of modern science, seems often to pay the price of forcing completeness in spite of acknowledging subjectivity and its workings.

This libidinal materialism of object *a* suggests, rather, a schema in which the whole of the manifestations of pleasure—or, all its possible forms/diagrams—is accounted for due to the idea of sublimation. Here, however, a theoretical proviso on this notion is needed.

The common view on sublimation (especially the Freudian one) is that of a transformation of sexuality into the higher demands of specific cultural forms. Paradigmatically, it is art or artistic practice which is chosen to represent the place for such operation. Sublimation would then mean the transformation of the sexual into an activity of creation.

However, Lacan's position on the matter is far more radical and, compared to this ordinary account, far harder to accept.

In one crucial passage from his seminars, Lacan doesn't refrain from giving a clear outspoken (and explicit) claim on the issue of sublimation, a passage which is worth quoting in its full extent:

> […] for the moment, I am not fucking, I am talking to you. Well! I can have exactly the same satisfaction as if I was fucking. This is what it means. That which poses, in any case, the question of *knowing if I'm effectively fucking.* […] The use of the drive's function has to do with doubting what is *satisfaction*. (Lacan 2003: 161–162, our italics)

This passage works to show how the previously outlined account of sublimation does not really correspond to the novelty of psychoanalysis. Lacan's view is that in *language* or *speech* as such lies already sexuality. Language, in all its possible actualizations, is *already* satisfactory (i.e. sexually satisfactory). A point which, to be fair, illuminates the peculiar Kantianism of psychoanalysis in that here Lacan seems to come close to the philosophical positions of Kantians like John McDowell: in short, to positions defending the idea of an unavoidable *conceptual* character of cognitive functions, where *conceptual* is here to be taken as standing for 'language-based'.

This explicit passage is used to explain that the goal (*Ziel*) of the drive is satisfaction, but that nonetheless this satisfaction occurs through *mentalization*.

For example, drive, in the case of the oral drive, goes around its object—the breast—but it is not in the order of the *need*; it is not a matter of physically filling up one's mouth. It is the «pleasure of the mouth» (Lacan 2003: 164) itself which gains the status of an autonomous activity. It is not "this mouth" which enjoys but, rather, an enjoyment which is—to use a neologism—a "mouth-ing" (a term which curiously resembles the meaning of "kissing"). Or, to state it in a more sophisticated way, in the oral drive there is in play a *mouth*-diagram: a particular set of possible operations with particular physico-geometrical constraints and possibilities.

It is thus repetition which paves the way for fantasy; it is the repetition of this putting-into-form (or deformity) of object small *a* which generates forms from other forms; Lacan uses here the expression of the «repeated reproduction of this *enforme*» (Lacan 2006b: 394). Enjoyment is, as such, what «remains sideways to what it reaches», that is, to reproduction (Lacan 2011b: 115).

Because of that, the plethora of sublimations includes *thinking* as another way of *missing* the target of reproduction. Enjoyment, in the speaking animal, is always *misunderstood* (ibid.); all these diagrammatizations of objects *a* portray enjoyment as giving rise to a cornucopia of possible ways of satisfaction which are already, so to speak, slipping out of a possible social acquisition. There's no room here for Aristotle's hierarchy of pleasures: a hierarchy between 'lowest' and 'higher' pleasures or between the *noble* and the *low*.

To use Mario Perniola's reflections, enjoyment (along its objects) is already something slipping out of life (and, *a fortiori*, of vitalism): it has to do with the *inorganic* life of pleasure (Perniola 2004: 178–179). Or, more precisely, with the *inorganic* side of the *organic* (a theme Freud famously acknowledges through the death drive).

This schema of an object which is not transparently accessible to the subject but that nonetheless exercises a diagrammatic or forming capacity is what Lacan condenses in the formula of an object which is excluded from the subject because of its extreme proximity: the subject, as he puts it, «is in *internal exclusion* to its object» (Lacan 2002: 865). A schema that can be thought via the notion of *extimité*, something which is outside the subject because it is placed in its farthest interiority.

The *great outside* (the 'grand dehors' of Meillassoux) is *extime*: it is a an outside of subjectivity which is graspable only by looking at its peculiar unfoldings. In the general theoretical economy of Lacanianism, it is this element which sets the ground for the topological moment: the subject and the object play this game of a dynamic interplay between the unfolding of the series caused by language (and desire) and the concomitant folding of these upon the hard kernel of object *a*.

We may recall here our argument on the Real as a texture of attractors and repulsors (see Chapter 1); this hard kernel is only backwardly revealed de facto; that is, «through the effects of the return of the signifier in our lives» (Friedman 2016: 173). It is the Mœbian topology itself, or that of the topological torus, which already comprises the idea of a place within, a place which is internally excluded (or externally included).

From this comes the proviso on the insufficiency of analytical/synthetical judgements when facing this *extime* reality of the object. Its reality can be grasped, or asymptotically *deduced*, only by the failures of the drive; failures which are, once again, *constitutive* of drive itself. These productive failures of the drive are what is revealed in psychoanalysis via the notion of sublimation.

6 The Object of the Real: The Two Asymmetries of the Lacanian Registers

So far, we've been following the suggestion of a Borromean partition of objects. By treating the Lacanian registers as tools to isolate specific types of entities, we are consequently led to describe what kind of entities are the objects in the Real. If symbolic objects are values and imaginary objects are gestures, matters become more complicated when trying to portray real objects as autonomous entities. The difficulty here arises for a specific reason which is already to be found in Lacan's corpus in its entirety, notably the way in which this register is slowly introduced and elaborated by the psychoanalyst.

We should point out that it is with the 'latest' Lacan (the Lacan of the One, the sinthome and topology) that the Real rises to its highest conceptualization. Prior to that, the Real is treated as subordinated to the other two registers, the Symbolic and the Imaginary. However, I would like to recall here our argument on the asymmetry of the symbolic if taken with the other two registers (see Chapter 1). That is, in *naming* them, the three registers are forced into their symbolic abstraction, thus losing their peculiar character. The point to be underlined here is that as one moves on to the latest Lacan, this asymmetry is *not* resolved by placing the three registers *on equal footing*, but rather by repeating another kind of asymmetry that this time puts the Real as 'special' amongst the whole of the three registers. As such, if we were to summarize Lacan's placing on his Borromean plateaus—by taking it as a whole—we could grasp that his move toward the productive and topological Real of his latest works is not simply to substitute the democracy of the three registers with a *new* psychoanalytical theory *tout court*. Rather, it is more the case that this partial emancipation of the Real in the topological moment is due to a willingness to maintain the idea of a Real as pertaining at the same time to a democratic ontology of the three registers and, complementarily, to what can be thought of (and lived by) the subject as a potentially autonomous register. That is, Lacan reproposes the asymmetry schema of the *nomination* by shifting the prerogatives of the three registers and by allowing *another* 'asymmetrization'; this time, however, producing an asymmetry which, contrary to the first (which was via nomination), places the Real as autonomous both in regard to theoretical investigation (thus the shift from structure to topology) and to the *lived* experience of subjectivity (thus the paradigmatic case of James Joyce or of artistic creativity in general). As such, the Real is not tantamount to the *materiality* of objects, nor it is the theoretical erasing of the other two registers. I argue that the Real, instead, lies in a specific place which is to be put in the middle of this 'false' distinction between the materiality of an object and the Real qua new regime of existence. That is, the reason for the new asymmetry is that the Real, by being in this *limbo* between an autonomous regime and one constituted by the other three registers, brings an unavoidable *tension*. That's the reason why Lacan's latest theorization doesn't point toward a 'liberal' ontology of the three registers—a position which is hardly compatible with the idea of the drive itself—but rather toward a dynamic (i.e. topological) reconceptualization of them.

As such, then, the Real of Lacan is likely to be conceived as an invitation, both theoretical and clinical, to dynamically consider the shift or passage from the *first-order* asymmetry (nomination) to the *second-order* asymmetry (the Real).

In pursuing this passage there's still no room, I suggest, to consider real objects as object-oriented ontology does (in their materiality): the paradigmatic shift of the asymmetry of the registers suggests, instead, a passage from a correlationist moment on the objects to an elevation of subjectivity itself to the Real object. There are traces of Lacan's willingness to make this shift in the whole of the seminars.

For example, during the first seminar, the real is still conceived as the result of the «junction of the symbolic and the imaginary» (Lacan 2014: 90). And Jacques Alain Miller has pointed out that it is arguably with the sixth seminar that the possibility of the passage from the first-order asymmetry to the second-order one is set. He notes that while, in that seminar, Lacan conceives the object as accessible only through fantasy, a few pages later Lacan acknowledges a basic «*difference between drive and fantasy*» (Miller 2014: 22). That is, Lacan can be accused of correlationism only until he will admit the existence of objects as belonging to the Imaginary alone, or—as Miller underlines—as objects coming from the mirror stage. These objects, Miller pinpoints, are objects coming from the image of the other, that is, «the image of one's own body» (ibid.); indeed, if we recall here our Borromean partition, these are still objects as gestures, gratifications from simulated actions which involve the body image.

However, if we compare this key moment which involves the splitting or gap between fantasy and drive to the previous Real as junction of the Symbolic and the Imaginary and, at the same time, to the latest Real as a dynamic non-phantasmatic thing, it is possible to grasp the overall schema that the latest asymmetry will take. These passages testify to the positioning of a post-phantasmatic thing as a matter of rethinking the subject's own position not as having to do with the symbolic automaton or with imaginary (i.e. phantasmal and correlationist) objects, but as acknowledging itself as *the* Real thing.

And, accordingly, it is here where the conundrum with philosophical realism arises (especially if we consider its object-oriented side). This is because the passage from the first-order to the second-order asymmetry, via the reevaluation of the Real 'upon' the Symbolic and the Imaginary, involves more the subject in its bodily and real existence than the mere external objects.

The anti-correlationist could here reproach psychoanalysis for not being able to conceive the Real of objects themselves: indeed, it seems that in the passage from the first scenario to the second, the appointment with objects as material or non-phantasmatic entities is missed.

One could expect Lacan to deliver, in the passage from the object as merely imaginary (fantasy) to the object as Real (in the subjective sense) a middle-stage theorization of objects in their concrete materiality.

Instead, the Real of Lacan ends up revolving around subjectivity (and its lived and bodily enjoyment) as *the Real* thing, thus suggesting the idea that psychoanalysis has little or nothing to do with objects in their mundane causal agency. As I will argue later on, we have plenty of reasons to stick to this Lacanian type of realism rather than conceiving realism as having to do with material objects. This is a position I will defend on the grounds of a basic anti-humanist stance of psychoanalysis, an anti-humanist stance that, indeed, hardly fits the correlationism or anthropocentrism usually ascribed to psychoanalysis.

For now, I will focus on the Real in its first appearance, that of a junction or collapse of the Symbolic and the Imaginary.

There's a short story by Thomas Ligotti which helps us in portraying this dynamic of the Real as the point in which the Symbolic and the Imaginary meet. It is a story about Lucian Dregler, an ancient history scholar obsessed with the mythical figure of the Medusa, a feminine mythical monster with a snake-covered head. A mythical figure whose power is, notoriously, to cause every man who looks directly at her to be turned into a lifeless statue.

The main character is portrayed as looking for the secret of the Medusa. He collects traces and information, he writes in his notebook in his grueling work of research. He takes up books and files to satisfy his obsession with the mythical figure. An obsession which, as Ligotti underlines, has more to do with the conflation of the attraction to the Woman (with capital 'W') and what Dregler himself calls "True Horror". Indeed, in leafing through the different sources, he crystallizes the idea of the Medusa as something belonging to a «psychic underworld where she serve[s] as the image par excellence of romantic panic» (Ligotti 2017: 29).

We are able to find, already in the initial passages of the story, the idea that «the real and the unreal lovingly cohabit in our terror, the only "sphere" that matters» (ibid.: 22). However, it is crucial, in the general economy of Ligotti's story, to see the way in which this trope of terror is conveyed through Dregler's research and the gaze of the Medusa.

Dregler's insatiable curiosity is then epitomized in a quotation he finds in one of the books: «Ah, to be a thing without eyes. What a break to be born a stone!» (ibid.: 28).

What we want to suggest here is that we can treat Dregler's research and the gaze of the Medusa (and *on* the Medusa) as standing for the Symbolic and the Imaginary respectively. That is, the whole of the fiction works by staging the line of the symbolic machinery, exemplified in Dregler jumbling words together in the form of dialogues, interrogations, notes, etc., and by announcing the possible encounter with the Medusa as such.

In fact, the narrative dispositive works so that, at the end, Ligotti describes the encounter itself. The ending is set so to portray the collapse of the Symbolic and the Imaginary in the actual sight of the Medusa which, out of nowhere, finds Dregler unprepared.

Dismayed as he is, «he barely recognized this face, this naked and paralyzed form which he had all but forgotten, except as a lurid figure of speech he once used to describe the uncanny condition of his soul. But it was no longer a charming image of the imagination. Reflection [on the mirror] had given it charm, made it acceptable to sanity» (ibid.: 46–47).

The eyes of the Medusa finally encounter Dregler's, and in a play of mirrors, Ligotti describes the progressive petrification from the lived perspective of Dregler himself: «Deep in the mirror opened another pair of eyes the color of wine-mixed water, and through a dark tangled mass they glared. The eyes met his, but not in a mirror. And the mouth was screaming, but made no sound. Finally, he was reunited, in the worst possible way, with the thing within the room» (ibid.: 47).

A final encounter that Ligotti doesn't refrain from describing as an event in which «[Dregler's] horror had at last found him» (ibid.).

Of course, to most of the Lacanian scholars, this story appears to portray one of the key tropes of the Real as something which is, in turn, the *ungraspable*, the *remainder*, the *unaccountable*, etc., a theme resurfacing here and there especially in Žižekian and/or Badiouian types of reading.

And, accordingly, this is still *not* the Real of the object*s* but it is instead a Real as the collapse of the seriality (qua machinery) of

Symbolization and the Imaginary as object of the body which is, in this case, the gaze of the other.

This reading of Ligotti's story is useful, then, to convey the meaning of what we called second-stage asymmetry; that is, we maintain that one of the *effects* or *ways* of the Real is that of an abrupt closeness to the cause of the desire (object small *a*), which is what manifested through the experience of horror or terror. Real objects are conceivable, if taken as Symbolico-Imaginary collapses, as events. As pinpointed by Julien: «[…]the event» is an «encounter with the *real*» (Julien 2008: 70).

But of course, the Real of Dregler is that of the cause of desire; just remember, concerning this question, the attractiveness (and repulsion alike) of the Medusa concealed in Dregler's words of 'romantic panic'.

The main character freezes because both its ongoing symbolization (exemplified in his theoretical research) and imaginarization suddenly fail. In the gaze of the Medusa the two registers collapse simultaneously: neither seen nor symbolized. The face-to-face encounter with the medusa implies an impasse of both discourse and eye contact: *if you see it, the seeing itself ceases to exist.*

It is an example of a petrifying beauty, as in the case of the sight of the Peafowl's tail; it is as if the Real here blocks both the descriptive and the pragmatic routes of perception (which are, incidentally, already neurologically grounded in the ventral and dorsal pathways respectively).

Anxiety is, to summarize, the (logical) proximity to the cause of desire (object *a*, in Lacan's parlance); that is, desire when it is divested of its phantasmatic support. The gaze of the Medusa is, in this case, what exemplifies the *event* of the rupture itself.

The *mise-en-scène* of Ligotti's tale works precisely because it plays with this impossibility. It stages a "saying", a symbolic machinery, in order to let a Real negatively emerge due to this impossibility of the saying. Horror, as a genre, plays with this evental character of the Real by *short-circuiting communication* deliberately. It 'knows' it can't but short-circuit communication of the Real, but it short-circuits it *better*; the negation of the Symbolic is achieved purposely. Since the Symbolic can't be but the negation of the thing, the horrific machinery works by acknowledging this annihilating character of the Symbolic while at the same time directing it towards its impossibility, the impossibility of saying *all*, of saying *everything*. In this sense, we could also suggest that horror works only if it allows for the un-said to break through the said. But of course, as Ligotti's example shows, it is a very fine art.

7 Object-Oriented Ontology and Fetishism

As I've been stating, the introduction of the Real is pursued through a theoretical strategy which involves a *continuous* dynamic as well as a clear-cut paradigm *shift*. I tried to convey the idea that this peculiar two-sided elaboration on the Real is not theoretically irrelevant and, as such, it should be treated as revealing an intrinsic feature of the Real as such. To summarize once again, the dynamic of the Real is a pattern which involves a passage from the Real as 'subordinated' or 'derivable' from the two other registers (the junction) to the Real as *the Thing* of the subject (or subjectivity as Real).

The anti-correlationist or object-oriented philosopher could here lament that this passage—which is already embedded in the subjective field as a constitutive dynamic—leaves the question of the object per se open and, to some extent, blatantly neglected.

Indeed, what psychoanalysis seems to leave behind in its development is the object in its peculiar (that is, ontologically independent) nature.

What is at stake here is nothing but the position of psychoanalysis within the plateau of concomitant discourses on the human and/or its relationships to other non-human entities. However, already at this level, it is possible to notice a psychoanalytical plea for a post-humanism of the subject.

One of the inaugural moves of object-oriented ontologies is, in fact, that of portraying the landscape of human and non-human objects by reorganizing their hierarchies and—at the same time—by restoring the importance of the agency of non-human things.

It is in this precise intersection where these ontological dispositives intervene so that any anthropocentric or logocentric type of theory is forced to acknowledge its insufficiency. The point, of course, is not to get rid of the importance of signifiers or language, but to acknowledge that philosophical investigation needs to go back to the long-forgotten things in themselves.

For instance, Levi Bryant justly laments that «traditional social and political thought» ignore the domain of the non-human by focusing all too much on «ideology critique, questions of identity, political economy, and so on» (Bryant 2014: 207).

In other words, «while humans are certainly exceptional, for us they are not *ontologically exceptional*. [...] They are beings that dwell among other beings, that act on them and that are acted upon by them» (ibid.: 215). The core of the argument is then of acknowledging that «we are intimately bound up with other entities of the world, coupled and conditioned by them in all sorts of ways» (ibid.: 216).

Now, despite the fact that psychoanalysis deals with subjects and language in their idiosyncratic entanglements, there are plenty of reasons to portray psychoanalysis as an already non-humanist, and hence 'realist', endeavor. All the emphases put on the symptomatic rather than will, the ego, etc., are to be taken as corollaries of the peculiar position of psychoanalytical knowledge as such. A knowledge which, as Lacan recalls, plays a position which eschews (or *should* eschew) the official character of what Foucault calls *episteme*. As such, then, the non-adaptationist core of psychoanalysis is to be understood *also* as its proper placing against the different *savoirs* of, say, economy, psychology, health, etc., in their intra-discursive interplay.

If we look closely to object-oriented philosophical positions, one of the key arguments for such a return to the agency of objects is that of, for instance, climate change. In short, the problem of logocentric (or discourse-centric) philosophical positions is that they are unable to uncover the effects of the agency of objects themselves. The human, so to speak, has left something *behind*: the fact that objects or things, in their assemblages, seem to display an active role in shaping the assemblages themselves; a role which is a constitutive ontological surplus with unpredictable (and often pernicious) outcomes. Indeed, if we are not able to trace the workings of objects/things, this ontological unpredictability of matter will eventually manifest itself in a way that affects the precise place we usually ascribe to the human itself.

However, this argument can hardly be used as a picklock against psychoanalysis (leaving the other possible targets aside). In one passage from the 9th seminar (February the 28th, 1962), Lacan makes some quick remarks on the space explorations made, at that time, by Soviet cosmonauts.

Lacan is there talking about the role of the symbolic machinery, geometries of time and space and the Kantian view on the position of the human within the cosmos. Leaving this detail aside for a moment, what is curious to notice is the hermeneutical turn proposed by Lacan on these crucial events of human history. The modern soul could foresee, in them, the quintessence of the human mastery over nature; that is, the event of space exploration is spontaneously taken as a monument to the human project in its complete appropriation of nature. Lacan's comment on the event suggests, quite on the contrary, that the figure of the cosmonaut precisely shatters the anthropocentric edifice from top to bottom. I won't enter the full details of the argumentation, but I will summarize the argument for such a reversal.

As I underlined, the example of space exploration is introduced in the context of the general relation of Kantianism and psychoanalysis. Lacan takes the event itself to corroborate what I've been calling his "accelerated Kantianism" or his peculiar "anti-Kantianism".

The aim of Lacan is to reconsider Kant's sensible intuition, along with its peculiar account of space and time. The historical event of space exploration, pursued by specific human beings, gives Lacan the opportunity to reconsider the role of the body in regard to Kant's *pure reason* itself.

As I specified above, Lacan refuses the possibility of ascribing the role of synthesis to subjectivity. This trope about the psychoanalytical displacement of synthesis in favor of the structuration of the unconscious resurfaces in Lacan's commentary on space exploration.

He underlines that, for that event to be possible at all, a key shift must occur in the conception of the body itself: the body paradigmatically exemplified in that of the astronaut.

His body is now something like a «shellfish» (ibid.); it is a weakened body, in the guise of a «living pulp» surrounded by a carapace. This emphasis put on the precariousness of the (human) body of the astronaut is made to underline that the *unity* of reason and its categories has now become something like an «exteriorized relation». To cut short, Lacan is here underlining the contrast between the lived and pulsing body and the whole of the symbolic apparatuses which were necessary for that even to occur.

The automaton of repetition, the symbolic machinery, the signifying chain, etc., are now tropes that point towards the idea of *knowledge* as something which commands subjectivity rather than the opposite. Indeed, a few passages later, Lacan states that there's a «contrast» between this body image (as something vulnerable, a 'mollusk') and the idea of a pure «machine which reasons, this *pure reason* [raison pure]» (ibid.).

That is the reason why Lacan puts the emphasis on the fact that all the cosmonaut has to do is «to push a button». This event alone is, for Lacan, an occasion to reestablish that the still too humanist worldview of Kant's space-time intuition is a «false geometry». The fact that the human has accomplished such a thing as exploring outer space is *not* the final proof of its anthropocentrism, but rather—as in the unconscious structured like a language—the proof of the opposite: the human is, and always was, *already* 'post-human'. It is because of the combinatorial logic of the symbolic and the mathematico-scientific apparatuses built upon it that that 'raw' flesh ('the mollusk in the carapace') could be launched into space.

Once again, to use Lacan's own words, «nothing is in common between the subject of knowledge and the subject of the signifier» (Lacan 2001: 53). The emphasis is, then, on the propelling force of that *disembodied* knowledge pursued by signifiers rather than on the intrinsic grandiose events of human history. That's why Lacan often underlines the combinatorial and organizing agency of what is generally ascribable to the artifice: be it implemented in techniques for agriculture, geometry, industry, work, etc. The leitmotiv underlying this line of reasoning is that of a double-sided (or parallel view) history of the *discrete* (taken here to stand for the signifier) over the *manageable*. And, as such, the human is, for psychoanalysis, *already* post-human in that it is caught in its former insufficiency as something manageable by the logic of the symbolic machinery. In underlying this, the view that jumps to the fore is rather the one portrayed by object-oriented philosopher Timothy Morton: the anthropocene, or the prominence of human activity to the detriment of all the rest, is already active in the very first moment of *sapiens*' management of nature.

Morton suggests the idea that it was with agrilogistics (the logistics of agriculture) that human communities began to «trace distinctions between the human and the non-human» (Morton 2018: 47). Distinctions which are coeval with the internal distinctions pursued by structure in the kinship.

For his part, then, Lacan's own 'object-oriented' position suggests a much more radical view of the human. This intrinsic 'non-humanity' (and hence, arbitrariness) of the signifier could be taken to portray the human as a real traumatism of nature. Thus, language is not really interpreted as a mere human product amongst others but, instead, it is what signals the hosting, in nature itself, of this element of imbalance, something like an out-of-control logic of signifiers.

By and large, this should already dissuade the philosopher from placing psychoanalysis within the postmodernist trope of a free proliferation of equipollent symbols: the materiality of signifiers is as much a cornucopia as it is a cage with its own rules and constraints (its combinatorial capacity).

This already-post-human character of the symbolic machinery is what compels us to acknowledge the disrupting force of enjoyment as an agency that vertically intersects linearity as such.

Lacan describes that horizontal logic by often recurring to the image of the circle or of circularity. This going around in circles of «the signifier, the Other, knowledge, the signifier, the Other, knowledge, etc.» is, for the psychoanalyst, the place in which «*enjoyment*» intersects the apparatus (Lacan 2001: 8).

This invitation to escape the cage of circularity, by reaching the 'object itself' (object *a*), doesn't equate to becoming realists of *things* but, rather, to acknowledge the Real as an ethical repositioning of the subject to itself; it is a *reductio* of the Other to object *a* (or, from capital 'O' to the small '*a*').

This reduction is directly linked to the body: a body which is not 'regained' or 'reconquered' through a synthetic operation (neither through a re-appropriative Aufhebung), but instead through a change in the position of the subject itself to its object.

It is for this kind of 'realism'—which I call 'ethical' in lack of better denominations—that holds a particularly important position when facing the issue of the object (or of 'objects') when trying to align Lacanianism with philosophical materialisms (especially in its immanentist versions).

As such, to flatten everything to the level of things/objects would imply, more or less, charging them with an energetic or causal value, which Lacan (reading Freud)—reserves instead to object *a*, to the remainder of the workings of signifiers themselves.

To speak about an intrinsic generative power of the object itself shows rather the fantasy of abandoning the distinction between the artifice and its differential and combinatorial dynamic (the 'post-human' machinery) along with the remainder altogether. In this way, the object-oriented scenario seems to flatten everything to a single level in which the object itself must engage in a fight between utilitarian anthropomorphization and its autonomous agency.

As such, then, the psychoanalytical realism is not in complete disregard of objects, but instead replaces them in a peculiar logic from which it is possible to speak about a Real of the subject itself. The latter Real is, to borrow from Zupančič, «that which traditional ontology had to cut off in order to be able to speak of "being *qua* being"» (Zupančič 2017: 44).

And, for its part, object-oriented ontology can be read indeed as a symptomatic attempt to illuminate the very logic of signifiers. As noted by Felice Cimatti: «[…] even if *speculative realism* wants to get rid of the linguistic turn, it fails. It fails because it isn't aware of how much [object-oriented ontology] depends on the lexicon of languages» used in its pursuit (Cimatti 2018: 25).

To be precise, Cimatti concludes that already in «speaking about simple *things* we are completely within the field of language» (ibid.). Indeed, considering the side of speculative or object-oriented scenarios, it isn't hard to notice that, quite often, the ontological plurality (and 'democracy' thereof) of objects is performed by rattling off a plethora of things and by making a plea for their common ontological dignity.

Thus, a chair, a dog, a poem, an earthquake, etc., are often examples of what is at stake with OOO. The confusion then arises between *things* themselves and the lexicon we implement to isolate them.

Along these lines, Cimatti clarifies this internal problem by pinpointing the presence, in these philosophical propositions, of a confusion between *names* and *things*. In the case of Bryant, where things are «differences», it seems that the name is not a way to mark an already given thing, but instead a way to isolate something in the world and transform it into something that we can conceive as *something*; the name becomes equivalent to a «procedure» (ibid.: 27). It produces the thing, in that it makes it thinkable as an autonomous and self-sufficient entity. The Other as a *place* or *treasure* of language means exactly this: I receive a set of instructions to read *my own being* as a thing. But, as I've already underlined, for Lacan it is this insufficiency or incompleteness of the Other which makes the subject's self-correspondence impossible: the object of subjectivity is not to be found in the lexicon nor in the Other, it is an excess or negentropic remainder of the activity of language as such.

Cimatti's critique can be read along the lines of what Lezra is trying to convey when speaking about abstraction in the Marxist tradition: «I refer to a mug, a potato, a table, a phrase, virginity, labor, a rose among other roses, conscience, and each one, ever so different from all the other roses, potatoes, virginities, and so on, is like every other inasmuch, and only inasmuch, as each individual I point to, here and now, can be converted into an abstract (Marx: the "ideal") form» (Lezra 2018: 70).

The reason behind the emphasis on the 'ethical' realism *versus* the 'ontological' one is due, then, to this peculiar feature of ontology to confuse things/objects with their abstractions or—in our case—with the lexicon.

Since I propose to read this possibility as a symptomatic manifestation of ontology itself, I will expose how this basic confusion between ontology and lexicon is at work in one possible drift acknowledged by psychoanalysis itself: namely, the category of *fetishism*.

In his 1970 intervention on the matter (*Inadequate substitutes of the sexual object*) Freud sets the basic axioms for a definition of fetishism.

The fetish is the result of two concomitant operations: that of *repression* and that of *idealization*. On the one hand, the original object, as in the case of the mother, must be repressed; on the other hand, it must be idealized. At first glance, it seems that these two operations are contradictory to one another. At the same time, it is taken in a negative dynamic which glorifies it.

The paradigmatic case is that of the object of the mother as a first source of pleasure and satisfaction. What happens in fetishism as a pathological outcome is that the desire of the fetish is fixated as a substitution of the normal goal: or, as Freud says, when «the fetish detached from the given person becomes the only sexual object» (Freud 2011: 4).

Freud analyses *en passant* all the possible concurrent explanations of the fetish, thus rejecting Iwan Bloch's idea that the fetish can be extracted from any stimulus coming from the woman, such as «the breast, the eyes, the hair, etc.» (ibid.: 8). However, Freud opposes the idea according to which the fetish is strictly linked to feminine stimulations. His conception is grounded in a more general economy which comprises cases in which the concrete bodily stimulation is not prominent.

Instead, the double-sided operation of fetishism can be clarified by a historical example mentioned by Freud himself, namely that of Christianity: the Middle Ages, according to him, began to «repress sexuality and to belittle the woman figure» because it idealized the mother as the Virgin Mary at the same time (ibid.: 10).

The case of the Virgin Mary is paradigmatic in that it shows how, in order to have a fetish, the basic operation is that of a sexual repression along with a concomitant idealization of the repressed object.

As such, this dynamic is already present in the Christian idea of parthenogenesis: the idea according to which the mother can maintain her reproductive capacity without gaining sexual pleasure from it. Parthenogenesis is a *maquillage* of the primary scene. It is the quintessential form of fetishism. In it, the subject's own position in regard to the primary scene is reorganized through a repression of the sexuality of the object and its idealization into a desexualized holy figure.

By all means fetishism decrees an unavoidable unbalanced economy of violence and/or hatred, since the first sexual object is idealized into an untouchable object. An untouchable object which is consequently accessible only through a disproportionate amount of sexual charge in the form of both worship and/or hatred.

However, this dynamic of fetishism, as a basic perverted repositioning of the subject-object relation, discloses the possibility of its application to diversified domains. And, curiously enough, Freud makes the case of a patient who became a «speculative philosopher» and for whom «names have the greatest importance» (ibid.: 9). For this patient, Freud underlines, something «in the intellectual field happened that is analogous to what happened in the field of eroticism: he took his interest away from *things* and directed it to *words*» (ibid., our italics). A passage worth noting which echoes the Lacanian conception of sublimation as having to do with a kind of 'exaptation'.

It is a dynamic in which the organ pleasure is tantamount to the power of the signifier to cut pieces of the body (the foot, the mouth, the fur, etc.) out of the overall picture: an operation which, as I already underlined, involves a negative operation of repression of the object as source of satisfaction, and its concomitant idealization. That is, since the object isn't accessible as a whole (the mother), the part is charged as a negation of the whole to which it belongs and subsequently taken as the one and only relic of the repressed object.

The scenario of fetishism is, arguably, a scenario ruled by a strict negation of intersubjectivity, for the part which is withdrawn from the whole cuts off the Other as such.

I'm not here following Galloway's reading of object-oriented ontologies as a de facto ideological conceptualization of Marx' fetishism. I'm rather advocating the possibility of reading OOO as a 'litmus test' to enlighten 'philosophical enjoyment' as such. One may argue here that this operation ends up being a pathologization of reason, a possibility which I'm far from suggesting. It is rather the reopening of the question of pleasure as a way to re-inscribe the *forms* of thought into their *sensuous* (and bodily) component (see Chapter 3 where I develop this in full detail); or, one may say, to conceive *speculation*—or the *speculative*—in the Hegelian sense of an unfolding of subjects and objects alike.

However, it is undeniable that (if we take our notion of 'Symbolic objects') by making fetishes of the symbolic objects, capitalism carries out a *mise en abîme* of the symbolic register. Via its utilitarian premonitory symptom, as Lacan argues, and the juridical support of the concept of usufruct (the temporal use without the *possessing*), capitalism could be interpreted as the material realization of philosophical ontology, especially if one looks at the particular financial and/or volatile facet of its late-stage phase. The gadget, the detached and absolute object, along with their material relations, make the world a material One.

However, it must be specified that I don't take the realist or object-oriented moments to stand simply for the pathological; instead, in a pure Hegelian fashion, I take them to be moments of the thing *as such* (where 'the thing' here stands for that compound notion which comprises subject and object alike).

As noted by Le Gaufey, indeed, Lacan's object *a* gains a particular relevance in fetishism itself. He underlines that the fetishist is a classic example of someone who doesn't enjoy the fetish *itself*, but someone who, instead, uses the fetish as a means for a much more mundane goal, that of genital enjoyment (Le Gaufey 2012: 64). Le Gaufey underlines, then, that we are all, to some extent, in the position of the pervert. A statement which can be interpreted (in a 'speculative twist') as meaning that thought itself can host an object-oriented moment.

Another corollary of the fetish is that once the object is dispossessed from the other, it also enters the realm of exchangeability (and, hence, of the artifice). It is a dynamic masterfully displayed in Dominique Aury's erotic novel *Histoire d'O* (written under the name of Pauline Réage).

It tells the story of a girl, O, who is persuaded by her lover to give herself as an instrument of pleasure in a Sadeian scenario. This almost spontaneous dispossession of her own body implies a kind of commodification of its parts: «Her hands are not hers, neither her breasts, neither—especially—the orifices of her body» (Réage 2014: 38).

And Lacan doesn't hesitate to speak of the body as an «inheritance held in usufruct» (Lacan 2011a: 4); subsequently stating this in legal terms such as «[the] division, distribution, retribution» of «enjoyment» (ibid.).

As such, this *usufruct*-like nature of the body of the Other is what Lacan synthesizes in the term *amur* (see above), a term which comprises the idea of the body as something like a patchwork of traces (ibid.: 6).

Alongside the Freudian double-dynamic of the fetish it is necessary, then, to introduce the element of the artifice, the legal, the exchangeable.

Already at the semantic level, the word 'fetish' comprises this feature of exchangeability. The word 'Fetiço' comes from the Latin 'facticius', which means 'artificial', but it can also have the meaning of 'sorcery' (Iacono 2001: 37). The meaning of the fetish is split into the artificiality of exchange (or the human traffic) and the charm of the absolute. As such, the genealogy of the fetish is what demands, Iacono underlines, the necessity to trace the «symbolic process of substitution» which makes it possible.

This means that the absolute enjoyment of the fetish, or its charming power, doesn't strictly depend on bodily stimulation, but that it can take any object as its support. It can be a whole place, as Combray for Proust (Schuster 2016: 59). It is more a matter of the parts/whole relation along with the geography (taken in its broader sense) they imply.

Lacan's distinction between organ enjoyment (as the only outcome of phallic enjoyment) is not to be understood as an impossibility of love *tout court*. Rather, the non-existence of the sexual relation is meant to be understood as acknowledging that the non-relation between sexes is not simply erased through love (such as Plato's fantasies of the Two-in-One), but instead *displayed* by it.

Something happens which resembles physics' indeterminacy principle: an oscillation between parts and whole which is constitutive of this non-relation.

Another key word which helps us in understanding this relation between the piece and the whole is the word 'porn'.

As such, the word 'porn' has its roots in the Greek 'πόρνη', which is translatable as 'prostitute'. However, πόρνη comes from the verb 'πέρνημι', 'I sell'. That is, the feminine figure of the 'Porneous' Venus doesn't simply stand for a woman who sells her body, but—more deeply—it ascribes a given value to different pieces of the body, making them 'social'. The 'graphing' (graphein) of the salable literally implies that once a piece of body is evaluated per se it enters the artificial realm of exchangeability. Porno-graphy reveals the non-existence of the sexual relation by writing down the single detached objects of the body. At the opposite of courtly love, it shows that while you can't enjoy the *relation*, you surely can enjoy the *sexual* (but without the relation). However, it is a sexual conceived as the possibility of enjoying singular objects, detached and valuable parts.

The logion «there's no sexual relation» is therefore conceivable not as the mere—and empirically false—fact that there is no sexual *intercourse*, but that «sexual relation», in order to exist, behaves as an oscillating entity. It shows a pattern which resembles Heisenberg's uncertainty principle. That is, the fact that if you measure the position of a given particle, you miss the information regarding its speed. Conversely, if you measure its speed, you miss its position. Thus, measuring one of them gives you information on one aspect but precludes access to the other. In the same fashion, «there's no sexual relation» implies that there's no "mesoscopic" level of description, nor any middle space, between the shifting from the "courtly" to the "detached piece". «There's no sexual relation» just means that sexual relation is a matter of a continuous (and always changing) oscillatory pattern between the romance of a distant enchantment of the object and the enjoyment of the non-personal (because it is detached) object.

If we merge this dynamic into the Freudian schema of subject-to-object relation, we have that love is what ascribes dignity to comedy. It elevates the non-relation of the Two to the impossible of the One.

I argue that it is exactly in these attempts of object-oriented ontologies to re-enchant the world that lies the conundrum between psychoanalysis and philosophy. For example, Levi Bryant states that «it has become fashionable to argue that an object is *nothing but* its relations», a position traditionally held by «French structuralism» and inspired by «Hegelian thought» (Bryant 2011: 270).

According to Bryant, what is wrong here is that if we put everything in the Procrustean bed of «differential relations» (Lacan's artifice, exchangeability, etc.) we're missing the positivity of substance as such.

What I've been trying to show is that even the problem of substance and the opposition between differentiality and positivity must be understood through the lens of Lacan's parts-to-whole relation. That is, even the philosopher is not immune from trying to 'pacify' the non-existence of the sexual relation. The emphasis on the Hegelian meaning of the speculative is used here to counterbalance the very position from which a subject is 'speculating'. Speculation, inasmuch as it involves the positing of the 'parts-to-whole' dynamic object, must be understood in a framework which includes the subject-to-object relation in its sensuous economy.

8 Speculation and the Thing-Body

The idea according to which speculation is an incarnation of the subject-to-object relation taken on the side (this time) of the sensuous is by no means meant to undertake objectivity. Here lies, in fact, another possible counterargument against the *ordo desiderandi* (*vs. ordo cognoscendi*) of such a conception of the object. That is, the idea according to which one's reflection on the relation itself taken as an object invalidates realism (or objectivity). I argue, instead, that *both* this supposedly correlationism of psychoanalysis and the realism of philosophical speculation are to be understood in a pluralistic way: that is, they are two subtropes or developments of the subject-object relation itself. Something which resembles what Hegel refers to as 'the Absolute'. A concept which doesn't stand for a closed totality, as the traditional 'Vulgate' presupposes. It rather presupposes an endless work of overcoming(s), reductions, openings, etc. which can be read as the proof of an unavoidable lack of ultimate sense or meaning (the 'Other' as incomplete).

For its part, indeed, psychoanalysis is not the attempt to reach a final equilibrium in the form of an absence of tension; it is neither a peace between the subject and its own Other nor a flattening into a homeostatic beatitude. It can be stated, instead, that the only goal of psychoanalysis is to fail: that is, to show that there's never an end-point in which linguistic satisfaction ceases to exist.

What Freud and Lacan opened up is the possibility of a reopening of the Thing and, by the same token, a reopening of the relation between the subject and the object.

This peculiar psychoanalytical conception of the object as an open entity owes a lot to the particular way in which Lacan reads Hegel. Or, at least, it is a conception which is symptomatic of the relation of Lacan to Hegel in general.

It can be stated that, on the one hand, Lacan's theoretical debt to Hegel seems to vanish if one reads the whole Lacanian corpus in its temporal progression. On the other hand, however, the general picture, namely the one comprising the first Lacan of desire and recognition and the 'Joycean' Lacan, rather shows the peculiar psychoanalytical torsion of Hegel himself. Let's see why.

The 6th and 10th Seminars, for example, are key places where it is possible to find a clear formulation of desire in terms of recognition by the Other. The subject, Lacan states, wants to be «recognized» by the Other (Lacan 2007: 27). By demanding to be recognized by the Other, the subject wants to become an object in the eyes of the Other itself.

Lacan's latest effort, instead, was to free psychoanalysis from the coordinates of recognition or from Hegel himself. This time, the problem of the subject is not so much that of escaping the struggle for recognition, but rather a matter of *installing* and subsequently *de-installing* the Name-of-the-Father, this concept standing for a function of 'socialization' of the subject's desire against the backdrop of a not-yet (or incomplete) detachment from the object of the mother. This operation hardly fits within the scenario of psychoanalysis as a pan-Œdipal dispositive. It is an operation in which, thanks to this 'downbeat and upbeat' rhythm of the Name-of-the-Father, the subject recognizes at the same time its necessity and its futility (or the possibility of getting rid of it).

In this operation, it is the subject *alone* with its enjoyment that counts; that is, it is the moment in which the subject acknowledges the necessity of the artifice and its contingent and creative—so to speak—nature.

This emancipation or detachment from the unity of the mother's body pursued by the Name-of-the-Father is already, we must underline, an operation which involves a linguistic and a bodily element. It is a passage which has, however, a linguistic/bodily precondition that the psychoanalyst Piera Aulagnier describes in these terms:

> The only necessary condition for the psyche to become active is that to the work of the infant's psyche is added the prosthetic function of the mother's psyche, a prosthesis that, for me, is comparable to that of the breast, in so far as it is an extension of one's own body, because it is an

> object whose juncture with the mouth is a vital necessity, but also because it is an object that gives erogenous pleasure, which is a *vital necessity* for its psychical functioning. (Aulagnier 2001: 14)

It is a moment in which the bodily and the psychic are already entangled and co-dependent. And it is this very codependence that unfolds, later on, in the pleasure of the object per se, or of the 'speculative' in our sense.

However, it is interesting to underline what lies in the middle of these two Lacanian moments, namely the 'recognition moment' and the latest one of the sinthome. One of the main reasons (if not the only one) for the psychoanalytical abandonment of Hegel is the rejection of the possibility of synthesis.

It should be already noted that this rejection has a particular psychoanalytical reason that other philosophical anti-Hegelianisms (such as Deleuze's) do not share.

Fredric Jameson has noted that there's a peculiar misunderstanding in reading Hegel's triad of thesis-antithesis-synthesis; that is, a vulgarization of it in the form of a method or development (Jameson 2010: 18).

In other words, it is commonly read as a stubborn systematization on the part of Hegel himself. He also pinpoints that it is with psychoanalysis that the well-known dialectic has its elements displaced or shifted in their order. It is precisely to get rid of the nightmare of closure (being it in the form of the Absolute or of synthesis) that «contemporary philosophy» or «Freud» tend to «reverse this order and to affirm that is the antithesis which produces the thesis in the first place, in order to generate the ideological illusion of the synthesis as such» (ibid.).

And, as we noted, even Lacan can't escape this operation. Psychoanalysis modifies the dialectical scenario by giving antithesis the role of commencement. At the beginning lies a fundamental rupture or non-coincidence of subjectivity: the subject is already alienated in that language creates ab initio the condition for the struggle for recognition. In other words, at the beginning there's the Other as incomplete and the subject's objectification through the recognition it demands.

Lacan starts from the premises of this Hegelian recognition of/by the Other, but then falls prey to the idea that the dialectic implies systematic closure. Indeed, for him the Absolute is the abolition of enjoyment (Lacan 2001: 36). While Hegel can function as a first-stage 'tool' to acknowledge the state of subjectivity, it must be later on put down due to the perils of systematic closure or—even worse—teleology.

However, even if Lacan is generally keen to avoid this outcome, the overall route from the antithesis to the final 'unstable' synthesis of the dynamic of the Name-of-the-Father allows us to portray a much more refined schema.

The progression goes from the antithesis as recognition (or 'master-slave') moment, then passes through the materialization of Hegel with the more 'Marxist' Lacan (Seminar 17th), and ends up in a moment in which at the place of the Other we find the Name-of-the-Father.

I would like to suggest that this scenario suggests a much refined dialectic, a dialectic which is not one of re-appropriation or systematicity, but rather of a *minor synthesis*; a psychoanalytical minor synthesis which maintains the object (as in the Hegel of the *Logic*) as entertaining with the subject a constitutive ambivalent and hence dynamic relationship. This *unfulfilled* synthesis (of Joyce in regard to his father, for example) in its double 'upbeat-downbeat' rhythm corresponds to a double dynamic of appropriation and abandonment.

The sinthome (the term with which Lacan names this new subjective position) is what allows for an openness to creativity and novelty; and, I want to underline, it is not a kind of 'weak synthesis', but rather a re-commencement, always renewable, on the side of the subject.

This third Lacanian moment is not a spiral folding of the two preceding moments; it is instead a possibility for the subject to become one-with-the-thing, an entity which is *directly* productive, this last term meaning here the broad meaning of *art* in the Lacanian context.

Prior to this possibility, the subject is still at odds with its own enjoyment. Indeed, in the second moment (that between recognition and sinthome), Lacan portrays the relationship between signifiers/repetition and enjoyment as having to do, this time, with the economical.

This is why, amongst the numerous mathemes and formulas left by the psychoanalyst, it seems that—*ipse dixit*—his object *a* holds a peculiar and special position.

During Seminar XVII, as we already pinpointed, Lacan explicitly reveals the deep link between his object *a* and Marx' *Mehrwert*, plus-value (Lacan 2001: 130–131). The underground matrix underlying both plus-value and object small *a* is the homology they show in relation to the concept of 'work'. That is, the two concepts share the feature of being a remainder of some type of work carried out in some specific domain. Thus every time there's 'work', there's always a part or piece left out. Lacan famously ascribes this general property of work to the theoretical legacy of thermodynamics, namely, to entropy.

For this reason—and following the basic laws of thermodynamics—anything ascribed to the category of 'work' is constitutively the herald of parts *en plus*, whether it is the case of the mechanical work of factory workers or the work of signifiers. Every time there's work, you get a remainder, a detached piece.

The *automaton* and the automaton of the machine are homologous in that they are always hiding object small *a*—the remainder—as both their most inner cause and their inevitable outcome. Which is why enjoyment, in this schema, is a matter of dispersion.

And Lacan quickly links this basic dispersion of enjoyment (in repetition) to the issue of masochism, as a prototypical subjective stance (Lacan 2001: 51). That's where the third moment is supposed to take place: namely to overcome the basic masochism of a subject stuck in its will to re-collect or reappropriate the dispersion.

As such, then, this failed attempt is what unfolds the possibility of a 'reduction' into a productive scarcity (sinthome). An event or possibility which is, as one may notice, directly linked to the body.

It is a passage which implies neither a *discovery* nor a more intricate *understanding* (Cimatti 2016: 130). To summarize, it is more about *seeing* what was already there in the first place, and seeing it for what it is, a «thing-body» (ibid.).

It is a thing-body, to use Cimatti's parlance, in which knowledge (or the craving thereof) has rounded the mark. It is a position which results from traveling on the Mœbian strip and from the acknowledgment of the autonomous agency of language.

To express this in other words, it is a moment of auto-nomy as the opposite of hetero-nomy: a law which doesn't come from the Other, but from '*a*' (or 'other' in small letters).

This repositioning of the subject as a thing (or, as 'the Thing') comes really close to Hegel's own anti-correlationism. In the second preface to the *Logic*, for example, Hegel makes it clear that the idea according to which *thoughts* are put between *us* and *things* simply reduces things themselves to «empty abstractions» (Hegel 1981: 15).

This anti-Kantian critique implies that the Thing, for Hegel, is already an ontologically rich entity and that 'content' always contains 'forms' and their possibilities. Indeed, after making this anti-correlationist point, he pinpoints that there's a logic («natural logic») which silently interweaves «all the representations, the goals, the interests and the actions» (ibid.).

This becoming thing-body of the subject is a matter of acknowledging that the Real of the subject is a place of infinite variations (or, of variations on variations).

It's a traversing of the subject's own material (fantasies, symptoms, etc.) in order to lose the dream of an ultimate reappropriation and embody, instead, this Thing that he/she is.

This reworking of the speculative finds its roots, again, in the Hegelian distinction between things/objects («*Dinge*») and the essence of things («*die Sache*»). It is when differentiating form and content that Hegel warns us not to disregard the latter by privileging the first. That is, it is a plea not to fall prey to reason's instrumental use of logic, such as in the case of the principle of non-contradiction. Against this mechanic and detached stance of reason, it is content (object small *a*, we may say) which is already *in-formed*. And it is its concept that opens the space for its development(s).

Psychoanalysis is, for its part, the attempt to rethink the 'object' of subjectivity, the real cause of desire, as what silently underlies its unfoldings.

References

Arribas, S., & Rouse, H. (2011). *Egocracy: Marx, Freud and Lacan*. Chicago and London: University of Chicago Press.

Aulagnier, P. (2001). *The Violence of Interpretation: From Pictogram to Statement*. Hove: Brunner and Routledge.

Balmès, F. (2011). *Structure, logique, aliénation: Recherches en psychanalyse*. Paris: ERES.

Benveniste, É. (2010). *Problemi di linguistica generale*. Milano: Il Saggiatore.

Bryant, L. (2011). The Ontic Principle: Outline of an Object-Oriented Ontology. In L. Bryant, N. Srnicek, & G. Harman (Eds.), *The Speculative Turn* (pp. 261–278). Melbourne: re.press.

Bryant, L. (2014). *Onto-Cartography: An Ontology of Machines and Media*. Edinburgh: Edinburgh University Press.

Cimatti, F. (2016). Divenire Cosa, Divenire Corpo. *Atque materiali tra filosofia e psicoterapia, 18*, 107–132.

Cimatti, F. (2018). *Cose: Per una filosofia del reale*. Torino: Bollati Boringhieri.

Deleuze, G. (2010). Che cos'è un dispositivo? In D. Borca (Ed.), *Due regimi di folli e altri scritti (Testi e interviste 1975–1995)* (pp. 279–287). Torino: Einaudi.

Deleuze, G., & Guattari, F. (2017). *Millepiani: Capitalismo e schizofrenia*. Napoli and Salerno: Orthotes.

Didi-Huberman, G. (2016). *Davanti all'Immagine: Domanda posta ai fini di una storia dell'arte*. Milano and Udine: Mimesis.

Falk, D. (2015). *Lingua madre: Cure materne e origini del linguaggio*. Torino: Bollati Boringhieri.

Freud, S. (2001). Per la genesi del feticismo. In S. Misura (Ed.), *Figure del feticismo* (pp. 6–18). Torino: Einaudi.

Friedman, M. (2016). Torus and Identification: The Beginning of Lacanian Mathematics. In M. Friedman & S. Tomšič (Eds.), *Psychoanalysis: Topological Perspectives* (pp. 153–190). Bielefeld: Transcript.

Galloway, A. (2013). The Poverty of Philosophy: Realism and Post-Fordism. *Critical Inquiry, 39*, 347–366.

Hegel, G. F. (1981). *Scienza della logica*. Roma-Bari: Laterza.

Iacono, A. M. (2001). L'ambiguo oggetto sostituto. Il feticismo di Marx e Freud. In S. Mistura (Ed.), *Figure del feticismo* (pp. 35–59). Torino: Einaudi.

Jeannerod, M. (2006). *Motor Cognition: What Actions Tell to the Self.* Oxford: Oxford University Press.

Julien, P. (2008). Du Nom-du-Père au Père-du-Nom comme sinthome. In P. Julien (Eds.), *Psychose, Perversion, névrose: La lecture de Jacques Lacan* (pp. 67–77). Toulouse: ERES.

Kant, I. (2006). *Prolegomeni ad ogni futura metafisica.* Bari: Laterza.

Kiarina Kordela, A. (2007), *$urplus: Spinoza, Lacan.* Albany: State University of New York Press.

Kiarina Kordela, A. (2017). *Essere, Tempo, Bios: Capitalismo e ontologia.* Verona: ombre corte.

Lacan, J. (2001). *Il Seminario Libro XVII: Il rovescio della psicoanalisi (1969–1970).* Torino: Einaudi.

Lacan, J. (2002). *Scritti.* Torino: Einaudi.

Lacan, J. (2003). *Il Seminario Libro XI: I quattro concetti fondamentali della psicoanalisi (1964).* Torino: Einaudi.

Lacan, J. (2006a). *Il Seminario Libro II: L'io nella teoria di Freud e nella tecnica della psicoanalisi (1954–1955).* Torino: Einaudi.

Lacan, J. (2006b). *Le Séminaire Livre XVI: D'un Autre à l'autre (1968–1969).* Paris: Seuil.

Lacan, J. (2007). *Il Seminario Libro X: L'angoscia (1962–1963).* Torino: Einaudi.

Lacan, J. (2008). *Il Seminario Libro VII: L'etica della psicoanalisi (1959–1960).* Torino: Einaudi.

Lacan, J. (2011a). *Le Séminaire Livre XIX: …ou pire (1971–1972).* Paris: Seuil.

Lacan, J. (2011b). *Il Seminario Libro XX: Ancora (1972–1973).* Torino: Einaudi.

Lacan, J. (2013). *Altri scritti.* Torino: Einaudi.

Lacan, J. (2014). *Il Seminario Libro I: Gli scritti tecnici di Freud (1953–1954).* Torino: Einaudi.

Lacan, J. (2016). *Il Seminario Libro VI: Il desiderio e la sua interpretazione (1958–1959).* Torino: Einaudi.

La Mantia, F. (2017). L'altro e l'uncino. Su un aspetto del pronome "Tu" in Lacan. *La psicoanalisi, 62*, 88–104.

Le Gaufey, G. (2012). *L'objet a: Approches de l'invention de Lacan.* Paris: EPEL.

Lew, R. (2013). Identité de structure entre le schématisme de Marx et celui de Freud. In S. Lippi & P. Landman (Eds.), *Marx, Lacan: L'Acte révolutionnaire et l'acte analytique* (pp. 131–150). Paris: ERES.

Lezra, J. (2018). *On the Nature of Marx's Things: Translation as Necrophilology*. New York: Fordham University Press.
Ligotti, T. (2017). *Nottuario*. Milano: Il Saggiatore.
Marrou, É. (2016). La bouche qui dit «Nous»: De l'intentionnalité collective à l'autorité en première personne du pluriel. In *Klesis, 2016*(34), 14–37.
Marx, K. (2013). *Il Capitale: Libro primo*. Torino: UTET.
Menninghaus, W. (2013). *La promessa della bellezza* (S. Tedesco, Ed.). Palermo: Aesthetica Edizioni.
Miller, J. A. (2014). Il filo del fantasma. In *La Psicoanalisi, 55*, 19–33. Roma: Astrolabio.
Morton, T. (2018). *Noi, esseri ecologici*. Roma and Bari: Laterza.
Nietzsche, F. (2018). *Genealogia della morale: Uno scritto polemico*. Milano: Adelphi.
Rastier, F. (2003). *Arti e scienze del testo: Per una semiotica delle culture*. Roma: Meltemi.
Perniola, M. (2004). *Il Sex Appeal dell'Inorganico*. Torino: Einaudi.
Réage, P. (2014). *Histoire d'O*. Milano: Bompiani.
Sasso, G. (1999). *Struttura dell'oggetto e della rappresentazione*. Roma: Astrolabio.
Schuster, A. (2016). *The Trouble with Pleasure: Deleuze and Psychoanalysis*. Cambridge and London: MIT Press.
Serres, M. (2007). *The Parasite*. Minneapolis and London: University of Minnesota Press.
Skriabine, P. (2004). Clinic and Topology: The Flaw in the Universe. In E. Ragland & D. Milovanovic (Eds.), *Lacan: Topologically Speaking* (p. 81). New York: Other Press.
Soler, C. (2016). *Gli affetti lacaniani*. Milano: FrancoAngeli.
Tomšič, S. (2015). *The Capitalist Unconscious: Marx and Lacan*. London: Verso books.
von Uexküll, J. (2010). *Ambienti animali e ambienti umani: Una passeggiata in mondi sconosciuti e invisibili*. Macerata: Quodlibet.
von Uexküll, J. (2013). Come vediamo la natura e come la natura vede se stessa? In A. Pinotti & S. Tedesco (Eds.), *Estetica e science della vita* (pp. 39–81). Milano: Raffaello Cortina.
Zupančič, A. (2017). *What Is Sex?* Cambridge and London: MIT Press.

3

The Real of the Body: *Fantasies and Intimate Diagrams*

Previously, I suggested that the Real of the Lacanian Thing must be understood as having to do with the body itself (or the 'thing-body'). The speculative, in this sense, has less to do with the material and autonomous agency of things/objects than it has with the (Hegelian-like) character of the Thing as a place in which the the subject-object relation is considered as One. In other words, it is a plea for a Real of subjectivity in which the speculative moment is already inscribed in its unfolding. It is a trope which, as I mentioned, gets rid of the hard distinction between form and content. Or, rather, gets rid of the idea that the content of such a Thing is to be separated from its actual unfoldings and developments. It is in such a scenario that the Real as the 'Real of the body' makes its entrance.

This speculative Thing must be thought of as an always developing entity which reassures the prominence of the body as its first source. However, it is a body which has gone through the signifiers.

Given this conception of the body, a problem arises. As noted by some scholars, when «[r]esponding to the accusation that Lacan's revision of Freud idealizes the signifier at the expense of the biological and the material, Lacanians will frequently make use of allusions to the body

Y. Di Liberto, *Being and Contemporary Psychoanalysis*,
The Palgrave Lacan Series, https://doi.org/10.1007/978-3-030-18476-6_3

as 'written by the signifier', but systematic attempts to reconstruct a Lacanian theory of the body are rare» (Eyers 2012: 129).

Indeed, it is a common reading (and sometimes an easy escape) to state that the body is written or 'covered' with signifiers. One may posit here a critique of Lacanianism more broadly, and claim that within his works themselves it is hard to find any conception of the body.

However, I will work out this problem by underlining, on the contrary, all the concrete traces of a Lacanian Real of the body. As Eyers further suggests, «the Lacanian body [is] not as the 'material' or substance that is gradually taken up within the idealizations of the signifying chain, but rather as a complex materiality that complements and subverts the signifier that *it nonetheless relies upon*, constituting and undermining the field of signification in a logic familiar to us as that of the Real, of the function of the paradox of constitutivity and dissolution» (ibid., our italics).

The emphasis must be put here on the relying of the body upon the signifier. Indeed, as I previously suggested, it is with the latest Lacan that the asymmetry between the three registers takes the shape of a new asymmetry in which the Real (of the Borromean taken as a whole) has the primacy.

In doing this, I align this 'asymmetrical' account of the Real to Duane Rousselle's plea for a Lacanian Realism. Rousselle takes on the famous Freudian logion '*Wo es war soll, Ich werden*', then reframed by Lacan as 'I must come to the place where the id was', as having to do with a *before* that stands for the 'it' of the Real. This 'before', he pinpoints, «could, in turn, be linked to the arche-fossil of Meillassoux's philosophy» (Rousselle 2018: 172). And, as our asymmetrical hypothesis claims, it is a moment in which «the symbolic and imaginary orders, which appear to us to be uniquely human […], *must* come from the 'it' of the real, that is, the pre-historic place of things or animals» (ibid.).

However, while I agree with Rousselle on the prominence of the 'it' (the Real) as an inscription *tabula* for the whole of the three registers, I suggest that psychoanalysis is the practice by which the subject is moved to uncover a Real as *post-historical* rather than *pre-historical*. That is, I still maintain the fact that such a pre-historic Real is a result of the entering of the human into the *presence-absence* oscillation (Freud's *fort-da*); and, as such, it is a mythical Real. For this reason, what I propose is instead—but aligning myself with Rousselle's final plea—the idea that the *post-historical* (or post-correlational) Real is something which breaks with the 'three' of the Borromean knot.

This suggests, in short, the idea of a Real of bodily subjectivity stuffed with creative (and authentically *new*) possibilities.

It is, to borrow from the previous chapter, the acknowledging of the speculative movement as a movement of the Real; or, in other words, as the subjective possibility of gravitating around object small *a* in a way which unfolds novelty.

Indeed, in order to do so the subject must overcome the idea of the object qua correlate. To translate this in psychoanalytical terms, it is the idea of the object as non-imaginary and non-phantasmatic.

It is a possibility already inscribed in what we've been calling imaginary objects or simulated bodily gestures. This new bodily Real is what overcomes the correlational subjectivity: «[…] for Lacan the limits of the real of the body exceed the limits of the specular body, as the real of the body opens onto the dimension of the spatiality of being, a spatiality which includes the object which is *extimate* to the body of the subject» (Cohen 2016: 246).

It is a repositioning of subject's relation to drive itself, not as an endless (and circular) correlation, but as a recognition of a Real which «exceeds the corporeal imaginary limits of the body» (ibid.). It is, in other words, what I've been calling the 'speculative': a possibility of reading drive itself as a productive and creative dynamic.

In order to portray this overall picture, I will borrow some key concepts from the physico-geometrical notion of the *diagram* (as it is found in Gilles Châtelet), the idea of incarnated fantasies (Didier Anzieu) and the idea that the body is a surface of inscriptions for signifiers. This last element is hidden in plain sight in the teachings of Lacan himself. But, in any case, it doesn't suggest the idea of the body as essentially equal to a still piece of matter. The logical—or the *topological*—nature of this Real points instead to an openness to creativity. A creativity which is not a simple 'once-and-for-all' arbitrary inscription of signifiers upon the body, but that unleashes all its possibilities as tropes of the body itself. It is a matter, to summarize, of space and geometry and how these are involved with the diagrammatization of enjoyment.

1 The Body Is No-Thing

If we take a look into modern anatomy, it is baffling to see how it started. Although there are already traces of anatomical schemata in the Middle Ages, it is with the meticulous work of anatomists such as Andreas Vesalius (sixteenth century) that an *interest* on the body took place. It is the birth of a particular type of gaze. But if we look closely on the nature of this anatomical gaze, he will bow to a self-contradictory fact. That is, *anatomy started by tearing out the skin*. As the psychoanalyst Didier Anzieu accurately remarks, the (often) unspoken epistemology of scientific discourses regarding the body simply revolves around the «surface/nucleus» distinction (Anzieu 2017: 9).

One has to remove the outside to see the inside or, remove the "cortex" to see the "substance".

It is as if the true object of enquiry has to be ripped away from its *first* part: the skin. In order to say something about the body's composition, the anatomical gaze gets rid of one of its constitutive organs.

Psychoanalytically, then, the discourse on the *anatomical* Real of the body started with a «mutilation fantasy» (ibid.: 20). It is worth to notice that things didn't change a lot since then. Amongst psychoanalysts themselves, there's an ongoing theoretical trend by which any discourse on the body (without signifiers/language) begins by speculating on drive (Lacan's object small *a*), lessening the importance of fantasy. In other words, it is as if the Real of the body can be investigated without the *shape* it takes in fantasy. The main result of such approaches is that «it seems that we renew the body from the side of the real, but conceived as the real of medicine» (Tyszler 2013: 265) or—which is the same—as the real of physiology. Once mutilated, once deprived of its dynamic form (fantasy), the body keeps running out of our grasp. Even though Lacan famously claimed that the constitution of the body as a whole is both imaginary and symbolic (we're referring here to the *Mirror stage*), he nonetheless puts a lot of effort in underlining the Real of the *fantasy*. The body is first and foremost an «instrument of enjoyment [*jouissance*]» (ibid.: 271), hence the importance of the fantasy (*fantasme*).

In 1961, during one of his seminars (session of March the 22nd, 1961), Lacan claims that «body's fragmentation [*morcellement*]» is the most basic fantasy. The "first" gaze, as the all-too-famous mirror stage explains, has precisely the function of overcoming this basic fragmentation of the body by giving to it an imaginary *one-ness*. This imaginary oneness also involves a symbolic dimension, for the reflected image on the mirror is made *one* only after the symbolic "authentication" made by the Other: «Look! It's you! How cute!», says the caregiver.

The jubilant event only sets the roots for fantasy in its general structure. If the body is the instrument of enjoyment and if it is nonetheless an always *reconfiguring* entity (by the gaze), it follows that fantasy must inherit this very *configuration* as well. Drives are «echoes in the body of the fact that there's a saying» (Lacan 2006: 16). This *silent* saying is the invisible imperative of enjoyment carried out by the phantasmal structure. More important, though, is the fact that just after the mentioned statement, Lacan claims that for this *echo* (fantasy) to resonate, a «sensible body» (ibid.) is needed. The two key senses mentioned by Lacan are *hearing* and the *gaze*, the two main ingredients of the mirror stage: the "symbolic certification" by the Other (*hearing*) and the imaginarization of a Body-made-One (*gaze*). This view is far from pacificatory, for what Lacan seems to suggest—at first—is the fantasy of the body as *sack*. The forming capacity of the gaze gives us only the *sack*: a Oneness, but nonetheless empty. He further remarks that «nonetheless, an empty sack is still a sack, the *one that is imaginable only because of the ex-sistence and the consistency of the body as sack*. [...] The Imaginary shows here its homogeneity to the real, and that this homogeneity depends only on the *number* as it is binary, 1 or 0» (ibid.: 17). That is, «Body» is *d'emblée* what can be One or Nothing.

Still, we didn't move any further: Lacan seems just to shift from the mentioned "mutilation fantasy" to the "sack fantasy". And, indeed, the point is exactly this one! The game can change the results every time, for if it is true that the body is this forgotten entity that endlessly exercises its «capturing power» (ibid.: 16), what gives shape to it is the always ongoing activity of *fantasy*, which at the same time creates the possibility for the *dynamization* of the cause of desire (object small *a*) and its unavoidable crystallization into unique singularities (i.e., *subjects*).

This is why Lacan abandons the image of the sack, as Tyszler so clearly remarks:

> There's a certain embarrassment with Freud, that is, the sack of the body. Freud maintains in his way, regarding his conception of the body, the idea of a *sack*, what is inside and what is outside of the body. [...] Lacan's topological work was meant to detach the body from this imaginary of the sack. [...] We ourselves think with our feet, we think with our body. (Tyszler 2013: 269, 270, our italics)

In order to think about the body you have to pass through the category of fantasy. The opposite is also true: to think about fantasy you have to pass through the body. We are already *performatively* halfway in our theoretical journey: we encountered already two different body-fantasies, namely the "mutilated body" and the "body-sack". This is indicative of the fact that if you want to talk about the body you have to look for the *way*(s) by which it enjoys (*fantasy*). Before we develop this precise theme in more theoretical detail—the body-fantasy relation—it is worthwhile to shed some light on an epistemological conundrum which affects psychoanalysis from both the inside and the outside.

This problem involves two different kinds of critiques: (1) Lacan gives an *unhappy* and *empty* account of desire and, (2) Lacan denies the body. It is surprising to discover how fierce these critiques can be in contemporary reflections on human subjectivity. Both of these accusations are paradigmatically represented in Rosi Braidotti's plea for an affirmative politics. While underlining the importance of *embodied* subjectivities, she claims that there are «no traces, [...], in Lacan, of positive vision of desire as *fullness* and *abundance*» (Braidotti 2017: 32–33). She then follows adding that, in Lacanian psychoanalysis, there's a «*denial* of the body» (ibid.: 33, our italics). Both these types of critique fail due to a structural confusion between *ontological* and *epistemological* statements.

Let's address the second critique. During a session of the XIXth seminar, Lacan claims that «What Freud introduces, what they imagine that *I disavow because I talk about the signifier*, it's the return on that fundament which lies in the body, and which makes that, fully independently from the signifiers where it is articulated, it's the four poles that are determined by the emergence of enjoyment[...]» (Lacan 2011: 226, our italics). The «four poles» he's talking about are, notably, the four symbols by which he famously articulated his theory of discourses: S_1, S_2, $\$$ and *a*.

What's important here to notice, however, it's the *hierarchical* order Lacan is portraying. It's not simply that body is *denied* or theoretically irrelevant; it is rather the case of finding a *new* jargon to speak about it.

In psychoanalysis the body was always already there. What these kind of critiques are missing is that the true problem lies *not* in the nature of *ontological* claims but, rather, in *epistemological* ones. That is, Lacan always talked about bodies; the problem was to critically avoid the jargons of psychiatry, biology, physiology and so on. Why is it that when humanity speculated on the body it gave rise—at the same time—to the most peculiar *fantasies* (the sack, the mutilated, etc.)?

On the background of fantasies lies the already mentioned risk of confusing the Real of the Body with the Real of medicine or the Real of anatomy. The object of psychoanalysis is the body, the main entrance to its nature is *through* language (signifiers and structured discourses). Put more simply, that «through» suggests more an epistemological strategy than an ontological description. While conceiving the body as a «support» (ibid.: 225) for discourses, Lacan at the same time warns us from the perils of claiming that the support of discourses is simply «the body». This is because, in his words, «that's not necessarily *one* body. Since we start from enjoyment [*jouissance*], this means that the body isn't all alone, that there's another» (ibid.). However, this isn't equal to saying that enjoyment is sexual (and bodily) enjoyment *tout court*. It means that if there's enjoyment it is *because* of relations (Symbolic, Imaginary and Real) that exist prior to the body, to *this* body. Yet the goal of psychoanalysis is (and always was) the overcoming of this basic anthropological dispositive towards the sinthome (*vs.* 'the symptoms'), an entity which is not characterized as a *painful* or *unhappy* repetition, but as the affirmation of the subject's singularity (to answer the first critique). By the same token, Lacan is also keen to refuse what Jacques-Alain Miller calls the *DSM-Utopia* (Miller 2017: 117). In other words, any *nosological hypostatization* of mental disease reveals the ideal of an *ultimate classification* of humans into their pathologies or cognitive malfunctions. That's precisely what's impossible from a Lacanian point of view: *to each one his own symptoms!*

Before returning, then, to the intimate and structural bond between body and fantasy, we would like to underline another weak point of affirmative critiques against psychoanalysis. Just after stating that in Lacan there's no *body* whatsoever, nor any *positive* account of desire, Braidotti quickly remarks that, today, millions of women undergo *esthetic surgery* (sic.), and other millions of men and women are using anti-depressant drugs. Instead of reading these two social symptoms as manifestations of the victory of narcissistic-related neuroses and the neoliberal treatment of psychic suffering as *neurological* malfunctioning respectively, she's more inclined to take these facts as proofs that body's «direct physical prominence and vulnerability» (Braidotti 2017: 33) are again at the center of the stage (!). In a way that is quite opposite to Braidotti's reading, it seems that, as suggested by Adrian Johnston, «words, thoughts and fantasies (all involving signifier-like *Vorstellungen*), although semblances, are not mere semblances as inconsequential fictions» (Johnston 2014: 70). In other words, these examples show how «signifying materials» do play a crucial role in one's life.

«The practical-clinical implications», Johnston further underlines, are that there's no possible *bracketing* of language or—as Lacan says—*there's no metalanguage*. The philosophical dream of affirmation is then equal to this type of operation: *to surgically modify my body has nothing to do with my fantasy, it is just something 'I' want to do!*

At best, one could say that these large-scale data bear witness to the fact that *Acting-Out* is becoming the general rule of our societies: «Beauty? Buy it. Anxiety? Cure it». That is, we already encounter a third fantasy: beside the mutilation fantasy and the sack fantasy, here we witness the *plastic* fantasy. It isn't more nor less "truer" than the other two; it's just another way of enjoying the body through another fantasy. If we inductively discovered the Symbolic-Imaginary *entanglements* constituting these fantasies concerning the body, we're still far from saying anything about the Real of the body. To put our argument *upside-down*, then, would also mean to take this *transformative* and *discourse-dependent* nature of the body enjoyment as the very departing point.

Indeed, this is the strategy we would like to follow, for explaining the body-fantasy conceptual bond, a *genetical explanation of the contingent fantasies "belonging" to each subjectivity* is needed. As Tyszler remarks: «Fantasy is the window on the Real».

Another common critique toward Lacanian psychoanalysis is directly linked to the first two. Namely, the idea according to which Lacan refrains from giving any account of affective life (as discussed by Malabou in Johnston and Malabou 2013: 150). In order to counterbalance those type of critiques, Lacanians often point out to the seminar on anxiety. As noted by Malabou, it would be quite reductive to portray the whole of human affective life by speaking of anxiety only.

And, indeed, this is also the case for Lacan himself, for he's not saying that anxiety is the only affect worth to explore but, rather, he proposes a key psychoanalytical distinction between affects (on one side) and emotions/feelings (on the other). A key distinction also embedded in Freud, who distinguished *Affekt*, *Gefühl* and *Empfindung*.

And that's for a structural departing point belonging to psychoanalysis: what we might call "the problem of "trust" (or "self-trust"). It's the trust one puts—or not—in what he's saying or what he's experiencing. That is, for the same clinical reason for which subjects tend to "bracket" some of their utterances arbitrarily as "unimportant" or "meaningless", one should never be too hasty in trusting his own descriptions of affective life. Lacan was so precise in underlining this point, which inherit its significance from the same DSM-utopia mentioned above. As he said once: no matter how much can you fit two different individuals under the same category of *obsessional neurosis*, they will be of no use for one another. This example maintains its importance for two linked reasons: (1) there are limits in nosological taxonomies; and (2) the phenomenological description of my own anxiety (for instance) doesn't affect the true reason behind it, nor the possible "healing" of it.

What's wrong with self-descriptions of one's affective states?

From a Lacanian point of view, what the psychoanalyst wants to avoid at all costs «is the temptation to try to read into and conceptualize affective experience, or to assume that, of themselves, affects might have some fundamental existential meaning to disclose» (Robertson 2015: 71–72). As Robertson accurately underlines, Lacan is here referring to Heidegger's phenomenology of *Stimmungen* (moods) as «modes of existential "attunement"» (ibid.). That is, phenomenological or existentialist descriptions of affects all too often suggest the idea of an "unmediated" access to subject's reality. As if there's "safe space" of theory within which the subject can, without disillusion, give a reason for her symptoms.

But the attempt to fit *Stimmungen* into linguistic descriptions of Being-in-the-World means no more or no less than transforming them into concepts, that is, into signifiers. Thus one is necessarily in need of something else than mere "I-feel-like" sort of descriptions. Moreover, it is not that affective life doesn't count. On the contrary, the basic idea of psychoanalytical undertakings of affectivity is to show that *the truth* of my moods lies—and is always reactivated—in the signifying chains and semblants coming out in relation to the Other. Or, for example, when the transfert appears, either inside the clinical setting (as its precondition) or in everyday life.

In order to eschew these self-delusional mystical descriptions, one has to focus on the overall economy of the subject's psychic life. In other words, one has to focus on subject's *fantasy* (*fantasme*). Thus the three bones of contention—body, desire, affects—are to be engaged through a theory which gives an account of the *forms* of *enjoyment*. And the forms of enjoyment are always corporeal. The point is, however, to rethink what this last term (corporeal) really implies, for the human being is soon enough in his development *taught* to speak of his body as "a property": «This is my body». Coeval to this event is the already mentioned birth of *fantasy*, the structuring of *enjoyment* into fixed "phrases". This brings us to yet another heated contention, the portrayal of the *fantasy* as a scene. Anti-Lacanian and anti-Freudian stances all too often consider the shape of desire described by psychoanalysis as an always ongoing *theatrical scene*. The Œdipal complex is nothing but a narration among the others, but for some reason some psychoanalyst seems to be able to say something interesting only by reducing everything to "mom and dad".

That's precisely the idea Lacan abandoned. It is remarkable to notice how the very first "anti-Œdipic" was no other than Lacan himself, for he clearly portrays the Œdipus complex as «a symptom» which can be «eluded» (Lacan 2006: 21) (and in fact, it is).

By the same token, Lacan approaches fantasy from a *logic* point of view, rather than a *scenic* one. Hence his well-known matheme of the (*logique du*) *fantasme*: "barred subject punch [*poinçon*] object *a*", the subject in her "relation" to her lost object: $\$\diamond a$.

As Tyszler points out:

> Lacan always suggests [against Freud] to break away from the scenic, from the imaginary of the scene, so that we can appropriate what he indicates as *object a*, object of the arithmetics. What he wants to produce is the research of these enjoyments [*jouissances*], not in the memory of the body, but in literality, in the way by which the games of the letter [*jeu des lettres*] contaminate the unconscious of this very memory. (Tyszler 2013: 275)

It's this *phrasal crystallization* of enjoyment which is beyond subject's direct cognition, as in the classic Freudian case of 'A child is being beaten'. The phrasal crystal by which we can approach particular fantasies synthesizes the ways in which the subject takes pleasure or suffering from her relation to the world. Fantasy determines both the pleasure and the displeasure. It is a structure, resulting from the effects of language on the body, which determines the "paths of least resistance" available to the subject in his pursuit of pleasure. By the same token, it nonetheless determines the repetition of "painful" or "unhappy" outcomes.

Since fantasy is a multilayered entity all by itself (permeable to discourses, bodily and phrasal), "body enjoyment" seems to be a pleonastic expression; there's no enjoyment outside body enjoyment. Fantasy is a complexity-laden concept in that it manifests the hybridization of humanity as both *nurtured* and *cultured*. As Malabou emphasizes, «nowhere are the consequences of humanity's abandonment to a limbo that is neither natural nor antinatural more apparent than in the peculiarities of human beings' emotional lives» (Johnston and Malabou 2013: 184). The problems arise then in saying something about the body tout court. And, indeed, our strategy will be to propose a model for fantasy formation, which is the entrance to any discourse about the body.

However, the watchful eyes of the contemporary reader could already envisage a cryptic plea for what Badiou calls «democratic materialism», the axiom of contemporary conviction by which «there are only bodies and languages» (Badiou 2009: 1). This is clearly *not* the case of our enquiry, for what is "Being", properly speaking, is a matter of language and, moreover, what stands next to (1) bodies and (2) languages are (3) the immanent truths of fantasy formation. Although Lacan distinguished between «truth» and «Real», fantasy does show aspects of both the notions. On the one hand, fantasy is Real in that it shapes subjects' lives in repetitive fashion and it is, therefore, "clinically true". On the other hand, however, it falls out of the true/false distinction because it is Real in the sense of *pure* repetition of an invisible and forgotten phrasal crystallization.

Therefore, to the ideology of the Two which suggests "body+language" ontologies, we strongly oppose a theory of the Three. Reacting accordingly, Badiou claims that:

> It is then legitimate to counter democratic materialism—this sovereignty of the Two (bodies and languages)—with a materialist dialectic, if by 'materialist dialectic' we understand the following statement, in which the Three supplements the reality of the Two: There are only bodies and languages, *except that there are truths*. (ibid.: 4, our italics)

Despite the fact that Badiou's route is quite different from ours, his plea for a theory of the Three against the Two is certainly held up in the context of fantasy formation. The point of contention would be, then, to give (or not) room for the possibility of a traversing of the fantasy. That is, which possibilities are there for the subject to overcome the Real but "un-true" (and hence contingent) essence of fantasy?

2 A Philosophy of the Skin: Nudity—Mirror—Phantom

The body is a paradoxical entity. On one side it seems to be the most intimate thing we have but, on the other—as we already pointed out—it seems to be also the very first victim of the most odd discourses. Then, as a coherent starting point, it would be mandatory to start from the most apparent of its features. That is: we are born—as non-human animals—*naked*.

The body is first and foremost without clothes. There is a boundless set of historical traces which testify this starting point, both as a pedagogical-anthropological discourse and also in the form of mythemes. As the story of Adam and Eve tells, nudity is something *which is discovered*. Before the "sinful" Fall, although they were naked (*árûmmîn* in hebrew), they didn't feel any shame. That is, Genesis 2:25 starts stating the fact that they were naked but without feeling so.

After the well-known taking of the prohibited fruit «the eyes of them both were opened, and they knew that they were naked (*ê|rummìn hëm*); and they sewed fig-leaves together, and made themselves girdles» (Genesis 3:7). As the tale goes on, Adam hides from the gaze of the other because he «was afraid» of him being *êröm*, naked.

Finally, God himself asks: «Who told thee that thou wast naked?». The scenario apparently comprises two statuses one after the other. At the beginning Adam and Eve are *really* naked, although they don't *know* that yet. At a second point, after their disobedience, they start to *know* their being naked, although nothing materially changed in respect to the first departing point. It is at this point that God himself makes them dresses to wear. Thus, it would seem that the Adamic progression is structured so that *real/material* clothes are the final step of a scenario in which the former *nakedness* is only metaphysical. And indeed, as Agamben points out in his analysis of nudity, the departing point of the tale is not nudity *qua* animal nudity. Instead, they're already «covered in a grace robe clinging to them as a glorious suit» (Agamben 2009: 85). His critical departing point, aimed at the «theological signature» (or *dispositive*) which shaped our way to think about nudity, ends up in a strong ontologico-political *sabotage* which opposes a monistic nudity qua immediately-apparent to the dualism of the western tradition. As he further remarks:

> [...]Nudity is only negatively accounted, as a privation of the grace robe and as omen of the shining glory suit which the blessed ones will receive in Heaven. A *full nudity* is given maybe only in Hell, in the bodies of the damned irremissibly offered to the eternal torments of divine justice. There isn't any theology of nudity in Christianity, only a theology of the dress. (ibid.: 87)

According to him, theology sets the theoretical roots for a nudity which is ever only conceivable in a *negative* way. The primacy of the (glorious) dress is what foreshadows the bare nakedness of men as corruptible flesh. The apparently *two-steps* structured tale of Adam and Eve is actually made of three parts. The nakedness only appear at the juncture between the first *grace dress* and the second God-made *material* one.

Agamben further synthesizes, borrowing from Erik Peterson's *Theologie des Kleides*, two types of nudity as *absence of dressing—Unbekleidetheit*—and *nudity—Nacktheit*. He then remarks that the difference between the two is that while *Unbekleidetheit* passes unnoticed, *Nacktheit* is what happens when one realizes it. That is, the bare body is not nude as a natural (i.e. unproblematic) state, but instead it is so only under the gaze, the opening of a gaze. In short, while nudity as *Nacktheit* belongs to the register of the event, nudity as *Unbekleidetheit* belongs to a state which is *before* any nude/non-nude distinction. As in the case of the infant or the non-human animal, nudity as *Unbekleidetheit* is unproblematic. To put it roughly, it is not important because it is not *yet* an issue. The Adamic condition is then equivalent to the state of animality, although with the theological ingredient of an invisible dress made of pure grace. It is only with the Fall that animality *qua* Nature becomes synonymous with sin, guilt and so on. "Sin" is nothing but the name which is negatively given to the losing of the grace. Indeed, Agamben is accurate in describing this event not as a real «metaphysical transformation» (ibid.: 89).

What Agamben is aiming at in his deconstructive approach is this theological dispositive. As he claims: if the post-Fall «libido» is characterized by the impossibility of «controlling the genitals», then «the grace state will consist in a perfect control of will over the sexual parts» (ibid.: 101).

Leaving Agamben's critical framework aside, the Adamic scenario effectively tells us something about the true nature of nudity in the speaking animal. The development of the infant's life arguably resembles the basic teaching of the biblical tale. In his former state of dereliction the infant doesn't problematize his body as naked. That is, like non-human animals, the absence of dresses is not even acknowledged; he/she stands *before* the naked/un-naked possibility and, therefore, before the presence/absence of shame. As he grows up he *discovers* his nudity and starts to worry about covering his body parts. He renders certain pertinent body parts as what could be under the gaze of the other (Augustin's *pudenda* and *glorianda*). By this token, nudity becomes a real "problem". But as the three-steps theological scenario shows, the ontogenetic level at which the infant reproduces the myth suggests a different appraisal. The short circuit is the one concerning the very beginning, for what is acknowledged as a *grace state* in the theological dispositive becomes, in the case of the infant, a mere natural *qua* animal state. In other words, it's the placing of the category of «Nature» which changes in the two scenarios. While in the case of Adam and Eve «Nature» is nothing but the *junction* between two types of dresses (the *grace* and the *artificial* one), in the case of the infant «Nature» is placeable only at the beginning, when the naked body of the newly born human is no different from the naked body of any animal whatsoever. To borrow from Agamben once again, the infant is in the register of *Unbekleidetheit*, an unproblematic and *shameless* nudity. But it is nonetheless a *bare* nudity, a pure piece of moving flesh. The Adamic state portrays, on the other hand, a *shameless* nudity but describing it due to the presence of an invisible grace dress. However, the principle of nudity qua *event* is what interests us in both the scenarios (the infant's and the Adamic). "Nudity" has to be discovered, it's a *Nackthteit* which is possible only under the gaze of a *Symbolic* or *Imaginary* Other.

Jacques Lacan does face the problem from his psychoanalytical standpoint. It comes as no surprise that when he asks if «nudity is purely and simply a natural phenomenon», he quickly answers saying that «the whole of psychoanalytic thought is designed to prove it isn't» (Lacan 1992: 227).

Immediately after this claim he suggest a very Agamben-like move: «The thing that is particularly exalting about it and significant in its own right is that there is *a beyond of nudity that nudity hides*» (ibid., our italics).

Lacan quotes then the Adam and Eve case in order to eschew any *phenomenological* account of nudity:

> But we don't need to engage in phenomenology; I prefer fables. The fable on this occasion concerns Adam and Eve, with the proviso that the dimension of the signifier also be present, the signifier as introduced by the father in the benevolent directions he gives: "Adam, you must give names to everything around you." Here is Adam, then, and here is the famous hair of an Eve that we hope is worthy of the beauty that this first gesture evokes. Adam pulls out one of her hairs. Everything I am trying to show you here turns on a hair, a frog's hair. Adam pulls out a hair from the woman who is given to him as his wife, who has been expected for the whole of eternity, and the next day she comes back with a mink coat over her shoulders. Therein lies the power of the nature of cloth. It's not because man has less hair than other animals that we have to check out everything that down the ages will burst forth from his industry. If we are to believe the linguists, the problem of different goods is raised within a structure. At the beginning everything is structured as a signifier, even if only a chain of hairs is involved. (ibid.)

While Agamben is so poignant in underlining the first departing point of the scene, criticizing it as belonging to a theology of the dress (*vs.* a theology of nudity), Lacan is more interested in the artificial and *productive* aspect of the human-made cloths. De-naturalizing the dress as *not* something coming out from the *biological lack* of hair, he states that the «industry» of dresses itself allows the human to enter in the realm of «goods» and, simultaneously, of «values». But both values and goods are only given in a structure: *there's value only in a differential structure.* The welcoming of the infant in the realm of signifiers actually sets up the possibility of being covered with signifiers; human beings started to give things a name. The emphasis must be put, then, on the fact that the making of the dresses subsequent to the naked state, once and forever puts the human into a realm of *changes* caused by *time value*:

> In the beginning there is the producer's inventiveness, namely, the fact that man - and why he alone? - begins to weave something, something that isn't in the form of a covering or cocoon for his own body, but something that as cloth is going to take off on its own in the world, is going to move around. Why? Because this cloth has time value. That's what distinguishes it from any form of natural production. (ibid.: 227–228)

The entrance into structure sets the roots for the subject dependence on the discourse of the Other and, conversely, it sets up the very possibility of *shame*; shame which is, we must now add, nothing natural. And this is also a point somehow touched by Agamben's approach. For him there's nothing natural in nudity, for it is dependent on the theological dispositive of dressed (in *grace*) or naked (in *sin*). As Agamben recalls, even twentieth century's nudism movements, in proposing their return to the naturism of the naked body, fell too quickly in advocating a *Lichtkleid*—a "robe of light", basically restating the theological dispositive of a primary grace garment.

But there's also nothing natural in being dressed, for the naked/dressed distinction holds only for the speaking animal. In other words, the binary switch of theology is valid only under the constraints of a *sinful* conception of humanity. Being naked is nothing but the removal of a grace-involucre, due to the forbidden fruit.

Although Agamben coherently makes a plea for a nudity which stands beyond this dispositive, we would like to emphasize some key aspects that Agamben seems to undervalue.

It is certainly true that the theologization of the human body revolves around the always renewable possibility of the "fall from grace". However, the Adam and Eve portrayal sheds precious light into aspects which are accountable only if we take a psychoanalytical framework as a starting point.

That is, the phenomenon of nudity—both as the "event of denudation" or as a continuous state, is directly linked to the affect of *shame* and, moreover, to a possible *gaze*. The nakedness of the human being makes sense only after a virtual or real gaze of something other-than-me. The concept of nudity makes little sense if examined out of its "inter-subjective" matrix. For if I was alone in the whole Earth, it would make no sense to feel naked at all.

This being *alone* is not, however, the mere fact of being materially alone, for this is precisely what Lacan cannot give room for. The entering into the realm of discourses is due to the differential grid of *values-signifiers* to which the subject must appeal.

Thus, following Lacan, we can acknowledge the departing point of the infant's life as both something which is *before* any naked/un-naked distinction and *before* any differential grid of values. «Values» which have signifiers as their unavoidable precondition. As Lacan so insistingly remarked through his career, it is the Symbolic which sets all the *dichotomies* and *binarism*: «man-woman», «good-bad», «black-white», etc. While the Real is—*par opposition*—what stands *before* or *after* this realm of differences.

Dresses (artificial cloths) cover the body with signifiers (Symbolic), although co-generating at the same time an unaccountable remainder (Real).

We already distinguished, then, the difference between a nudity conceived as "post-Symbolic" and a nudity as "pre-Symbolic". In other words, we have a nudity as the always (uncanny) possibility of "feeling naked under the gaze of the other" (*Nackheit*) and a nudity which is *before* the artificial covering by signifiers/cloths, hence an almost unaccountable and animal nudity.

The desirable political outcome of such analysis is, for Agamben, «the deactivation of the dispositive», which «is retroactive both upon nature and the grace, both upon nudity and the dress, freeing them of their theological signature» (Agamben 2009: 128). In a Lacanian framework, one would pessimistically argue that there isn't such a possibility, for a full de-alienated coincidence with the Real *qua* post-Symbolic would be quite different from a mere backward return to animality. And indeed, both for Lacan's latest plea for a *symphôme* as for Deleuzian concepts of *becoming-animal*, it's not the case of a dreamful and—one would say—impossible return to pre-Symbolic purity. We will sift this possibility later on. For now we must go through another key distinction concerning nudity: nudity as *partial* or as *total*.

In his *The Animal That Therefore I Am*, Derrida describes the experience of the encounter with a cat which catches him in the nude. He's standing naked in front of the animal's gaze. He takes this experience as a departing point for reflections on animals, vulnerability and human anthropocentrism.

What he's aiming at can be connected to the ontologico-political aim of Agamben's discourse. While the latter hopes for a sabotage of the dress *vs.* an ennoblement of non-dualistic nudity, Derrida is more focused on denouncing the Western Philosophy's vice of reducing the animal to a mere lacking-version of the human species. As Khandker underlines:

> The terms and designations according to which the lives of animals tend to be judged are inescapably humanist or anthropocentric (questions of rights, subjectivity and agency), while moral philosophy, in its dealings with moral agents and moral patients, is already defined in terms of certain human characteristics (rationality, symbolic use of language, etc.) to which non-human animals inevitably fail to conform. Therefore, we must conclude, other animals are simply not worthy of moral consideration. (Khandker 2014: 57)

It seems that the animal is only negatively accounted as something which stands in a realm of pre-Symbolic nudity. That is, anthropocentric discourses elicit violence toward the animal in their very conceptual appraisals: the animal *doesn't have* language, *doesn't have* shame, etc.

As Derrida describes the experience of the cat's gaze on his naked body, he claims that:

> In the optic center of such reflection one could find the thing and, to my view, the focal point of the incomparable experience which we call *nudity*, which is supposed to be proper to men, therefore irrelevant to animals, although they're naked and, as we think, without the slightest awareness of being so. Shame of what and naked in front of whom? Why one must be caught into shame? And why this shame which is ashamed of being ashamed? (Derrida 2006: 38)

As in the case of the Adamic myth and the ontogenic account of infant's nakedness, Derrida directly links nudity to the *event* of the «awareness» of being naked. It is as if the animal, which stands before the Symbolic dimension of dressing and before any cognition of the nakedness/un-nakedness of its body, is traditionally conceived to be one step below human kind. This Derridean Ur-Nudity of the animal is the theoretical fulcrum around which humanity built up its conceited anthropocentrism:

> This 'unprecedented' degree of subjection of the animal, Derrida writes, amounts to *violence*, and he goes on to compare this large-scale subjection of animal life to examples of genocide, and the death camps. Rather than simply making this comparison in order to elicit an emotional response, or to evoke *pathos*, Derrida draws attention to what has become the centre of moral philosophising about the status of animals, namely, the capacity to suffer, as originally put forward by Jeremy Bentham. (Khandker 2014: 59)

It seems that the ennobling of mankind has to rely upon the ontological mortification of the animal. Derrida further remarks that this shame experienced by the human is «the shame of being naked as a beast». The problem is then immediately linked by Derrida to the missed conceptualization, in western thought, of the act of the *dressing*:

> In theory no animal, beside men, ever thought to dress itself. The dress is a peculiarity of men, one of his «features». The «dressing» is inseparable from all the other figures of «human feature», although there's less talking about it compared to language or reason, to *logos*, to history, to laughter, to mourning, to sepolture, to gift, etc. (Derrida 2006: 39)

And indeed it's astonishing to notice how poor is the state of affairs concerning the *dressing* as a first and foremost anthropological feature. Although theology, for Agamben, is ever only a theology of dress, it seems that for Derrida what is needed is a *philosophy of dress*. That is, what is missing from Agamben's point of view—a non-theological account of *nudity*—is exactly the opposite in the case of Derrida, who would rather prefer a non-anthropocentric account of *dressing*.

From a Lacanian point of view, there can be no theory of the one without the other; more accurately, the psychoanalytical account of nudity can't be approached without considering (1) the mirror stage as the departing point of that mentioned «awareness», and (2) the fact that structures and signifiers are not portrayed as our anthropological merits. Language, the Other and the marking of the signifiers upon the skin, all are effects of the same dispositive, whose functioning is already active before our biological birth.

It is no surprise that Derrida puts Lacan amongst the protagonists of such anthropocentric discourses. The philosophical tradition he's arguing against comprises Lacanian psychoanalysis.

The problem of including Lacan in this discourse is that psychoanalysis does give an account *not* of plain (*total*) nudity, but instead an account of *how* it becomes possible for this thing we call «our body» to be fragmented and structured into "shame-points" and, by the same token, "gaze objects".

In other words, it seems that what Derrida is really aiming at is a concept of nudity qua *total* nudity, as if the nakedness of the human being can be conceived as belonging to a strict «dressed/naked» binarism. His critique towards western philosophical tradition is undermined by this fixed opposition. He criticizes Lacan for being not able to give an account of this type of nudity (i.e. *total nudity*), therefore stating that Lacan thinks about the animal as a mere being *without* language. It seems that, following Derrida, Lacan merely gives a negative account of animality, conceived as what you get from *subtracting* language from a natural being whatsoever. Add language to an animal and you get humans, subtract it from humans and you get animals.

However, this reading of Lacan holds only if it is taken as a consequence of the «dressed/naked» *strong* opposition. What's really at work in the psychoanalyst is rather that one is never *completely* nude. The subject's body is always naked in certain points.

The problem must be then shifted from the strong binarism to the «total/partial» distinction. This mandatory theoretical shift is due to the fact that Lacan was more keen to *isolate* certain body objects as more pertinent to the «dressed/naked» couple in respect to others.

It's the pertinentization of certain objects that activates—upon them—the «naked/non-naked» "switch". In short, one has to look, first and foremost, at the encoded body zones to which the nakedness could apply. *Shame* is nothing natural, because it depends on the virtual symbolization of body objects. The main difference between Lacan and Derrida, on this theme, is that while the psychoanalyst gives room for a dynamic and topological account of nudity, the philosopher seems to understand the body as what can be either completely naked or completely dressed. Since nudity cannot be comprehended, from a Lacanian point of view at least, without considering it as the other side of the Other's gaze, it follows that nudity is subject to the *pertinentization* of objects/parts isolable from the body. Moreover (as we will show later on), it is a matter of individuating the shapes of the signifying involucre which covers the human body from the mirror stage on.

This is another way to say that what we name as "my body" is actually an *already-shaped* configuration which involves the Symbolic, the Imaginary and the Real. One is never *completely naked*, for being naked always involves the sudden covering of certain body parts instead of others.

Starting then from the two-sided distinction of «naked/dressed», we would like to suggest that to follow Lacan also means to add a third element of the distinction: the *neutral*. Hence what we get in the end is the couple constituted by pertinent objects and neutral zones. These latter zones are nothing but the remainder of the symbolic "packaging" of the body into isolable naked or non-naked objects. In short, the final result is a set composed by *naked zones*, *un-naked zones* and *neutral zones*. The neutral zone inherits the dynamic and signifying features belonging to the first two. That is, it is identifiable only starting from the first two parts as their unavoidable remainder. The *neutral* is nothing other than the *non-body*, what is foreign to the body itself, a property which becomes sadly apparent in *phantom limbs* types of failed proprioception. As the body makes its entrance into the desire of the Other, the gaze to which it is subject (and "subjected") determines the very core of what can be named as belonging to my body *tout court*.

Thus, what Derrida calls Pathos, this feature which seems common to both human and non-human animals, must be diversified. That is, the pathos of the speaking animal is deranged by the effects of the linguistic material. The sensible body of the speaking animal is foremost subjected to a first "clothing ceremony" which dresses its apparently bare skin in a signifying patchwork. The *trait unaire* constitutes the first stitching of its entrance in the realm of desire. This does not, however, guide us toward an anthropocentrism. Rather, what the phenomenon of language at best shows it's the moving of the human subject from the "center" to the "periphery".

Although there's already a copious literature on the well known Mirror Stage, it is worth to re-engage its key features, for they clearly show how matters concerning bodily proprioception, fantasy and the phenomenon of *shame* are engendered by the same dynamic. What follows will be, then, more a theoretical re-actualization of the mirror object rather than a simple explanation of its prima facie importance in psychoanalytic discourse.

There are multiple things at stake in the mirror stage. Surely, the most apparent one is the self-recognition and the formation of a body image which is validated symbolically by the Other. Curiously enough, the Greeks and the Romans believed that the reflection of oneself into water showed the *soul* of the subject. That is, the reflection was the most inner truth of the subject. And, for the same reason, a distorted reflection was read as a bad omen.

Lacan does borrow a lot of the key ingredients for his mirror stage from previous ethological and psychological theories.

The mirror stage portraits a scenario in which the infant sees his/her image reflected on the mirror:

> [...] at an age in which, for a short time, he's surpassed in instrumental intelligence by the chimpanzee, he recognizes already his own image in the mirror. Recognition which is displayed by the enlightening mimic of the *Aha-Erlebnis* [...]. (Lacan 2002: 87)

That is, the infant experiences the *Aha!* experience (*Erlebnis*); he starts to play and enjoy the game of the matching between his own movements and the corresponding reflected images.

> [the child] playfully put the relation between movements in the image and the reflected environment to the test, and between this virtual complex and the reality which it doubles, in other words his own body and the people, or the objects standing nearby. (ibid.)

This playful mirroring is what, according to Lacan, gives a pre-social—in its *Écrits* version—Gestalt of the I. In other words, it is what first and foremost constitutes a seed of subjectivity:

> The important thing is that this form situates the *I* instance, before its social determination, in a line of fiction, forever irreducible for the single individual or, rather, which will only asymptotically reach the subject's becoming, despite the success of the dialectic syntheses by which he - as an *I* - has to resolve the discordance with his own reality. (ibid.: 88–89)

The developmental function of the mirror stage serves the purpose of symbolizing «the mental permanence of the *I* and at the same time prefigur[ing] its alienating destination» (ibid.: 89).

The mirror stage furnishes the infant with an imaginary corporeal totality (and *one-ness*). As we already noted, this event overcomes the basic *fragmentation* fantasy of the infant body, which is synonymous to saying his *basic psychosis*. However, the mirror stage also sets the roots for alienation for it implies, next to this Gestaltic-Imaginary dimension, a Symbolic one. In other words, it involves the *validation* or *certification* of the Other, who looks both at the reflected image and at the infant. The infant's *Aha!* is "completed" by the Symbolic recognition of the Other, which validates the matching by crystallizing the always changing reflection in a stable symbolic *anchorage*. As Lacan says in a session of his first seminar: «The whole problem is then the one of the junction of the symbolic and the imaginary in the constitution of the real» (Lacan 2014: 90).

Moreover, he adds that the mirror stage:

> [it is also responsible] of the correspondences which unite the *I* with the statue upon which the men projects himself, with the phantoms dominating him, and at last with the automaton in which he resolves in the ambiguous relation with the world he fabricates. (Lacan 2002: 89)

At a glance it is possible to recognize the (phenomenological) implications of this experience. Lacan doesn't refrain from linking the mirror stage to libido, ontology and fantasy:

> [T]he *mirror stage* is a drama whose internal push precipitates from *insufficiency* to *anticipation*, and that for the subject taken in the trickery of *spatial identification*, plots *phantômes* [fantasies] which proceed from a fragmented body image to an orthopedic form of its totality [...]. (ibid.: 91, our italics)

The insufficiency of *détresse* is partially overcome by *anticipation*, which involves a passage from the identification of body-in-space to the creation of fantasy. The sense of the mirror stage is not reducible, then, to the mere dimension of self-recognition and recognition by the Other, but instead «reveals a *libidinal dynamism* which is, until then, problematic, and also *an ontological structure of the human world which becomes part of our reflections on paranoid cognition* [*connaissance*]» (ibid.: 88, our italics)

We will face the *paranoid* condition as an embedded ontological outcome later on. For now we must focus on the triangulation between Symbolic, Imaginary and Real.

Lacan retakes the mirror stage during the first seminar, adding a model which is an ersatz of the former version. The optic model which follows is to show that the mirror stage «is not just a step in development» but, instead, it has an «exemplary function», for it mediates and reveals the relations between the subject and its image as *Urbild* of the ego (Lacan 2014: 90).

This newly underlined function is meant to extend the already mentioned (*Écrits*) «spatial identification». That is, «in order to have an optic, every point given in real space must corresponds to only one point in another space, which is the imaginary space» (ibid.: 93). This is the main reason for which in the context of optics Lacan refrain from referring to the Real with capital 'R' (as transcribed by Miller). This is due to the fact that, coming from the ontological claims of the paranoid *connaissance* embedded in the mirror stage, Lacan is referring to the real qua reality, which is—at least in this period—superimposed to the Imaginary.

In later years (Seminar VII) he will more and more suggest that the entering into the symbolic involves the loss of the Thing. Or, to be more precise, it involves a Kantian making of the *preconditions for the loss itself*:

> I am trying to show you how Freudian aesthetics, in the broadest meaning of the term - which means the analysis of the whole economy of signifiers - reveals that the Thing is inaccessible. That needs to be placed right at the start of the problem, so as to be able to articulate its consequences,

> and especially the question of idealization. In any case, you saw last time, in connection with the sublimation involved in the moral code of courtly love, the beginnings of the emergence of an ideal type. (Lacan 1992: 159–160)

Moreover, then, the lost object, which is the remainder of the mirror *function* (not just 'stage'), will be put in a Real as synonymous to the "back-and-forth" event of the encounter (*tyche*) (Lacan 2003: 52). An encounter which breaks suddenly from the *automaton* of signifying chains.

Another key element of the Mirror Stage Conference jumps here to the fore. Namely the dual linking between—on one side—the mirror image and "sense of reality" and,—on the other side—the mirror stage and «the sense of beauty as *formative* and *erogenous*». It is no surprise, as we will show later on when we will encounter the phenomenon of the *mimicry*, that the conceptual chain portrayed by the mirror stage is made so: *body-image-symbolic-beauty-reality-erogenicity*. That is, the mirror stage simultaneously involves a *cognitive* function and an *aesthetic* one. Beauty and the horror of the body fantasy are due to the same underlying pattern. Reality begins with the enjoyment of cognition.

To sum up our conclusions we can say that the Other is, to put it roughly, a function. It is the empty slot into which the image finds its name and, at the same time, creates the double anchorage between what the subject says and the order into which this saying belongs. The Other seems to hold *me* in my entrance into the world of human kind. But although this «holding» could be depicted as a grandiose and happy event (*Aha-Erlebnis*; "That's me!"), it carries nonetheless the truth of the basic misrecognition involved in it. Recognition and misrecognition are one and the same thing. That's the main reason behind Lacan's abandonment of any (Hegelian) dialectical pacificatory appraisal of subject-formation.

We spoke at length about mirrors, bodies, images, etc. Now we must ask: how are these elements linked to fantasy formation and to nudity?

Nudity can't but be conceived as the *showing of pudenda*, the *showing of erotizable objects*. At the same time, however, nudity is also the *gaze* of the Other. To be more precise, we should add that nudity is *in* the gaze of the Other. Thus, nudity as event implies two aspects: the body as a map of *erotizable objects* and the bare eye of the Other.

The ingredients are set for the Lacanian acknowledgment of the remainder of the scopic scene, that is, what he calls object small *a*. The Imaginary-Symbolic entanglement leaves this piece out of the frame.

During the Seminar on the *Four fundamental concepts*, Lacan reengages the problem of the remainder in this optical scenario by giving it a clear conceptualization: the gaze is the object *a*.

He surprisingly ends up telling his audience a personal anecdote in order to explain the link between object *a* and the spatial condition in which the subject finds herself.

He was on a boat with a family of fishermen. Suddenly John, one of the fishermen, draws Lacan's attention to a floating tin of sardines. It was floating on the water, sparkling at the sun. Suddenly John asks him: «*Do you see that tin? Do you? Well, it doesn't see you!*» (ibid.: 94).

Although John appeared to be amused by the thing, Lacan recalls being not so amused. He tried to understand why he wasn't amused by this, and he came up with an explanation which is directly linked to the *gaze*.

In short, the social discrepancy between him as a «young intellectual» and the fishermen's belonging to the working class played a crucial role.

He tells us that, compared to the hard lives of the fishermen, he was «showing off» (ibid.). As he says: «I was the blot on the painting». And it is at this point that Lacan draws the most important theoretical conclusions.

> I am not simply that dot-like being which orients itself in respect to the geometral point from which perspective is caught. Undoubtedly, the painting is drawn deep down in my eye. The painting is certainly in my eye. But I, *I am in the painting*. (ibid.: 94–95, our italics)

The meaning of «I am in the painting» must be understood so: the experience of being the *blot* in the painting breaks with any concept of space as a mere *geometrical space*. What's more important and evident in the case of the relationship between the subject and the gaze is the «point of view», the point of view of the *overall picture/scenario* catches me not as the protagonist of a possible crossing of the passageway but, rather, as the «screen» (sic.) that light must pierce through in order to have any image formation whatsoever. That is, I'm not the protagonist of a free walking in a geometrical space. Rather, the sparkling of the tin is exactly what distorts this "primacy of the geometrical" by making me *screen*.

This is the main reason for which Lacan underlines *en passant* that he's not talking about «the constructed relationship, the object of the philosopher» (ibid.: 95). The mirroring or representative function is superseded by the idea of the *screen*.

The gaze is an object *a*, a philosophical ungraspable remainder, for it constitutes the subject as orientable screen and not as a mirroring-rappresenting *tabula*: I am watched!. I'm not, for the same line of reasoning, the empty angular spot from which the world is given. I'm one part comprised in the scenario itself. Thus, I'm not mirroring the outside, I'm an orientable and deformable surface—screen—which is watched before my watching itself. As Cézanne said in front of the Sainte-Victoire mountain: «The mountain is watching me».

Yet the more straightforward conclusion to draw, to answer Derrida's portrayal of the cat's gaze as denuding gaze, is that things are much more intricate than it may appear. The «I'm watched» experience belongs to a realm which stands before any *animate/inanimate* distinction. The pernicious anthropocentric outcome portrayed by Derrida is nonetheless the inheritance of this former imbalance, for "inanimate objects", "Nature", and so on, are no different from their animate and moving counterparts. Yet Lacan underlines also an *aesthetic* function comprised in the mirror stage. This is what brings us to the link between mirror stage and narcissism. Lacan acknowledges the theoretical problem faced by Freud concerning the issue of libido, namely the fact that at Freud's time there was little or no scientific appraisal of an *energie* belonging to the realm of living beings. Although Freud seems to maintain a weak link to Weissmann's theory, he nonetheless uses it as an instrumental departing point for further psychoanalytical explorations. Drawing from this, Lacan portrays sexual libido as centered to the imaginary function. Ethologists, recalls Lacan, prove the «prevalence of an image, […] a transitory phenotype», whose appearance functions as a constructed signal, a «Gestalt». He follows adding that «the mechanical insertion of sexual instinct is crystallized upon a relation between images» (Lacan 2014: 145).

It is in this context that Lacan re-engages the problem of the two narcissisms through his optic theory alongside his mirror stage. The first narcissism is the one carried out by the «body image» (ibid.: 149). But the main difference between this first narcissism and the second one lies in the passage through the mirror stage, a step which «manifests a new noetic possibility», namely the possibility (forbidden to the non-human animal) of *anticipation*. The other has a captivating value for he/she anticipates the unitary image of both the mirror and of any fellow human.

The second narcissism seamlessly carries out a double operation in which the subject-world connection is both *libidinal* and *imaginary*. That's why, from the point of view of psychoanalysis, the *gaze* is never just an exploring gaze, nor a speculative one, but rather always and already an *enjoyed one*. Or, as we already said, both cognition and the philosopher's "thinking" are ways of enjoyment.

Yet this passages from Seminar I are also the occasion, for Lacan, to shed some light into the subject-object *love* relation. If the other becomes *captivating*, hence becoming the *Ich-Ideal*, the object of love is nothing else but its coincidence to the Ego ideal. It is the case of a "I-love-me-through-the-other" situation. That's why Lacan is quite critical of the link some psychoanalysts make between genital maturation and constitution of reality, as if a «libidinal ascesis» into affective communion was the final resolution for the human adulthood. Although Lacan doesn't exclude this possibility, he nonetheless distinguishes between two types of love corresponding to the two types of narcissism: Eros and Agape.

However, what's important here for us is the theoretical routes the concept of narcissism has taken. Freud portrays narcissism as both a normal result of child's development and as a possible pathological outcome. On this theme, Lacan also seems to acknowledge narcissism as an inevitable outcome of the body image. However, he also maintains that *love* is not always the "self-love" but distinguishes between two different love experiences.

The history of Freud's never solved dilemma (pathological *vs.* developmental) ends up in Ego Psychology, a theoretical position Lacan viciously criticized, and for the best reasons.

In the reconstruction of the history of narcissism, Lunbeck underlines that Freud's "oscillating" understandings of it «made this all more difficult» (Lunbeck 2014: 252), hence giving room to Ego psychologists' theory of a *healthy* and *adaptive* narcissism as one of the possible outcomes.

Ego psychologists pushed Heinz Kohut's (optimistic) conception of an adaptive and functional narcissism to its extreme theoretical consequences. In order to solve the problem of classical (i.e. Freudian) accounts of narcissism as both *developmental* and as a *dormant pathological outcome*, ego psychologists took the de-pathologizing route plotted by Kohut. That is, they isolated the idea of a «healthy narcissism» (ibid.: 254). Since then, for example, political demagogy on economic growth seemed to absorb more and more the lexicon of a *narcissistization of the Nation-qua-Entrepreneur*: the individual selfish and self-empowering man can be useful to the grandiose ambitions of national economies. To paraphrase a popular saying: *"Healthy Egos in a Healthy Economy"*.

Lacan, for his part, seems to move beyond Freud's normal/pathological scheme, avoiding the idea of an adaptive healthy narcissism notwithstanding. The phenomenon by which the body image and the sexual libido are linked will bring us to the repercussions the mirror stage has on the understanding of the phantom limb phenomena. In short, the seamless link between libidinal, aesthetic and narcissistic aspects of subject's formation is blatant in contemporary understandings of failed body proprioception.

If we go back to the stage mirror conference, Lacan proceeds by underlining the historical moments in which the idea of body image's fragmentation became more apparent.

In particular, the exoscopy of the body is linked to Hieronymus Bosch's famous drawings of fragmented and assembled bodies. As we recalled at the beginning, Lacan is keen to fix «modern man's imaginary zenit» (Lacan 2002: 91) fifteenth century's fragmentation fantasies. However, the remarkable point is that these fragmented fantasies are «tangible[s] also at the organic level, in the *fragilization lines* which define phantasmatic anatomy [...]» (Lacan 2002: 91, our italics) As the uncanny anecdote of Kafka's *Odradek* shows (Kafka 2017: 130–132): the (paranoid-like) partialization of the body is the *conditio sine qua non* of later subjectivity (and hence, neuroses). Odradek is a whimsical creature. It has a body but it also seems human made. It is composed by artificial pieces but at the same time it seems to have a life of its own. It is at the same time a pleasant co-tenant and an uncanny out-of-this-world creature. Kafka's anxiety is due to its double facet of being purposeless and harmless at the same time: it *is*, nothing more and nothing less. In short, we are all Odradeks.

Yet some positions of the subject in respect to the mirror (and her later development) display a counterbalancing of the former *Imago* with an aggressiveness towards the mirror itself. The fantasy of the broken mirror is astonishing in showing how deep the *I-Other* bond goes.

The gesture of greedily breaking the mirror is a display of another fundamental feature Lacan ascribes to the Ego formation. Namely, the coeval birth, next to the jubilation of the «that's me!» experiene, of aggressiveness. Aggressiveness is yet another outcome of the mirror function, for it is comprised amongst the effects of the misrecognition. The mirror is the gaze of the Other, as it is also *just* the Other when it comes to narcissistic mortifications. In short, the anchoring of the Imaginary and Symbolic in the optic dispositive creates the preconditions for anger.

The breaking of the mirror seems, at first, to nullify its symbolic and certificating Other (the one who's looking at me). At the same time, though, its breaking corresponds to a misplaced desire of returning to the *morcelé*, to the fragmented, for if the subject was able to reset the initial conditions of the game it would be "much easier". The broken mirror, then, bears witness to the (ideological) semblant of purity, with the concomitant possibility of a renewed mirror stage. By consequence, it is the Other upon which the act of breaking the mirror reverberates who becomes the primary target. As the mirror breaks and falls into pieces, the disappearance of my body image co-generates the *presence of the Symbolic Other* as the only imaginable entity enjoying the spectacle. The emptying of the mirror space truly reinforces the symbolic dimension of the Other: "it ran out of the mirror just to put itself next to me". Yet according to Anzieu, fifteenth century begins with the anatomical fantasy of mutilation. How are these two fantasies connected? The mutilated and the fragmented body seems to overlap one another, and for an another phantasmal reason. That is, if the basic fantasy of the envelope gives birth to the content/containing diagram, the unlikely and uncanny possibility of a bodily dispersion of the organs is its direct consequence.

Whatever ontogenetic role these diagrams do exercise in subject's development, it seems that the pertinency of the mirror itself has taken a predominant role. That is, if modernity can be characterized by the fragmented body, post-modernity begins with the "broken mirror". That is, the mirror decays in its ruling and unifying function, leaving its integrating function to the workings of the Real.

For if modernity involves the *content/containing* and the *fragmented/integral* diagrams, the synthetic function of Kantian subjectivity holds the balance of the theoretical possibility that one has not to trust the mirror so easily.

In other words, although maintaining the *Ego*-formation role of the mirror, it seems that the "digestion" of modernity results in a bracketing of the mirror as an ambiguous and distorting object. If I cannot trust the mirror, the ruling function of the Symbolic-Imaginary bond carried out by it must be reconfigured in its hierarchies.

Moreover, the proliferation of images in their contemporary technological supports, testifies the fact that since bodily images are always partial and (indefinitely) technically reproducible, the workings of subjectivity revolve around the attempts to make all these imaginary fragments "one". However, this operation is fulfilled at the price of 'getting rid' of the Other; that is, as we emphasized in the breaking of the mirror, the true target of the breaking itself is the Symbolic order, the discourse of the Other.

«Mirror stage» becomes more and more synonymous with «Screen stage». Contemporaneity is—in part—the victory of the Imaginary register over the Symbolic one, of the screen over the mirror. The symptoms of this event are everywhere and it is not a surprise that Godard's 2014 movie, coherently entitled *Adieu au Language*—'Goodbye to Language'—was meant to be in 3D: the (spurious) contemporary abandonment of the Symbolic register says goodbye to language as it allows the image to settle the geometrical space by three-dimensionalizing the screen.

As the screen of Lacan's tale of the tin is portrayed as a 2D orienting and deformable surface, the 3D surpasses symptomatically the surface by *realizing*, so to speak, the Imaginary.

This is not equivalent to saying that three-dimensionality was only recently discovered. Or that space qua *geometrical spatialization* was only a recent invention. This theoretical urge for a conceptualization of the screen stage must be not mistaken for a de facto undervaluation of the flat two-dimensional space against the newly born three-dimensionality of the Imaginary. As Worringer so punctually remarked, the reading of Art History as progressive evolution towards the perfect mimesis has very little theoretical and historical bases. Moreover, this teleological reading of optics in their relation to geometrical space is often too easily keen in portraying the (2D) drawings in the caves as a proof of a pre-perspective naiveness of the old *Homo sapiens* (*vs.* the more sophisticated modern man of perspectives and three-dimensionalities) (Worringer 1997: 26–48).

This is clearly not the aim of Lacan's example of the tin of sardines. For three-dimensionality as a mandatory feature of spatial identification—the first outcome of the mirror stage—is secondary to the bi-dimensionality of the screen which allows light to pierce through and reach the retina. It's the "I'm watched" experience.

This quick emphasis on a supposed screen stage is then, no more no less, the acknowledgment that the material-technologic advent of screens and hence reproducible images, moves the fulcrum of the (Borromean) Symbolic-Imaginary-Real registers clockwise.

If "my body" is pixel, polygon, texture, patchwork, etc., the breaking of the mirror and its contemporary equivalent of the "resetting" become the always renewable purity I can achieve. The imaginary and symbolic effects of technologic materiality jump here in their evidence and suggest what Vigano rightly calls a *mediatic transfert* (Vigano 2009: 8). «If the screen of the computer takes the place of the gaze of the mother», he further claims, «the image which enters in the game of the infant won't be the ideal ego but, instead, an *avatar*» (ibid.). And we have indeed proofs of the reactualization of the fragmentation fantasy (the Lacanian *morcelé*), for example, in the paradigmatic work of Shelley Jackson's *Patchwork Girl*. It is an outstanding piece of work in which hypertextuality is pushed to its natural outcomes. It's the reactualization of *Frankenstein* in the form of a stitched girl's body.

The program of Shelley Jackson allows the user to move and modify the female body assemblage. The screen stage both conveys the possibilities of *indefinite reproduction*, *imaginary fragmentation* and *partialization*. It's not a surprise then that these three operations are isomorphic to their Symbolic counterparts: (1) indefinite reproduction becomes signifying chain (with its primacy of syntax over semantic), (2) imaginary fragmentation becomes the incompleteness of language as *there's no metalanguage*, and (3) *partialization* becomes metonimia and metaphor.

That is, the Imaginary overcoming of the other registers inherits some key features of the symbolic order, although translating them into their spatial counterparts. The post-modern *morcelé* is the birthplace of the body-as-assemblage fantasy, which is—we now can add—nothing but the fragmented body put to the fore without the Symbolic anchorage as its *validation*. Images validate themselves because we discovered the possibility of operations to articulate them. «There's no meta-image» will become our (paraphrased) *logion*.

Once again, when we speak of bodies we can't but at the same time speak about fantasy (*fantasme*). Because fantasy is the anchorage of the body to the linguistic. Epochal shifts in body fantasy are coeval to visions of the relationship between humans and world.

As we underlined in the case of the broken mirror—that is, from now on, synonymous with the *screen* mentioned in Seminar XI—the basic gesture it enables is a mythical fantasy of *re-birth*, which implies a birth of sexuality purified from the impossibility of the relationship between sexes (Vigano 2009: 12).

The victory of the Imaginary aspect upon the Symbolic one, in the mirror stage, reflects this tireless temptation to let the reflected image correspond to the other's gaze *tout court*; in other words, to superimpose them. It is not, strictly speaking, the case of a «manqué» mirror stage, as Dubost suggests in the case of narcissism (Dubost 2003: 5). It is, rather, the case of an *incomplete* mirror stage that, for its avoidance of the symbolic dimension (the Other), gives ultimate primacy to the Imaginary of the jubilant reflected image. However, Dubost is right in highlighting that what happens in the mirror stage is the «necessary difference [*écart*] between the reflection and the image», because the reflection is what will be lost, but the image will be maintained by the subject thanks to the Other's *parole* (ibid.: 6).

It's this maintaining power of the Other that finally becomes secondary if compared to the always potential repetition of the mirroring itself.

We come now to casting out nines. For if the Imaginary-Symbolic bond is the main entrance to the Real of the body, there's still a missing register: the Real itself.

There are phenomena of failed body perception which bear witness to the Real of fantasy. These phenomena—phantom limbs, supernumerary phantom limbs, surplus limbs (also known as *xenomelia*)—can shed some light into the third and "missing" component of the Borromean topology of subjects, the Real. By this token, Friedler puts forward the proposal of *phantom organs* and, from this starting point, makes a plea for a «grounding [*soubassement*] of fantasy» on the Real (Friedler 1995: 202). In short, the phenomenon of phantom limbs displays a crucial role in understanding how far the three Lacanian registers are topologically sustained one upon the other. Moreover, then, the anchorage of fantasy to its Borromean topology seems to corroborate the idea that «libido has preferential trajectories» (ibid.).

Although acknowledged in ancient times, the phenomenon of phantom limbs seems to disappear throughout history, only to resurface in recent times. Friedler rightly ascribes this theoretical oblivion to the difficulties this phenomena show when medically understood. Beside the recent neurological and psychiatric re-appraisals of it, the medical discourse was rather stubborn in accepting the idea of a part of the body which appears and disappears in such a way.

In short, phantom limb is the condition in which a subject experiences the permanence of a missing part of his body. The most popular examples are the amputated: they can still feel their missing limb. This "feeling" is conveyed by—usually—pain or tingling sensations.

In his historico-theoretical account, Friedler also points out that the complexity of the phenomenon requires a multidisciplinary approach which would at the same time comprise brain-related and psychoanalytical aspects.

In phantom limbs phenomena, the surgically removed limb still "exists" somehow. It is curious to find out that this very existence conveys some anomalies. For example, the phantom limb is usually not identical to the former amputated biological limb. The subject perceives it as being longer or shorter than the original one.

As noted by Élisabeth Grosz, phantom limb phenomena are the most convincing evidence of the existence of the body image (Grosz 1994: 70). Moreover, they are proofs of what we proposed by the syntagma «enjoyment of cognition», an aspect Lacan introduces in the mirror stage itself as the coeval birth of body ontology (fantasy) and aesthetics. Grosz further emphasizes that:

> Like hysteria, hypochondria, and sexuality itself [...], the phantom limb testifies to the pliability and fluidity of what is usually considered the inert, fixed, passive bio logical body. The biological body, if it exists at all, exists for the subject only through the mediation of an image or series of (social/cultural) images of the body and its capacity for movement and action. The phantom limb is a libidinally invested part of the body phantom, the image or *Doppelgänger* of the body the subject must develop if it is to be able to conceive of itself as an object and a body, and if it is to take on voluntary action in conceiving of itself as subject. (ibid.: 41–42)

This «libidinal investment» aspect of cognition *tout court* also plays a crucial role in the other two phenomena of failed proprioception: *supernumerary phantom limbs* and *xenomelia* (surplus-limb).

While in the case of the phantom limb the subject *still* perceives a non-existing part, in the case of *supernumerary phantom limbs* the subject experiences the phantom presence of a limb that *was never there in the first place*. That is, the subject "imagines" (broadly speaking) a supernumerary limb she never had: a sixth finger, a third leg, etc.

Xenomelia, finally, is the phenomenon by which the subject fails in recognizing a *real* part of her body as a part of it, hence trying to get rid of it by amputation.

All these phenomena not only suggest the importance of cultural norms of beauty, but also the involvement of the Image of the Other as the very grounding of narcissism and love.

As Brugger et al. shows in his social neuroscientific appraisal of xenomelia, «the main phenomenological correlates of the different forms of xenomelia concern the erotic attraction to amputees or paraplegics and the urge to simulate the desired state» (Brugger et al. 2013: 3).

That is: *change the body image* and you also change the shapes of erotic investments. The ontological becomes erogeneity.

Thus, reducing these types of phenomena to the Procrustean bed of «psychosis» would be rather rash and wouldn't tell anything relevant about their subjective experience. As Brugger emphasizes

> A full understanding of non-psychotic individuals' feeling of "being in the wrong body" and their desire to correct the mismatch between body and self by massive modifications of the prototypical, four-limbed corporeal morphology can only be reached by respecting the crosstalk between brain, mind, and society. (ibid.: 5)

Thus a patient with xenomelia could be heard saying things like «The soul feels as though it belongs to a body with only one leg. The body does not correspond to this inner reality».

Phantom limbs, xenomelia and supernumerary limbs all testify about the entanglements between different dimensions of their complexity. In the quoted study, Brugger ends up proposing a curious schema for understanding such complexity (Fig. 1).

Let's reengage the three different forms of failed body perception: phantom limb, supernumerary limb and xenomelia.

These experiences testify—before their neuroscientific appraisal—how much the Borromean topology of the Real-Symbolic-Imaginary registers could already disclose the dynamics involved in bodily and subjectivity formation.

Although we are not suggesting that there can be a psychoanalytic *clinique* of these phenomena, we would like to show how these very impasses of proprioception show, as an "empirical recoil", the stakes in giving any account of the body (or, more accurately: *body fantasies*). Phantom limbs, supernumerary phantom limbs and surplus-limbs (xenomelia), all bestow theoretical force to the argument for which what we call «our body» is really a vibrating and always reconfiguring

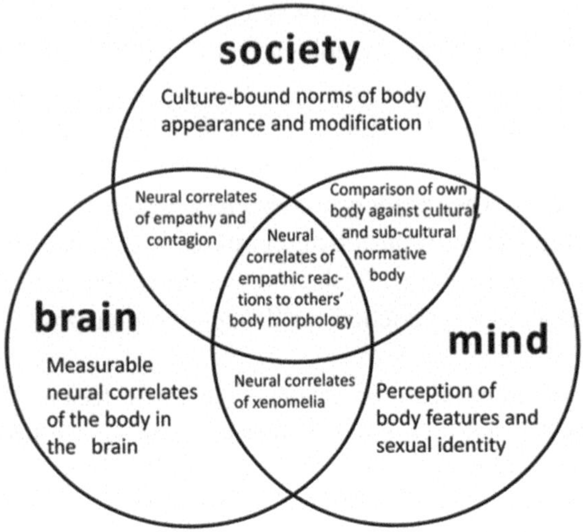

Fig. 1 Society, brain and mind schema for failed proprioception (Brugger et al. 2013)

entity; or, to say it more technically, the body is underdetermined by fantasy. These extremes point out to the Real of the body as both the *involucre* which contains a content and the body as a surface of (symbolic) *inscriptions*, along with their imaginary effects.

Rather than portraying plasticity as the end of psychoanalytical instruments as the keys of emotional life, the most likely conclusion to draw from it is that failed body proprioceptions truly reveal what happens when the Borromean knot falls apart. By the same token, extreme cases of body misrecognition reveal what happens when the relations between Symbolic, Imaginary and the Real are severed. In other words, the passage from a body fantasy to another—as showed in the case of *mutilation desires*—negatively validates the hypothesis of the Borromean topology. Cut one of the three registers and the whole structure falls apart; or, more precisely, let one of the registers fall and see how the other two are insufficient. In one case you have the overcoding of the Symbolic by the Real (phantom limb/pain), in another you have the overcoding of the Imaginary by the Symbolic (supernumerary phantom limb) and, finally, you have the overcoding of the Real by the Imaginary (xenomelia). However *ad hoc* this account may sound, it is worthwhile to underline that the *failures* of embodied subjectivity described by contemporary neuroscience negatively confirm the Borromean approach by showing what happens in extreme cases, rather then denying it *tout court.* While Malabou is right in making a plea for a Post-Lacanian "up-to-date" account of the self and emotional life, we suggest that it's quite rash to jump into *Anti*-Lacanian conclusions.

Failed proprioceptions would show, at the same time, the difficulties and the truth of a Borromean topology of the subject.

Hence, superimposable to the above tripartite diagram is the Borromean topology envisaged by Lacan: (Fig. 2).

The intersections between one register and the other become the body's fulcrums when the opposite register fails. Thus the trajectories of libidinal investment are put to work when the subject has to "recover" her body image despite the failure of one of the three registers and the potential (but theoretically impossible) misfortune of a Borromean breakdown.

The overlapping of body image and libidinal investments becomes blatant even in more ordinary cases. If one takes the example of anorexia, it is striking to notice how the subject "truly" experiences the

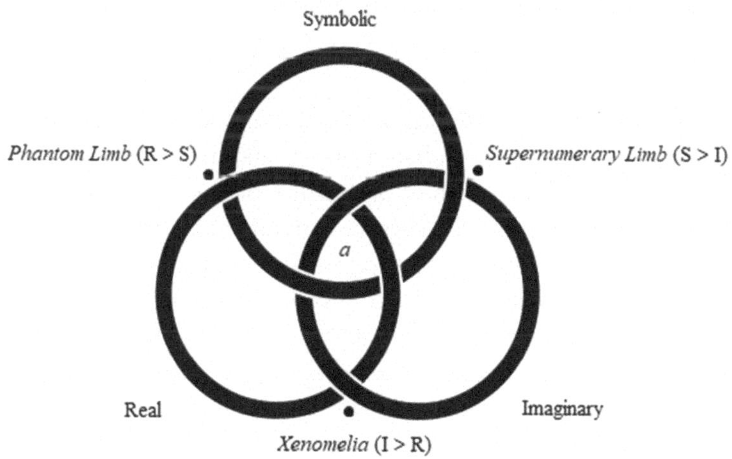

Fig. 2 Integration of the Borromean knot with failed proprioception

mirror as sending back an oversized or fat body. Thus, to recall our argument against phenomenological accounts of lived experience, nothing in the scene of the anorexic seems to suggest an indirect and unmediated relation of the subject to her bodily existence. The truth of my body is always, more or less, a "functional lie". This holds for the Ego as for the investments carried out in bodily attunements.

Next to our Odradek's analogy we should then put Friedler's *Golem*. As he says: «in the real, we have a Golem» (Friedler 1995: 195).

In his historical synthesis of the notion of «phantom limbs», Friedler comes to the theoretical acknowledgment of castration as a form of hallucination, further arguing that in the case of *hallucinated castration* (or *ablation*) what is produced is a «vanishing point on the real». It is a case in which the void «passes on the real» (ibid.: 185).

The next question is, however, how to give an account of the body-fantasy formation? How are the linguistic and cultural facets of the body entangled with bodily *Erlebnis*?

How is it that, «[…] a phantom [*fantôme*] of operation can produce a phantom organ; as in the case of castration»? (ibid.: 186). In the next section we will try to answer this questions.

3 A Philosophy of the Skin: Anzieu, Lacan and Fantasy

As we already envisaged in the context of Lacan's mirror stage, he makes an explicit use of the term «phantasmatic anatomy». That is, the *fantasme* is already at work in the *fragilization* of the body shape carried out at the organic level by the lines and "deformities" of the body itself. It's here that Anzieu's metapsychology of the skin and Fontaille's plea for an *incarnated semiosis* come as prolific co-operating frameworks. The body is a hybrid creature in which "map and territory" do mesh in a panoply of effects (what we'll call *diagrams*) embedded in particular singularities (subjects). Hence the *ways of pleasure/displeasure* share the properties inherited from the (René Thom's) *catastrophes* of subjectivity formation. Dynamics involving a symbolic dimension (signifying material and Anzieu's *formal signifiers*), an imaginary dimension (the image of the body and its possible deformations), and a real dimension (the return, or *tyche* [in Greek], of their pre-cognitive everyday effects). The Real of the body is graspable only through its phantasmal expression. As Lacan claims in his report of the 1966–1967 Seminar: «[…] for the subject there's no other entrance in the real than that of the fantasy» (Lacan 2013: 322). But we already underlined that from a Lacanian point of view it makes little sense to talk about enjoyment and fantasy formation without the support of a «sensible body». And as we noted in Friedler's account, there's plenty of somaesthetic [*somesthésique*] evidence to propose the concept of fantasies belonging to the Real or, more exactly, as readable through the Real.

However, it is at this point that the very conception of this sensibility becomes problematic. The theoretical hypothesis we would like to pursue, namely the reading of Anzieu through Lacan and vice versa, will be possible only after a historico-theoretical proviso.

Both the psychoanalysts had hostilities between each other which involved their biographical, theoretical and political lives. In order to succeed in our theoretical efforts an excursus on their relationship is required.

The apple of discord between them has very deep roots which can be dated back to—at least—Lacan's famous Aimée case (1931) and even, going earlier, to 1920.

Élizabeth Roudinesco, in her biography of Lacan, recalls the period in which he wasn't yet a "full-fledged" Freudian psychoanalyst nor still just a psychiatrist. After 1920

> there were two possible interpretations [of Freudism]: one was aimed at rehabilitating the primacy of the unconscious determination on the subject (the *id* "stronger" than the *ego*); the other, by contrary, tended to give to the ego a predominant role. (Roudinesco 1995: 53)

Although Lacan seems initially to adequate his reading to the IPA's route, namely the second one, he struggles very soon to «mediate between his own Freudian re-elaboration of the field of psychiatry and an adequate reading of the second topic» (ibid.: 54). Thus his entering the analytic couch of Loewenstein, in 1932, is not without relevance with this theoretical problem.

Moreover, this is the same period of time (1931, to be precise) in which Lacan took the famous Aimée case. This case is then reconstructed as clinical material in Lacan's *thèse de doctorat.* However, here begin the conflicting versions of the case. A case which will later on bring a *clinico-biographic* conundrum into feeding the quasi *ad personam* hates between Anzieu and Lacan. And that's for a very simple reason: Aimée was no one else than Marguerite Pantaine, Didier Anzieu's mother (!).

If we were to listen to Lacan himself, Aimée didn't receive any Freudian type of cure because of her "fault". That is, Lacan underlined, as Roudinesco claims, his complete innocence and absence of responsibility concerning the outcome of the case. However, Anzieu's later afterword to Jean Allouch's *Histoire de la psychanalyse en France* was a proof of the fact that it was Aimée (Marguerite) herself who refused to be analyzed by Lacan, a man she described as «too seductive and too foolish» (ibid.) to be analyzed by.

However, things got even worse when Anzieu himself became a patient of Lacan in 1949, «without knowing that Marguerite [his mother] was the [famous] Aimée case» (ibid.: 204).

It so happened that the already psychiatric inmate Marguerite/Aimée (at Sainte-Anne), decided to pay a visit to her son and his wife. She then told Didier Anzieu the truth behind the Aimée case. In other words, she told him about the analysis with Lacan and about the *thèse de doctorat* in which she appeared under the name of "Aimée". Suddenly Anzieu decided to read the *thèse* in order to discover more about that story.

When asked why he didn't recognize the last name of the patient ("Anzieu"), Lacan confessed he didn't know the true identity of Aimée until a certain point in the development of the cure. However, according to Roudinesco, the truth is that Lacan didn't ignore the real name, but instead he repressed it. Thus, Lacan didn't want to admit his fault in front of her son Didier.

This brief biographical excursus brings us to its institutional outcomes and, maybe even to the theoretical ones.

As the famous institutional disaster of the 1964–1965 period, in which the legitimated Freudian France was born, divided Anzieu and Lacan with (now) an institutional certification, all the ingredients for further theoretical conflicts were settled. In the *Quinzaine littéraire*, Didier Anzieu called his old analyst a «heretic» (ibid.: 355). Later on, Lacan had the occasion to retort by accusing Anzieu of «stealing his ideas» (ibid.: 356, Lacan was referring to Anzieu's book on Freud's auto-analysis).

Everything is soon done. Around the name of Aimée (Lacan's patient, Anzieu's mother) and, more importantly, around the likely inevitable transfert which occurred during Anzieu's analysis with Lacan, a theoretical "iron curtain" was the most likely outcome.

It is quite surprising to read Lacan's quick "memorandum" of the Aimée case and to notice that, according to him, «the fidelity to the symptom's *formal envelope*» brings to «literary effects» such as «involuntary poetry» (Lacan 2002: 62). That is, the symptom's *expressive* facet of the 'pre-analytical' Lacan is conceived as *passage à l'acte* (ibid.), a theoretical move Anzieu himself would refuse without a moment's hesitation.

We shouldn't jump, however, to a naive biographical appraisal of the reasons behind a supposedly incompatible treatment of *fantasy*. For this reason, we would like to suggest that the paths taken by the two psychoanalysts do interlace each other in some crucial points. Namely, the points from which it is possible to build up a model for fantasy formation. Despite the barbs of criticism moved toward Anzieu in the Rome Discourse (September the 26th, 1953), and despite the fact that Lacan abandoned pretty much every attempt in building a metapsychology (in contrast to Anzieu), there's a lot to be shared between the two concerning the concepts of "body" and "fantasy". In other words, in order to propose a model for fantasy formation, it is required to draw some key notions both from Anzieu's theory of the psychic envelope (skin-Ego) and Lacan's general account of fantasy and the effects of language on the human body.

There's an underlying path which allows us, passing through Lacan and Anzieu, to overcome their mutual incompatibilities.

One of the main points of contention between the two is the one regarding the putative role the mirror stage plays in carrying out subjectivity formation. In short, although Anzieu quotes Lacan in several points of his *The skin-Ego*, he's not so keen in considering the mirror stage as the *main* element for the ontogenic birth of subjectivity:

> [...] going back to the mirror stage, as it was conceived by Lacan, in which the Ego identifies itself as different upon the model of the specular image of the whole unified body, Winnicot described an earlier phase, that in which the mother's face and the environment's reactions provide the first mirror to the child constituting his Self starting from what is reflected in this way. But, like Lacan, Winnicot places emphasis on visual signals. I would like to underline the existence, even earlier on, of a resounding mirror, or of an auditive-phonic skin, and its function for the acquisition, by the psychic apparatus, of the capacity of signifying and then symbolizing. (Anzieu 2017: 161–162)

From the perspective of Anzieu it would be rush to reduce the Ego as a result of the jubilant experience of mirroring experienced by the child. There's something which stands *before* the mirror stage. Namely, the skin envelope as an already sensible surface capable of receiving stimuli from the outside and, at the same time, of constituting a sensorial interface which puts—already—the seeds for the acquisition of symbolic and signifying capacities.

For the same reason, it's the *placing* of the fantasy (*fantasme*) which inherits this basic difference in subjectivity's preconditions. While Anzieu's portrays fantasy as a directly skin-manifestation, Lacan tends to give—in a classical Freudian fashion—fantasy a *phrastic* structure. As Lacan will remark when speaking about his conception of *fantasme*: «fantasy is a phrase, on the model of *a child is being beaten* [...]» (Lacan 2013: 322).

At the same time, for Anzieu fantasies take the virtual and diagrammatic shapes of singular deformations of the envelope. The skin-Ego is that entity, very early constituted in the subject's development, which has the function of creating a content/containing structure, along the inside/outside distinction, the me/other difference, etc.

By this token, one of the first definition he gives to the skin-Ego is: «the establishment of the skin-Ego responds to the need of a narcissistic involucre and assures the psychic apparatus with the certainty and constancy of a basic wellbeing» (Anzieu 2017: 41).

And it's not a surprise that while Lacan's mirror stage has as its preconditions the fragmentation fantasy, Anzieu's skin-Ego is formulated upon the fantasy of the mutilation, of the horror of a skinless body indistinguishable from the body of the other (i.e. the mother's). While for Lacan the mirror stage conveys the body-as-one Gestalt, Anzieu gives more importance to the supposedly pre-mirror phase in which an individuation is carried out through the *fantasy of the skin-Ego* itself. As he says:

> The skin-Ego is a reality belonging to a phantasmal order: portrayed into fantasies, dreams, ordinary language, body attitudes, thought disturbances; and, at the same time, it furnishes the imaginary space constituting the fantasy, the dream, the reflection, any psychopathological organization. (ibid.: 4)

Yet both the psychoanalysts seem to start from the primacy of fantasy. However, while Lacan portrays the first fantasy as the fragmentation to be overcome, Anzieu puts the indistinct fantasy of a caregiver-child "collective" envelope, which will be later on split creating a skin—body-world interface—upon which the Ego is based.

Anzieu's plea for a re-habilitation of the skin as a respectable and worth exploring organ is due to this ontogenic primacy of the sensible («phonic envelop») over the linguistic (Lacan's Symbolic or, more precisely, *linguistérie*).

That is: in the beginning it was the *envelope*. Anzieu also claims that «the three bases of human thought, the skin, the cortex and sexual coupling correspond to three surface configurations: the envelope, the cap, the pouch» (ibid.: 10). In other words, the material skin (as sensible surface), as it constitutes the first relations between the body and the environment, carries out a series of «catastrophes» (in René Thom's meaning) which will take the child to the state of a thinking and "independent" individual.

Why is the skin so important? Because, among all the other organs «it is almost always available to receive signals, to comprise codes without them interfering with others. The skin *cannot refuse* a vibrotactile or electrotactile signal: it can't close the eyes or the mouth, neither it can stop its ears or nose» (ibid.: 14).

As the first and most prominent organ, the skin is also peculiar in that it is always available for exchanges with the outside. Another key point Anzieu doesn't wait to underline is the fact that the skin is also the first "place" or surface upon which *nudity* and *erogeneity* are constituted: «In its nudity it materializes our undressing, but also our sexual arousal» (ibid.: 17).

Considered all this theoretical premises, Anzieu describes fantasies as the contingent alteration of the skin-Ego. The skin-Ego conveys mainly two functions: it is an *envelope* in the sense of creating a self-other distinction and, also, it is a *surface of inscription* as it allows what is outside to leave traces on it. Here it's the description of a pervert masochist case:

> The failure of the containing function of the skin-Ego is not only materialized through the countless burn and cut scars all over the body, but through the planing of particular excrescences (right breast torn off, right little-toe cut with a steel saw), through the filling of particular sockets (belly button filled with melted lead), through the artificial enlargement of some orifices (anus, glans' chink). The function of the container is restored through the repetitive establishment of a suffering-envelope thanks to the wide diversity, cleverness and cruelty of the instruments and techniques of torture: the fantasy of the ripped off skin must be continuously reinvigorated by the pervert masochist so that he can regain a skin-Ego. (Anzieu 2017: 111)

Before going through in building a theoretical bridge between Lacan and Anzieu, it is mandatory to shed some light to the overall structure of Anzieu's discourse.

Although his arguments are clinically apparent, Anzieu is here victim of a misconception regarding the already discussed mirror stage, for he seems to undervalue one of its aspects. Lacan doesn't claim that the mirror stage is *just* the focal point after which the Ego is formed. The mirror stage has an imaginary facet (the reflection) and, also, a Symbolic one. What the mirror stage carries out it's the operation of the *anchorage* between the Imaginary body as one (the jubilant Ego) and the signifying chain (the signifiers in the uttering of the caregiver). Anzieu seems to foreshadow this second and crucial aspect. If we take this departing point as a mere "hermeneutic" short circuit, we are able to balance the accounts. For it is striking how the body-as-inscription-surface is both present in Lacan and Anzieu.

The problem is, from a Lacanian point of view, to introduce the ingredient of enjoyment (the object *a* in the matheme of the fantasy). But when he does underline the way this linguistic-sensible entanglement is carried out, he underlines an aspect of the body which is common to Anzieu's skin-Ego:

> With this connection to enjoyment we open the only ontic admissible by us. [...] We argued that the place of the Other is nowhere else than in the body, which is not intersubjectivity, but rather the *integumentary scars* on the body, peduncles inserting themselves upon its orifices to carry out an holding function, ancestral and technical artifices gnawing it. (Lacan 2013: 323)

That's how the body becomes the body. That is, by becoming a three-dimensional and textual map, by constituting erotizable objects, objects which are—we can now add—nothing but the points through which *pleasure* and *displeasure* can be achieved.

One key point we must underline here is that neither Lacan nor Anzieu conceived the body as an *undifferentiated monolithic block*. Thus, Lacan gives some remarks on erogenous zones, in Seminar XI, describing them as «edges», «hemming» (as the mouth) (Lacan 2004: 164), etc.

The problem is shifted then from the mere statement that the body is a sensible entity to *how* language and signifiers enter the scene. Thus, Lacan never denied sensibility, but ascribed to the Other the role of leaving signifying *scars* upon the teguments of the body. These scars or signifying materials do share the Janusian feature of the interface, doubling the body into points upon which this «peduncles» carry out a «holding function». That is, they *hold a text*.

Leclaire talks about a doubling of the body apropos of this kind of textuality. More precisely, he claims that the body is «*zonified*», thus achieving the aspect of a set of «literary spaces» (Leclaire 1971: 62).

He coherently underlines that matters of pleasure-displeasure are not *just* conceivable through the concept of «need», for pleasure has nothing to do with the organic (as the chainsmokers or the alcoholics show), but rather with the body as a set of *places* («lieux») and a conflictual order (ibid.), a conception a philosopher would easily link to a Nitzschean dynamic of forces.

If the body is not a monolithic block, but rather an already incarnated fantasy (Anzieu) or a map of tegumentary signifying scars (Lacan), it follows that the body is to be conceived as a *virtual surface dotted with Gibsonian affordances*. The body hosts the discourse of the Other by making it "flesh". That is, to borrow from Friedler's account of Real fantasy once gain, libido seems to have preferential trajectories. As we will later show, this is equal to the claim that *fantasy is diagrammatized enjoyment*. That is, the theme of a disconnection between the knowledge (*savoir*) of the body on the body itself reflects the idea of the body as a system which affords virtual operations. It is conceivable in itself as a locus of possibilities and impossibilities—paths and constraints—hosting symbolic representations of objects (such as the 'mouth-breast' object). In their 'comedy', these paths of possible/impossible enjoyment are not pursued at random.

Before entering into the details of this textual-surface account of the body, we should recall for a moment the argument about phantom limbs, for Lacan's acknowledges the existence of another fantasy before the fragmentation's one and even earlier to the Œdipus: the *castration fantasy*.

This basic «mutilation of a limb» (Lacan 2013: 48) (male member) is directly linked to the nudity we described in Lacan's reading of the Adamic myth. The uncanny nature of the castration fantasy is *not* due to the physical removal of a piece of the body per se. It's rather due to the fact that the detachment of a piece of body makes it *replaceable* and hence analogous to a social artifact. That's why Lacan is more interested to the fact that Adam and Eve begin to wear *made* dresses, the third and final act of the tale, for if they are artificial or human-made, they enter—as a consequence—the realm of exchangeability, values and the differential values of signifiers. That's the "uncanny" core of the detached-limb fantasy. As we underlined when we spoke about the social and aesthetic dimensions of failed proprioception, the fantasy of losing one's member is related to the *me/non-me* distinction or, moreover, to the *containing* function of Anzieu's skin-Ego.

To recall the concept of symbolic objects *qua* values we proposed previously, the mutilation fantasy (and horror) unleashes the idea that a piece of my own body becomes a value; or, more precisely, becomes *evaluable.* Hence, the achievement of a given value in a differential matrix is the imaginary risk through which the limb sets the axiom of sexuality in the social realm: the mere possibility of losing the phallus—'non-phallus'—is what performs the very genesis of desire in that the Other becomes not just what towards which my desire is aimed at, but also the instance that demands "my phallus" per se. Hence the castration fantasy is not a mere "fear" of materially losing a piece of my body: it is rather the very condition from which the desire of the Other is doubled. The Other asks the subject "to lose something" (symbolically) to enter the signifying chain and, reciprocally, the order of civilization.

4 A Philosophy of the Skin: Involucre, Inscription, Surface, Patchwork

Teguments—i.e. textures—cover the body in particular points, which are «peduncles» inserted into the *affordances*—in the Gibsonian sense—of the body. The holding function is nothing but the erotization of the body which is, we can now say, nothing but a playful and dynamic text.

In short, this idea implies that the body is to be conceived as an entity made up of portions which afford particular pieces of linguistically codified fragments. The resulting patchwork is, in turn, what is manifested with fantasy. As such, then, fantasies are to be considered as being both ontologically and causally prior to the second elaboration pursued by thought. To be more precise, it is more the case that thought itself is to be understood as emanating from fantasies conceived in this way.

In order to understand the body as a dynamic patchwork, the tattoo (along Lacan's use of it) can help us in grasping some of its main features.

Wiener envisages three possible facets of the tattoo. It involves, according to him, three different dimensions. The tattoo has the characters of (1) the *hieroglyph*, (2) the *trace* and (3) the *stigma*. In short, it has an (1) esthetic/beauty dimension (hieroglyph), a (2) mnemonic dimension (trace) and, finally, a (3) identification symbol (stigma).

The tattoo is a «real trace on the body which is situated in a bond between the symbolic and the imaginary registers. The imaginary, erotic dimension of the tattoo is linked to its visible aspect on the skin which appeals the gaze» (Wiener 2001: 35).

It draws at the same time the objects as imaginary supports of enjoyment (objects as correlates of the subject) and their already 'externalized' nature of being under the gaze of the Other.

Indeed, it is a cultural tool in which different functions are coevally executed: «it displays a will of incarnating beauty, art at the level of the body in a durable form. As trace [*empreinte*], its quasi indelible feature [...] confers to it the consistency of an archive, of a cicatricial memory. As stigma, initiation mark or totem, it constitutes an attempt of symbolization of the flesh» (ibid.: 36).

The emphasis here must be put on the word 'flesh'. Lacan's own reflection on the tattoo allows him to detach it from its direct anthropological or ethnic application in favor of a psychoanalytical reevaluation of its meaning.

He links the tattoo to the idea of 'virtual organs'; or, as we may put it, to virtual organs of enjoyment as particular subtexts of the body. Lacan underlines the fact that the 'organ of enjoyment' doesn't coincide with any actual organic counterpart. Instead, even their «being unreal doesn't prevent [organs] from incarnating [*de s'incarner*]»; and he continues saying that «one of the most ancient ways of incarnating this unreal organ on the body is the tattoo, the scarification. The carving has the utter function of situating the subject for the Other, marking its place in the field of group relations, between one and all the others. And, at the same time, it has evidently an *erotic function* which is perceived by everyone around» (Session of May the 27th, 1964, quoted in Wiener 2001: 37, our italics).

The tattoo is a living artifact which signals the prominence of an already 'intersubjective' self-acquisition of one's own body. It «exposes itself to the gaze» and «constitutes as well a source of enjoyment of the ink upon the skin. *The skin as corporeal envelope reflected on the mirror is a source of enjoyment*, particularly around its cuts (the mouth...) and its condensations (birthmarks, stains, tatoos)» (Wiener 2001: 38).

The body is the place of this ongoing outward *élan* towards the Other; it is with this constitutive operation that the Real of the body exceeds, during its formation, the demands of (and inscriptions into) the Other. The latter functions as a maieutic gravitational point which allows the body to articulate itself with what will later constitutes the whole of its patchworks.

It is at this point where the problem of the body *tout court* intersects with the body of psychoanalysis. For example, Jacques Fontanille underlines that «most current semiotics or semiologies of the body are traditionally gestural and mimo-gestural semiotics, which rightly don't speak about the actant-body [*corps-actant*]» (Fontanille 2011: 81). That is, most of the conceptualizations about the body treats the gesture as «a sort of somatic accompanying of the verbal communication» (ibid.). Rather than seeing the bodily as a mere substitute or completion of the verbal, Fontanille makes a plea for the body of psychoanalysis «which, far from being a simple instrument, it is itself the source and the site of energies (drives) from which psychic instances take their representations» (ibid.: 82).

We can borrow here the concept of imaginary objects as gestures. As we showed previously, represented actions inherit the possibilities and constraints of their concrete counterparts. However, the idea of virtual organs implies that this very 'mentalized' side of the action is already active in shaping the ways in which the subject relates (bodily) with the environment.

The actant-body shows «some recurrent and typical figures, which are, first and foremost, *the flesh in movement*, and the *corporeal envelope*» (ibid.: 83, our italics).

It is within the first mother-infant bodily interactions that all the subsequent catastrophes are set to take place. The «minimal experience of 'there's something which has a sense'»—which is what we've being calling 'thought' or the 'speculative'—«supposes an encounter between two movements: [...] the movement of the becoming world [...] and [...] that of the attentive body».

In the pre-split subjectivity, it is «our moving flesh, real or imaginary, from which the movement is carried out, modulated or opposed by the 'tendency lines' of being» (ibid.: 86).

These tendency lines are diagrams of the body which result from the virtualization of the organs. The tattoo, then, is not the concrete portion of ink, but indicates instead the taking (by the Other) of the subject into a scenario in which the body is rendered asymmetrical.

While I call these tendency lines 'diagrams', Fontanille uses the *icon*, a notion which is far from being incompatible with the first. This becoming iconic of the body is what affects «the articulation and reception of verbal language as well» (ibid.: 87).

Fontanille pinpoints, then, that the «Freudian barriers» have to be considered as «sorting operators [*opérateurs de tri*] which select, carrying out an incarnated axiologic modalization, what is good or bad, acceptable or intolerable, desirable or repugnant, vivifying or disruptive, etc.» (ibid.: 89).

The author further acknowledges this already 'intersubjective' facet of one's own body when he states that the «envelope, as interface between me and the other, can't be logically assimilated neither to the *I* nor the other. It's a different thing, therefore, in that it is constituted thanks to the stimulations emanating from another flesh; it is *mine* as well, for it manages the energies coming from the I». This envelope or set of patchworks has then, «literally the statute of a 'me-myself as another [*moi-même comme un autre*]» (ibid.: 89).

Anzieu's skin-Ego is what, accordingly, Fontanille rephrases as «Self-envelope [*Soi*-enveloppe]».

It is the connections and exchanges with the Other that gives existence to the interface. The fantasy, as what crystallizes the patchworks and asymmetries into their quasi-definitive state, is what arises from the transformation of the envelope into an inscription surface; that is, the body becomes erogenous because it synthesizes the paths of exchange from inside to outside (and vice versa) through what psychoanalysis calls fantasy. Indeed, that's why fantasies are also always anatomical. Or, to put it differently, that's why the subject's access to its own body comes often in the shape of a sophistry regarding the relationship between its supposed 'energetic' and 'anatomical' side.

As underlined by Fontanille:

> [...] The Self-envelope converts an amorphous flux of tensions and emotions in signifying figures, identifiable and distinctive, also inscribed in the form of sensible impressions. Thanks to clinical observations, D. Anzieu shows indeed how the envelope hosts the mark of «formal signifiers», expression which conceals certain typical configurations incarnating the states or the internal movements of the subject under care. The formal signifier or «configuration signifier» is the result of a coherent and recognizable deformation of the envelope. (ibid.: 93)

However, here a problem arises which touches directly the conundrum of metapsychology or of the speculative. It is the problem regarding the specific *way* to access these constructions or moving patchworks. It has to do with the strict opposition between the supposed sophistry of the body (anatomical fantasies) and the logicality of signifiers.

Moreover, this problem can be reinterpreted as standing also (but not totally) for the opposition between the reliability of the signifying chain and free association *versus* the arbitrary tendency lines of the envelope. We could here suggest that the sophistry of the latter is hardly suited for the analysis of the first.

I argue, instead of straight opposition, to treat the body as a place in which both sophistry and logicality are involved at the same time. In other words, the idea according to which the bodily is to be conceived as an object which eschews logical reasoning must be rejected or, at least, fairly softened.

It is the reason why I kept the notion of the diagram as a useful tool to grasp the problem of the Real of the body.

However, I also maintain that this opposition is not to be conceived as just a secondary reflection on the issue of the body but that it is, instead, *constitutive* of subjective life itself.

It is a trope which echoes in the paradigmatic figure of Antonin Artaud, a figure which can be taken as a counterpart of Lacan's Joyce.

Jacques Derrida underlines that, for Artaud, «*organization* is articulation, the conjunction of functions and limbs (artron, *artus*), the work and play of their differentiation» and that, therefore, he «doesn't trust the articulated body» just like he doesn't trust «articulated language» (Derrida 2002: 242).

The reason behind Artaud's idiosyncrasy is that «articulation is the structure of my body and structure is always expropriative structure» (ibid.). It is, as I already noted, an intrinsic possibility of the body which lies in the mirror stage. There's a game of a supposed totalization of the body and, contemporary to this, a grammatization of it; it becomes one but by opening the possibility for articulation which has to be found in the Other.

Derrida further remarks that such a view rejects the idea of the organ altogether (ibid.). Because, in short, the biological body corresponds to the alienating differentiation of its parts. It is, however, with Lacan's reflection on the tattoo and the virtual organs that another possibility arises.

Artaud's lamentation on the alienating function of linguistic articulation holds only if we consider the relationship between language and the body as having to do with a rigid axiomatization of the body in its early stages. Indeed, it seems that Artaud is against alienation in its first general organic aspect. For example, Derrida underlines that «the moment sex becomes an organ, it becomes alien to me, it abandons me, to get the arrogant autonomy of an inflated object» (ibid.: 243).

For this reason, it comes as no surprise that the tattoo is envisaged as something which «paralyses the gesture and kills the voice» (ibid.: 244). The tattoo is what kills the lived and corporeal experience of the flesh in its pre-organized form (ibid.).

The tattoo, according to this view, is something like a stagnant and motionless residue which is unsuited to grasp the living dynamic of the bodily. For this reason, Derrida underlines that, for Artaud, it is more a matter of stigmata rather than tattoos (ibid.: 245).

This view sheds a precious light on the sophistry-logicality dyad. In fact, what Lacan suggests via the 'peduncles' and the 'tattoo' is not to be understood as a 'logicalization' of the bodily into the signifying. It is rather the case of the interplay between the 'dotted' and the 'continuum': it is with language (Artaud's conception of alienation) that the dotting of the flesh becomes the place upon which further non-dotted (or moving) elements—as tendency lines or diagrams—are capable of arising.

It is with the tattoo, taken in Lacan's broad sense, that the Real is set in motion.

As Jacuqes Fontanille argues in the context of Didier Anzieu, the envelope is the functor of two functions: that of the *container* and that of the *inscription surface* (Fontanille 2011: 96).

The organizing function of the self (as distinguished from the other) is what sets in motion the possibility of the creative work of the patchwork to go beyond its prima facie baptism, namely that of sifnigiers. It is with the differentiation of the flesh that a former imbalance is set to produce the Real of the body.

5 Diagrams—Some Theoretical and Historical Remarks

The concept of the diagram has different but concomitant meanings. Its history begins with Charles Sanders Peirce and resurfaces throughout the works of Gilles Deleuze, Félix Guattari, Michel Foucault and Gilles Châtelet.

Peirce envisages diagrams as a subclass of icons. Icons are signs which display a factual similitude between the signifier and signified; for example, a similitude between a representation of an animal and the animal represented. The first is connected to the second via their resemblance.

Icons have, however, two subclasses: that of the image and that of the diagram. In the case of the image, the relation between the signifier and the signified is that of a similitude of qualities. In the diagram, instead, the similitude is about the relations between their parts.

As such, then, the diagram is a sign which displays a possible matching (despite being constitutively incomplete) between the objects and parts of the signifier and the objects and parts of the signified.

The basic difference lies in the fact that in diagrams it is the structural or spatial relations which matter, and not the intrinsic qualities of the elements put in conjunction.

However, it is most notably with Félix Guattari, as Claude Mercier underlines in his historical survey, that the concept of the diagram takes a non-anthropocentric and non-binary conceptual twist.

Guattari deemed it unfruitful for the philosopher to use scientific concepts in a metaphorical way. The peril is that of a mere imitation of the scientific jargon in an impressionistic fashion. Instead, he made a plea for a type of creative notions which are «fundamentally inexact and therefore rigorous» (quoted in Mercier 2012: 180).

That is, he envisaged diagrams as tools which can be used (by the philosopher or by the artist) despite—and *thanks to*—their constitutive degree of approximation. This key approximative content of the diagram is due to its *dynamic* nature: while the image rests on an anthropocentric schema which blocks the object within its qualities, the diagram is an open (or deterritorialized) way to portray objects along with their forces and developments.

As such, then, a diagram is always and essentially incomplete; it gives a picture of a portion of being which is isolable only because it is this portion *itself* which legitimate its objects.

Within the diagram, objects and their relations are—so to speak—ontologically co-dependent.

Indeed, as underlined by Mercier, «it is with the sign-diagram that one passes through the unconscious, the sign-diagram will be what remains after the operation of the signifier. Meaning escaped significations and the subject» (ibid.: 183).

A diagram is what is left after the baptism of the signifiers. They set the 'niche' of the body in motion as a set of constitutive imbalances and objects belonging to them.

It is the signifier when it is taken outside the realm of meaning or sense. It helps us to describe the post-historical Real of the topological Lacan; as Mercier pinpoints, the diagram «constructs a Real to come, a new type of reality» (ibid.).

The diagram, to put it differently, flattens the dyad of signifier/signified into the horizontal and open-ended flux of signifiers. It calls for an «a-signifying semiotic» (Watson 2009: 191).

If Guattari opened the possibility to read diagrams as maps of the configurations of the Real, it is with Foucault that the diagram comes close to its mathematical roots. When elaborating on the Panopticon in his *Discipline and Punish*, Foucault makes a quick remark on the fact that the Panopticon must not be confused with neither an oneiric edifice nor with its real and material counterpart. Instead, he pinpoints *en passant* that the Panopticon is, indeed, a diagram.

It is not simply an edifice in which one is constantly seen without seeing; the Panopticon is, broadly speaking, a diagram made of vectors and objects coming in and out of these vectors.

It is an «abstract machine which is defined through a pure function: *to see without being seen*; and through a pure matter: *any human multiplicity*» (Mercier 2012: 197).

That is, a diagram must not be confused with proto-temporal archetypes (as if one could enlist the whole plethora of diagrams); and it also doesn't equate with the material counterparts in which it is instantiated.

A concept here is at hand: that of the schema or the pattern. Diagrams are patterns that «emerge as meaningful structures for us chiefly at the level of our bodily movements through space, our manipulation of objects, and our perceptual interactions» (Johnson 1990: 28–29).

That is, a diagram comprises all the features of fantasy: it is an abstract bodily interface mediating the inside and the outside: as such, it distributes its objects by constituting them at the same time.

Of course, the type of things to which a diagram refers to are isolable only insofar as they take a temporary crystallized form.

And it is at this point where the physico-geometrical matrix of the diagram makes its entrance.

In fact, the implicit reference of these philosophical implementations of the concept is that of the works of mathematician Gilles Châtelet.

Since it has a pattern-like facet, Châtelet claims, «a diagram can immobilize a gesture» (Châtelet 1993: 33).

'A Panopticon' is, as such, the mental gesture which mobilizes vectors of forces in a radial way. It is easy to notice here that, because of this openness of the diagram, it can be implemented as a skeletal structure for subsequent and differentiated metaphors.

In this formal and mathematized version of the diagram, Châtelet claims, the diagram is a «swarming of virtual gestures» such as «pointing, closing, prolonging, streaking of the continuum» (quoted in Mercier 2012: 185).

It manifests an open creativity which is paradigmatic of poetry and its short-circuiting of language itself. Diagrams «are like the accomplices of the poetic metaphor» (Châtelet 1993: 33).

The non-static nature of the diagram is so that its existence comprises its genesis (ibid.). In other words, the objects of the diagram (being them the 'dot', 'the line', etc.) are *suggested* via the development of the diagram itself.

Just like imaginary objects (or simulated gestures), diagrams can be taken to stand for the possibility of a knowledge which explores the possibilities, constraints and transformations of gestures in the broad sense and, at the same time, of gestures in the sense of specific phantasmal forms.

6 The Diagrammatization of Enjoyment

In the Lacanian context, the tool which allows for an immanentist or deterritorrialized Real is that of topology. As noted by Rousselle, the strings of the Borromean knot «might be thought to reach out from the lines of vector-space toward infinity» (Rousselle 2018: 164). However, while he revolves around physics, I'm here suggesting to use the diagram (two routes which are likely similar in their aim). It is by using such a tool that Anzieu's idea of the formal signifier and Lacan's idea of fantasy come closer to one another.

Of course, such an operation is possible only with the proviso that Anzieu's concept of formal signifier, while it surely describes diagrams, lies beyond Saussurian linguistics and, as such, poses a certain number of problems and epistemological difficulties (Golse 2008: 110).

Another risk, which is is connected to the first, is that formal signifiers, unlike fantasies in the traditional psychoanalytical sense, are not constructed on the model of the phrase. That is, fantasy in the Freudian sense is posterior to the acquisition of language because of its very phrasal nature (such as in the case of 'a child is being beaten') (ibid.: 112).

I take nonetheless the risk of aligning this bodily account of the signifier as a set of textile or diagrammatic operations with Lacan's Real despite the apparent limitations.

In July the 24th, 1986, Didier Anzieu presented the concept of «Ego-skin» [*Moi-peau*] at a congress which was held in Paris. In a quick remark, he evoked the concept of formal signifier, giving a clear-cut definition of the notion. For him, «formal signifiers are about modifications of space and have a fundamental role in constituting psychic envelopes» (quoted in Golse 2008: 111–112). He further proceeds in enumerating some exemplars: «A portion of skin shrinks, a common skin is ripped off (classical fantasies), a volume flattens, a plane surface bends and swirls, a straight line turns, bends…» (ibid.).

Just like diagrams, formal signifiers are meant to indicate transformations (ibid.: 114). A formal signifier is, to put it roughly, a «representation of forms» (ibid.: 111).

As such, they have to do more with states of matter or with the psychic space taken as a development of tropes.

Although Lacan was explicitly against the idea of the *metaphor* as a tool for describing poetic creativity (unlike Anzieu, we must add), even psychoanalysts are divided on the issue of the use of metaphoric reasoning.

Starting from the case of Lacan himself, when speaking about the object of the *recess* [*recès*], Lacan explicitly says that any graphic-imaginary representation of it must be rejected in favor of a pure *logical* appraisal of it. He quickly adds that «the recourse to the *image* to explain the metaphor is always false» (Lacan 2006: 94, our italics). Indeed, it has to be done through the diagram.

To use our lexicon, Lacan would resolutely abstain from giving to the *image* of the recess any imaginary or graphic modelization of a given fantasy, thus being in perfect coherence with his idea that fantasy has to be grasped from a *logical* (or phrase-like) point of view.

We argue that this is one of the limits of portraying dynamic-bodily objects with *just* logical tools, for the expression of fantasy is nothing but living (enjoyable) metaphor (although the concept of diagram comprises broader aspects of the metaphor).

Here the theoretical proviso of an incompatibility between Anzieu and Lacan reestablishes its importance, although it may serve us well in depicting a possible *unificatory* outcome.

Although it is true that signifiers in their *chain-like* aspect (the *automaton*) shun any possibility of a pictorial or imaginary representation, it is also true that Anzieu's formal signifiers are different from mere representations.

For Golse formal signifiers are easily «metaphorizable» (Golse 2008: 115); so the main conundrum is to whether let the entity of formal signifier fit into Lacanian psychoanalysis or establish some hybrid account completely anew. We will abstain from taking a firm decision on this point, since we prefer to develop a coherent account of fantasy and let the reader decide whether the loyalty to one school or the other is a sufficient reason for rejecting our discourse *tout court*.

Just after the 'anti-image' remark made by Lacan, he follows adding that the metaphor is not an image but rather the «specular image of the body» (Lacan 2006: 94), a point we already encountered when speaking about the body image in the mirror stage.

But immediately after recalling the role of the metaphor as having to do with the specular image of the body, Lacan corroborates this claim by saying that this anthropomorphic image «masks the function of the orifices» (ibid.).

That's how the arguments about the non-monolithic character of the body and fantasy as a *textualizing* (diagrammatizing) of the body do converge. The Lacanian argument about tegumentary scars and body as a surface of *peduncles* upon which enjoyment hooks itself via the linguistic (and Gibsonian) affordances of these very edges and orifices, finally seems to hold the benefits of interpreting formal signifiers with body in the Lacanian sense. As Kiarina Kordela remarks: «[T]he symptom is signification in the sense of a Mark-of-the-*Vertretung*, a mark with an organic bond with the body-of-a-concept, a reason for which it can manifests itself not just at the level of discourse but also as body Mark [...] given to be decoded» (Kiarina Kordela 2017: 148).

However, here we encounter the two limits undermining the Lacanian approach. They can be synthesized in this way: (1) although Lacan famously envisaged a way to "overcome" the symptom by transforming it into *sinthome* (as in the paradigmatic case of James Joyce), he doesn't seem to develop any theory explaining *how* is this transformation achievable; (2) since this very transformation implies an unavoidable conceptualization of *creativity*, it is striking to notice how the issue of *creativity* itself is never thematized *per se*. One could say that Lacanian psychoanalysis does recognize the role played by signifiers and the Symbolic (more broadly) in—let's say—pictorial productions.

Nonetheless, it is discouraging to find out that the Real of *jouissance* supposedly carried out by the *sinthome* is never fully explained in the *concrete* and *practical* ways in which it manifests.

That's why, moreover, we preferred to join a *hybrid* route linking the insights of Lacan with those of Didier Anzieu. The latter, accordingly, devoted much of his efforts in proposing a theory for artistic creativity or creativity tout court. If it is the functioning of the fantasy that, put upside-down, turns into an occasion for *diagrammatizing* enjoyment into shapes and forms, how could we abstain from giving a hypothesis (at least) for how is this even possible?

The main reason why psychoanalysis had always to abstain from such descriptions is quite simple: *drive* (Freud's *Trieb*) was always acknowledged as the "myth" of psychoanalysis. That is, since the main difference between drive and desire is that the first *has* as its goal an *object* and the second is object-less, drive itself manifests to us *only* when it takes its peculiar *phantasmatic form* (fantasy) or when it is entangled with desire. To put it another way, since drive's «essence» is «to be undetermined» (Baas 2012: 24), then drive never manifests itself *empirically*.

Although it is methodically and clinically mandatory to distinguish between desire (*automaton* of the signifying chain) and drive (the *surplus* of object small *a*), we argue that very often psychoanalysis falls prey of a "normative" bias in favor of desire over drive. This is not surprising, for the very features of desire make it way more manageable than fantasy, an entity which always manifests itself as an arbitrary and "distorted" phrasal form. Although «for desire, the aim is determined by the object» whilst in the case of drive «the aim is undetermined» (ibid.: 23), we would like to avoid a deflationary account of this very undetermined nature.

For our part, in short, it is *not* true that fantasy (drive's shape) is without *any* object. While the aim of desire is an object, the aim of fantasy is a gesture. We want to suggest the possibility that, although one has to maintain desire and drive as different, it is impossible to give an account of what Lacan called the *sinthome* without considering fantasy in its theoretical dignity. Thus, evoking here the objectless character of drive is secondary if compared to the importance of trying to describe the *gesture* implied in concrete and individual fantasies. That's the reason behind our account of *fantasy* as diagrammatized enjoyment: one way or another (joyfully or painfully) *drive takes its places* (as Anzieu underlines). Moreover, if one doesn't deal with the proper nature of diagrammatic enjoyments, there's no room for describing any sort of *creative overcoming* of the symptom *a-là* Joyce.

It is worth, however, to underline the key elements surrounding the idea of a passage from symptom to the *sinthome*. The *sinthome* is a «way of enjoyment» (Nusinovici, in Chemama and Vandermersch 2004: 314–315) that becomes possible when the subject *abandon*—in a peculiar way—the unconscious. If desire is desire of the Other and if all that it takes to "desire" is nothing but inheriting the symbolic debt of entering the signifying chain, then the *sinthome* is precisely a way *not* to desire. Properly speaking, for Lacan, sinthome is when the subject is somehow able to invent something out of his own subjectivity. In the case of James Joyce, it was the absence of the father, the key aspect which gave rise to the inventiveness and to the artifice of Joyce's famous writings. It can be described as a kind of "overcoded-hacking" of the subject upon his/her desire, in order to make something out of it by paradoxically flattening himself to a single dimension of productivity. Every invention is carried out by this operation of the sinthome. Artistic creativity also falls into this category, but so does anything really new produced by a subject.

However, here we meet again with the two critical aspects underlined before: although Lacan gave a topological account of this operation, he never seems to go deep down to the very *raison d'être* of these types of idiosyncratic *know-hows*.

Yet Lacan, although refuses any biological or developmental theories of fantasy formation, he suggests nonetheless that fantasy is something which is always *hiding* and "hard to confess". This is due to the unavoidable embarrassment the subject experiences in getting too close to it. Thus Lacan acknowledges fantasy as something between «desire» and «comedy»:

> I will add […] that it's precisely this which explains to us retrospectively the particular quality by which the fantasy is covered - be it the perverted or not - when it is confessed, that is to say that type of embarrassment

> we have to name in its most extreme point and which often holds the subject from delivering fantasy. This ridicule side is explained only by the relationships [...] between the position of desire and the field of comedy. (Lacan 2016: 485)

Following Golse's reading once again, one is surprised to find out that formal signifiers shun any active/passive grammatical dichotomy. That is equal to say that, in the case of formal signifiers, it is not a matter of scenes in the theatrical sense, nor of scene[s] in the architectonic sense, but it is rather the case of «a transformation of a geometrical or physical body feature, or of a portion of space» (Golse 2008: 113). Just recall the reasons behind Foucault's quick portrayal of the «Panopticon» as a *diagram*. In that case, Foucault underlines the necessity of rejecting any *oneiric* (sic.) explanation or any reduction to the material edifices (i.e. architectural incarnations). Furthermore, Golse underlines how the transformations belonging to formal signifiers reveal first and foremost some types of «inside/outside» confusions. According to his reading, this is due to the fact that the *actions* represented in phantasmatic scenarios reveal a basic confusion between imaginary and real (ibid.: 114).

To summarize, then, fantasy is neither scenic nor theatrical (Lacan), neither oneiric nor architectural (Foucault), neither linguistic nor sensible (Fontanille). Although we should add: it can actualize itself in ways that can be scenic, theatrical, oneiric, architectural, linguistic and/or sensible. The plane of expression of fantasy is therefore polymorphic.

The reason behind our choice of the conceptual tool of the diagram is that it allows us to take in—at the same time—fantasies as *logical* (Lacan), *scenic* (Freud) and *epidermic* (Anzieu). That is, the diagram is 'loose' enough to host dynamic operations—Anzieu's panoply of body tropes—but, at the same time, it gets an 'inelastic' tone, thus being able to comprise the self-necessitating outcome of the «comedy» of fantasy.

That is, *fantasy has a diagrammatic core*. If its first property is to be diagrammatic, a second property of it emerges: the property of *intra-expressive veridiction*.

There are multiple ways in which a diagram is instantiated and multiple expressions of it. Thus, a diagram can be expressed cross-dimensionally:

Expression.: = {scene; theater; dream; architecture; language; senses; music; (…);}

The set of possible diagrams is always exceeding its actual expressions. If we group all the parts (and their combinations) of a given expression ('P(Exp.)'), the set of the diagrams ('D') is greater than its actual expressions.

$$P(Exp.)$$

$$D > P(Exp.)$$

It is with the intrinsic life of diagrams that a new manifestation can arise so that it is expressed into one or more dimensions.

However, we are not suggesting a return to the very familiar gesture of structuralism. In other words, what has to be avoided is the theoretical possibility of a strict juxtaposition between expressions as material reifications of underlying structures. Although it may seem so, the difference between (diagrammatic) fantasy and structure in its classical structuralist and post-structuralist facets, lies in one single property. That is, the fact that fantasy as the diagrammatization of enjoyment doesn't involve *prima facie* any "prepackaged" category (i.e. economy, parenthood, religion); if fantasy, in its *hic et nunc*, is the subset composed by picking up innumerable expressions, it follows, arguably, that there can be also "dormant" fantasies or, which is synonymous, "dormant" expressions of the same diagram.

In other words, these are diagrams/fantasies which picked up no element whatsoever amongst the possible expressions (the set we called '*Exp*'). Diagrams that *are there*, *virtually*, but that have no expression. The Symbolic and the Imaginary of fantasy are therefore always contingent and, in some way, arbitrary. This last feature, that of arbitrariness, has to be understood as the fact that there's no room for theoretical appraisals of "history" as something determined by cause-effect structures, for the deranging power of fantasy (i.e. its taking diagrammatic shapes) shows its synchronic affinity with other expressions (what we call *intra-expressive veridiction*) rather than diachronic "large scale" developments. Although, as we previously underlined, fantasy is somewhat permeable to social discourses (by the *poinçon*), this fact doesn't give any causative role to these discourses in a "hard" sense. Otherwise all we would obtain is just another «there are only bodies+language» thesis, to which we should now oppose «there are only bodies+language+*truths*». These truths are—as Badiou would say—immanent (they are not of outer space) and Real in that they involve *jouissance*. This last point should come as no surprise, for what we previously acknowledged through Lacan is the fact that fantasy at the same time furnishes the subject with an *enjoyable body* and a *sense of reality*. "To desire another body" is "to desire another world". Because fantasy is a double anchorage between the two.

The diagrams are fantasies in the psychoanalytical sense: there are subjects who enjoy "panoctically" (radial voyeurism), others who enjoy with their bodies in vertical suspension (pierced constriction), etc.

The creativity of fantasy is structurally bounded to the workings of diagrammatic creativity. The fundamental psychoanalytical concept of repetition must be acknowledged as the blind crystallization of diagrammatic enjoyments. As the extreme cases of seriality (in murderers, for example) shows, diagrams/fantasies of enjoyment stand before any self-comprehension by the subject acting them. Seriality and repetition are synonymous.

It comes as no surprise, then, that these extreme cases often show the presence of a "style", an "identification mark". Once the schema is crystallized into diagrammatic forms, the routes it can take are uncountable. But once it takes a (beyond self-comprehension) given route, it inherits its classic repetitive birthmark.

Forget about content, fantasy is the repetition of form. And it is with art in the Lacanian sense that an «aesthetization of the symptom» (Miller 2017: 120) into *sinthome* is possible. «Art», as Miller remarks, «makes use of the phantasmatic component of the symptom» (ibid.).

It is the Real of the body as a cornucopia of diagrams which allows the subject to translate the symptom into the sinthome.

References

Agamben, G. (2009). *Nudità*. Roma: nottetempo.

Anzieu, D. (2017). *L'Io-pelle*. Milano: RaffaelloCortina.

Baas, B. (2012). *Y a-t-il des psychanalystes sans-culottes? Philosophie, psychanalyse et politique*. Paris: ERES.

Badiou, A. (2009). *Logic of Worlds: Being and Event 2*. London and New York: Continuum.

Braidotti, R. (2017). *Per una Politica Affermativa*. Milano and Udine: Mimesis.

Brugger, P., Lenggenhager, B., & Giummarra, M. J. (2013). Xenomelia: A Social Neuroscience View of Altered Bodily Self-Consciousness. In U. Voss (Ed.), *Frontiers in Psychology, 4*(204) (online).

Châtelet, G. (1993). *Les Enjeux du Mobile*. Paris: Le Seuil.

Chemama, R., & Vandermersch, B. (2004). *Dizionario di Psicanalisi*. Roma: Gremese.

Cohen, R. (2016). The Spatiality of Being: Topology as Ontology in Lacan's Thinking of the Body. In M. Friedman & S. Tomšič (Eds.), *Psychoanalysis: Topological Perspectives* (pp. 227–249). Bielefeld: Transcript.

Derrida, J. (2002). *La scrittura e la differenza*. Torino: Einaudi.

Derrida, J. (2006). *L'animale che dunque sono*. Milano: JacaBook.

Dubost, M.-D. (2003). De l'archaïque: un refoulement possible ou un refoulement manqué. *Analyse Freudienne Presse, 8*(2), 109–115.

Eyers, T. (2012). *Lacan and the Concept of the 'Real'*. New York: Palgrave Macmillan.

Fontanille, J. (2011). *Corps et Sens*. Paris: Presses Universitaires de France.

Friedler, J. (1995). *Psychanalyse et neurosciences: La légende du Boiteux*. Paris: Presses Universitaires de France.

Golse, B. (2008). Les Signifiants Formels Comme un lointain écho du bébé que nous avons été. In D. Anzieu et al. (Eds.), *Didier Anzieu: le Moi-peau et la psychanalyse des limites* (pp. 103–122). Paris: ERES «Le Carnet psy».

Grosz, E. (1994). *Volatile Bodies: Toward a Corporeal Feminism*. Bloomington and Indianapolis: Indiana University Press.

Johnson, X. (1990). *The Body in the Mind: The Bodily Basis of Meaning, Imagination, and Reason*. Chicago and London: University of Chicago Press.

Johnston, A. (2014). *Adventures in Transcendental Materialism: Dialogues with Contemporary Thinkers*. Edinburgh: Edinburgh University Press.

Johnston, A., & Malabou, C. (2013). *Self and Emotional Life: Phylosophy, Psychoanalysis, and Neuroscience*. New York: Columbia University Press.

Kafka, F. (2017). Il Tormento del Capofamiglia. *La Metamorfosi e altri racconti* (pp. 130–132). Milano: Garzanti.

Khandker, W. (2014). *Philosophy, Animality and the Life Sciences*. Edinburgh: Edinburgh University Press.

Kiarina Kordela, A. (2017). *Essere, Tempo, Bios: Capitalismo e ontologia*. Verona: ombre corte.

Lacan, J. (1992). *The Seminar of Jacques Lacan: Book VII the Ethics of Psychoanalysis (1959–1960)* (D. Porter, Trans.). New York and London: Norton.

Lacan, J. (2002). *Scritti*. Torino: Einaudi.

Lacan, J. (2003). *Il Seminario Libro XI: I quattro concetti fondamentali della psicoanalisi (1964)*. Torino: Einaudi.

Lacan, J. (2004). *Il Seminario Libro V: Le formazioni dell'inconscio (1957–1958)*. Torino: Einaudi.

Lacan, J. (2006). *Il Seminario Libro II: L'io nella teoria di Freud e nella tecnica della psicoanalisi (1954–1955)*. Torino: Einaudi.

Lacan, J. (2011). *Le Séminaire Livre XIX: …ou pire (1971–1972)*. Paris: Seuil.

Lacan, J. (2013). *Altri scritti*. Torino: Einaudi.

Lacan, J. (2014). *Il Seminario Libro I: Gli scritti tecnici di Freud (1953–1954)*. Torino: Einaudi.

Lacan, J. (2016). *Il Seminario Libro VI: Il desiderio e la sua interpretazione (1958–1959)*. Torino: Einaudi.

Leclaire, S. (1971). *Démasquer le réel: Un essai sur l'objet en psychanalyse*. Paris: Seuil.

Lunbeck, E. (2014). *The Americanization of Narcissism*. Cambridge and London: Harvard University Press.

Mercier, C. (2012). L'intimité des diagrammes. *L'Unebévue, 29*, 179–206. Paris: L'unebévue.

Miller, J. A. (2017). La signature des symptômes. In *La Cause Du Désir, 2*(96), 112–120.

Robertson, B. (2015). *Lacanian Antiphilosophy and the Problem of Anxiety: An Uncanny Little Object*. Basingstoke and New York: Palgrave Macmillan.

Roudinesco, É. (1995). *Jacques Lacan: Profilo di una vita, storia di un sistema di pensiero*. Milano: Raffaello Cortina.

Rousselle, D. (2018). *Lacanian Realism*. London: Bloosmbury.

Tyszler, J. J. (2013). Le fantasme pour la psychanalyse ou comment le corps se sexualise. In H. Guilyardi (Ed.), *Qu'est ce que le corps dans la psychanalyse?* (pp. 259–278). Association Psychanalyse et Médecine «Hors Collection».

Vigano, C. (2009). Réalité virtuelle et réalité sexuelle. *La Cause Freudienne, 73*(3), 37–41.
Watson, J. (2009). *Guattari's Diagrammatic Thought: Writing Between Lacan and Deleuze*. London and New York: Continuum.
Wiener, S. (2001). Le tatouage, de la griffe ordinaire à la marque subjective. *Essaim, 2*(8), 35–49.
Worringer, W. (1997). *Abstraction and Empathy: A Contribution to the Psychology of Style* (M. Bullock, Trans.). Chicago: Elephant Paperbacks.

Conclusion: *A Nameless Nature*

In his poems on the *Herdsman*, Fernando Pessoa tells the story of a gaze: the gaze of the herdsman on things and nature. As he contemplates Nature in its totality, he acknowledges this totality as a bias of the mind: «Only Nature is divine and it's not divine…/If I speak about it as an entity/It is that to speak about it/I have to use human language/which attributes personality to things/and imposes names to things./But things have no personality nor name:/they exist, and the sky is big and earth is wide, /and our heart is large like our clenched fist…» (Pessoa 1984: 111).

It is the description of the impossibilities of the lexicon. It is a poem about the relationship between language and things.

By the time the herdsman acknowledges the limits of speaking about nature as an 'entity', he makes a deep ontological claim: «I saw there's no Nature,/that Nature doesn't exist,/that there are mountains, valleys, plains,/that there are trees, flowers, herbs,/that there are rivers and stones,/but that there isn't a whole to which all this belongs,/that a real and true whole/is a sickness of our ideas./Nature is parts without a whole.» (ibid.:133).

The statements about the weaknesses of language suggest here, for the author, an image of radical incompleteness. That is, what is first and foremost acknowledged as a symbolic incompleteness (the words,

Y. Di Liberto, *Being and Contemporary Psychoanalysis*,
The Palgrave Lacan Series, https://doi.org/10.1007/978-3-030-18476-6

the lexicon) is translated into the ontological claim that it is nature *itself* which doesn't allow for a comprehensive and totalizing Real.

'Nature doesn't exist' is here tantamount to saying that *things* do exist and, despite their existence, they don't give room to any 'whole'. It would seem that the herdsman's claims are about the disenchantment of Nature in a reductionist fashion; instead, it is quite on the contrary the attempt to rethink a materialist re-enchantment of the relationship between the Symbolic and the Real by maintaining nonetheless a distance from fantasies of the whole.

And, for our part, it is within the relationships between philosophy and psychoanalysis that the ontological problem transforms into a play of incompletenesses. The psychoanalytical Thing is the subject as lacking. But, exactly like Pessoa's Nature, it is a lack which is acknowledged only by trying to fulfill its demands.

Nature, in Pessoa's passage, doesn't know about any incompleteness, because it simply doesn't proclaim its own existence. Neither do trees, rocks, etc. Nature, as psychoanalyst Pierre Fedida underlines, «doesn't know the absent» (Fedida 1978: 10).

The incompleteness of the Other, the incompleteness of the Symbolic register, all points toward the idea that nature as such is devoid of any absence. We call nature what seems to be without holes, without lacks and *a fortiori* what doesn't put any effort in constituting its existence.

However, this 'lack of the lack' of nature is due to the fact that, in nature, there's no one to receive the letter: Nature knows no Other, to use a Lacanian category.

It would seem that the human Thing arises as an *excavation* of this plenitude. Indeed, it became fashionable to portray Lacan's implicit ontology as a double-level scenario: the plenitude of nature and the lack of the subject. It is only when the human enters the scene that the Other, and its absence, is set in motion.

The tale of the herdsman suggests us, quite surprisingly, another concomitant possibility. It is objects and things which exist, no nature and no subjects: it is the gaze of the human as an already all too anthropocentric dispositive which reveals something of the human itself (and, dialectically, to itself). That is, its tendency toward the transcendental.

The trope of a basic mismatch between nature's plenitude and the lack of subjectivity has been lately re-elaborated so as to acknowledge how the interplay between the 'natural'—broadly speaking—and the realm of the symbolic has to do with a play of concomitant incompletenesses (for example in the works of Adrian Johnston).

It is the view which I tried to suggest and that hopefully did emerge throughout the chapters: it is with 'nature' (without capital 'N') that we already find all the preconditions for the subject to emerge. The subject is, for its part, not an object among other objects, but precisely the locus in which lies a problematization of the object as such.

Indeed, the encounter between the Real of Speculation and the Real of psychoanalysis should be the one of *how* and *when* the intersection(s) of the truths of science and the truths of the subject do suggest the *miracle* of the human.

In other words, the problem lies in finding a Real of subjectivity which is neither tantamount to its biological concreteness nor to its mere identifications. But keeping nonetheless these elements as co-constituents.

As such, Pessoa's poem could be taken here as a warning not to speak about Nature but only about *natures*. In this second meaning, the concept of nature doesn't belong to the traditional dichotomy between the natural and the artificial. In its plural form (*natures*) it stands really for an equal footing of the functionings of things broadly taken.

It is for this purpose that I ended up proposing a Real of subjectivity as stuffed with diagrams of enjoyment. Here, the 'Speculative' takes another meaning: psychoanalysis is an invitation to speculate on the possibility of speculation itself. It is precisely because of a Real to be 'regained' or 'reached' that the subjective project comes close to the speculative one. The two share the question about the conditions of a subject of science in a material reality (1), and they both aim at a second-order reflection upon the possibility of saying something about the Real (2).

However, it is this particular Real which unfolds in its multiplicity when one sees through the lenses of philosophical metaphysics or through subjectivity itself.

In other words, it would seem that the two efforts differ in their task: while the first asks 'What is the Real of the world *without* the subject?', the second asks 'What is the Real of the subject *without* the world?'.

What I tried to show is that the two questions should be answered *within* their junction. They are two questions deeply rooted in philosophical investigation already in the form of the swinging between idealism and realism.

For Quentin Meillassoux, speculation on the Real is an opportunity to reopen the possibility of contingency and the necessity thereof. If «what is absolutely dead in the spirit of contemporary philosophers is the belief according to which things have a necessary reason to be what they are» (Meillassoux 2017: 61), it is only when plunging into the inner workings of subjectivity as such that one sees the same problem posed as urging an answer to the Real of the subject: 'What am I?' or 'What is the Real inhabiting me?'.

However, psychoanalysis warns us not to fall too easily into conceiving our Real as a biological Real of adaptation. Time, space, objects, causalities, etc., help us configuring a Real of the subject as something that slips out of a plain adaptationist account (Lacan 2006: 11).

Both second-order reflections on the Real and the concrete embodiment of one's own Real (Lacan's sinthome) are two sides of the same question.

But it is in posing such a question that psychoanalysis makes a plea for the acknowledgment of the historicity of subject's life. As Hélène Bonnaud remarks: «from the birth on, the child is taken in the signifiers of what will become his history, in other words he already has a certain place in the parents' discourse» (Bonnaud 2018: 32).

To some extent, then, this book was an invitation to re-engage the placing of the real effects of linguistic objects *within* the factual existence of subjectivity. To use Meillassoux' words, it is a matter of asking how the contingency of the signifiers turns into their necessity.

Against the backdrop of the chain of signifiers as something exercising a real agency upon subjective life, Lacan envisages a way out. It is not, as I tried to suggest, a clear-cut escape from the linguistic toward the material; it is a repositioning of the subject within its own Real, a Real which is stuffed with its own idiosyncratic forms.

It is not surprising, then, that philosophy and psychoanalysis do share some affinities in exploring the Real. As Badiou pinpoints, they are similar in that they «hold *truth* and *error* as intrinsic» (Badiou 1992: 281–282). It is in the pursuit of the 'speculative'—in the broader sense I suggested—that philosophy and psychoanalysis seem to share some features of their methodologies.

Neither 'Nature' with capital 'N', nor 'Truth' with capital 'T'; the Real of subjectivity guides us toward multiplicity and the necessity of what is contingent.

References

Badiou, A. (1992). *Conditions*. Paris: Le Seuil.

Bonnaud, H. (2018). *L'Inconscio del bambino: Dal sintomo al desiderio del sapere*. Macerata: Quodlibet.

Fedida, P. (1978). *L'absence*. Paris: Gallimard.

Lacan, J. (2006). *Il Seminario Libro II: L'io nella teoria di Freud e nella tecnica della psicoanalisi (1954–1955)*. Torino: Einaudi.

Meillassoux, Q. (2017). Metafisica, Speculazione, Correlazione. In D. Sanctis (Ed.), *I Nuovi Realismi* (pp. 61–86). Milano: Bompiani.

Bibliography

Agamben, G. (2009). *Nudità*. Roma: nottetempo.

Alliez, É., & Lazzarato, M. (2016). *Guerres et Capital*. Paris: Éditions Amsterdam.

Allouch, J. (2001). *Le Sexe du maître: L'érotisme d'après Lacan*. Paris: Exils.

Althusser, L. (2017). *Essere marxisti in filosofia*. Bari: Dedalo.

Anzieu, D. (1981). *Le Corps de Œuvre: Essais psychanalytiques sur le travail créateur*. Paris: Gallimard.

Anzieu, D. (1990). *A Skin for Thought: Interviews with Gilbert Tarrab on Psychology and Psychoanalysis*. London and New York: Karnac Books.

Anzieu, D. (1999). *Creare Distruggere*. Roma: Borla.

Anzieu, D. (2017). *L'Io-pelle*. Milano: RaffaelloCortina.

Arribas, S., & Rouse, H. (2011). *Egocracy: Marx, Freud and Lacan*. Chicago and London: University of Chicago Press.

Aulagnier, P. (2001). *The Violence of Interpretation: From Pictogram to Statement*. Hove: Brunner and Routledge.

Aulagnier, P. (2004). *L'apprenti-historien et le maître-sorcier: Du discours identifiant au discours délirant*. Paris: Presses Universitaires de France.

Austin, M. (2015). Time. In P. Gratton & P. J. Ennis (Eds.), *The Meillassoux Dictionary* (pp. 165–167). Edinburgh: Edinburgh University Press.

Baas, B. (2012). *Y a-t-il des psychanalystes sans-culottes? Philosophie, psychanalyse et politique*. Paris: ERES.

Y. Di Liberto, *Being and Contemporary Psychoanalysis*,
The Palgrave Lacan Series, https://doi.org/10.1007/978-3-030-18476-6

Badiou, A. (1992). *Conditions*. Paris: Le Seuil.
Badiou, A. (2009). *Logic of Worlds: Being and Event 2*. London and New York: Continuum.
Badiou, A. (2016). *Alla ricerca del reale perduto*. Milano and Udine: Mimesis.
Badiou, A. (2017). *Elogio delle matematiche*. Milano and Udine: Mimesis.
Balmès, F. (1999). *Ce que Lacan dit de l'être*. Paris: PUF.
Balmès, F. (2011). *Structure, logique, aliénation: Recherches en psychanalyse*. Paris: ERES.
Benoist, J. (2017). *L'adresse du réel*. Paris: Librairie Philosophique J. VRIN.
Benveniste, É. (2010). *Problemi di linguistica generale*. Milano: Il Saggiatore.
Berto, G. (2016). *Il male oscuro*. Vicenza: Neri Pozza.
Bonnaud, H. (2018). *L'Inconscio del bambino: Dal sintomo al desiderio del sapere*. Macerata: Quodlibet.
Brad, W. K. (2011). *Kuhn's Evolutionary Social Epistemology*. Cambridge: Cambridge University Press.
Braidotti, R. (2017). *Per una Politica Affermativa*. Milano and Udine: Mimesis.
Brassier, R. (2007). *Nihil Unbound: Enlightenment and Extinction*. New York: Palgrave Macmillan.
Brassier, R. (2011). Concepts, Objects, Gems. In J. Elliott & D. Attridge (Eds.), *Theory After Theory* (pp. 278–293). London and New York: Routledge.
Braudel, F. (2006). *Civiltà materiale, economia e capitalismo: Le strutture del quotidiano (secoli XV–XVIII)*. Torino: Einaudi.
Braver, L. (2007). *A Thing of This World: A History of Continental Anti-realism*. Evanston, IL: Northwestern University Press.
Bristow, D. (2017). *Joyce and Lacan: Reading, Writing and Psychoanalysis*. London and New York: Routledge.
Brugger, P., Lenggenhager, B., & Giummarra, M. J. (2013). Xenomelia: A Social Neuroscience View of Altered Bodily Self-Consciousness. In U. Voss (Ed.), *Frontiers in Psychology*, *4*(204) (online).
Bryant, L. (2011). The Ontic Principle: Outline of an Object-Oriented Ontology. In L. Bryant, N. Srnicek, & G. Harman (Eds.), *The Speculative Turn* (pp. 261–278). Melbourne: re.press.
Bryant, L. (2014). *Onto-Cartography: An Ontology of Machines and Media*. Edinburgh: Edinburgh University Press.
Bryant, L. (2015). Correlationism. In P. Gratton & P. J. Ennis (Eds.), *The Meillassoux Dictionary* (pp. 46–48). Edinburgh: Edinburgh University Press.
Bryant, L., Srnicek, N., & Harman, G. (2011). Towards a Speculative Philosophy. In L. Bryant, N. Srnicek, & G. Harman (Eds.), *The Speculative Turn* (pp. 1–18). Melbourne: re.press.

Catren, G. (2018). A Plea for Narcissus: On the *Transcendental Reflection* ∧ *Reflective Mediation* Tandem. In F. Gironi (Ed.), *The Legacy of Kant in Sellars and Meillassoux: Analytic and Continental Kantianism* (pp. 155–170). New York and London: Routledge.

Châtelet, G. (1993). *Les Enjeux du Mobile*. Paris: Le Seuil.

Châtelet, G. (2006). Interlacing the Singularity, the Diagram and the Metaphor. In S. Duffy (Ed.), *Virtual Mathematics: The Logic of Difference* (pp. 31–45). Manchester: Clinamen Press.

Chemama, R., & Vandermersch, B. (2004). *Dizionario di Psicanalisi*. Roma: Gremese.

Chiesa, L. (2014). Editorial Introduction: Towards a New Philosophical-Psychoanalytic Materialism and Realism. In L. Chiesa (Ed.), *Lacan and Philosophy: The New Generation* (pp. 1–19). Melbourne: re.press.

Churchland, P. (2012). *Neurobiologia della morale*. Milan: Raffaello Cortina.

Cimatti, F. (2016). Divenire Cosa, Divenire Corpo. *Atque materiali tra filosofia e psicoterapia, 18*, 107–132.

Cimatti, F. (2018). *Cose: Per una filosofia del reale*. Torino: Bollati Boringhieri.

Clemens, J. (2013). Vomit Apocalypse; Or Quentin Meillassoux's *After Finitude*. *Parrhesia, 18,* 57–67.

Coates, J. M., Gurnell, M., & Sarnyai, Z. (2014). From Molecule to Market: Steroid Hormones and Financial Risk-Taking. In R. Mackay (Ed.), *Collapse: Philosophical Research and Development* (Vol. VIII, pp. 417–461). Falmouth: Urbanomic.

Cohen, J. (2018). Speculating the Real: On Quentin Meillassoux's Philosophical Realism. In F. Gironi (Ed.), *The Legacy of Kant in Sellars and Meillassoux: Analytic and Continental Kantianism* (pp. 171–178). New York and London: Routledge.

Cohen, R. (2016). The Spatiality of Being: Topology as Ontology in Lacan's Thinking of the Body. In M. Friedman & S. Tomšič (Eds.), *Psychoanalysis: Topological Perspectives* (pp. 227–249). Bielefeld: Transcript.

Colletti, G. (2016). *The Psychoanalysis of Sense: Deleuze and the Lacanian School*. Edinburgh: Edinburgh University Press.

Corning, P. A. (2005). *Holistic Darwinism: Synergy, Cybernetics and the Bioeconomics of Evolution*. Chicago and London: University of Chicago Press.

de Mijolla-Mellor, S. (1992). *Le plaisir de pensée*. Paris: Presses Universitaires de France.

Deleuze, G. (1983). *Nietzsche and Philosophy*. Minneapolis: University of Minnesota Press.

Deleuze, G. (1986). *Foucault*. Paris: Minuit.
Deleuze, G. (2010a). Che cos'è un dispositivo? In D. Borca (Ed.), *Due regimi di folli e altri scritti (Testi e interviste 1975–1995)* (pp. 279–287). Torino: Einaudi.
Deleuze, G. (2010b). Quattro proposizioni sulla psicoanalisi. In D. Borca (Ed.), *Due regimi di folli e altri scritti: Testi e interviste 1975–1995* (pp. 58–65). Torino: Einaudi.
Deleuze, G. (2017). *L'immagine-tempo: Cinema 2*. Torino: Einaudi.
Deleuze, G., & Guattari, F. (2002). *L'anti-Edipo: Capitalismo e Schizofrenia*. Torino: Einaudi.
Deleuze, G., & Guattari, F. (2017). *Millepiani: Capitalismo e schizofrenia*. Napoli and Salerno: Orthotes.
Dennett, D. C. (2012). *Coscienza*. Laterza: Che cosa è.
Derrida, J. (2002). *La scrittura e la differenza*. Torino: Einaudi.
Derrida, J. (2006). *L'animale che dunque sono*. Milano: JacaBook.
Derrida, J. (2010). *La voce e il fenomeno: Introduzione al problema del segno nella fenomenologia di Husserl*. Milano: Jaca Book.
Descartes, R. (2010). *Discorso del metodo*. Milano: BUR.
Didi-Huberman, G. (2016). *Davati all'immagine: Domanda posta ai fini di unastoria dell'arte*. Milano and Udine: Mimesis.
Dreyfus, H. L. (2013). The Myth of the Pervasiveness of the Mental. In J. K. Schear (Ed.), *Mind, Reason and Being-in-the-World: The McDowell-Dreyfus Debate* (pp. 15–40). London and New York: Routledge.
Dubost, M.-D. (2003). De l'archaïque: un refoulement possible ou un refoulement manqué. *Analyse Freudienne Presse, 8*(2), 109–115.
Dupuy, J. P. (1999). Philosophy and Cognition: Historical Roots. In J. Petitot, F. J. Varela, & J. M. Pachoud (Eds.), *Naturalizing Phenomenology: Issues in Contemporary Phenomenology and Cognitive Science* (pp. 539–558). Stanford: Stanford University Press.
Esposito, R. (2006). *Communitas: Origine e destino della comunità*. Torino: Einaudi.
Esposito, R. (2018). *Politica e negazione: Per una filosofia affermativa*. Torino: Einaudi.
Eyers, T. (2012). *Lacan and the Concept of the 'Real'*. New York: Palgrave Macmillan.
Falk, D. (2015). *Lingua madre: Cure materne e origini del linguaggio*. Torino: Bollati Boringhieri.
Fedida, P. (1978). *L'absence*. Paris: Gallimard.

Fink, B. (2002). Knowledge and Science: Fantasies of the Whole. In J. Glynos & Y. Stavrakakis (Eds.), *Lacan & Science* (pp. 167–178). London: Karnac.
Fisher, C. (2007). Feminist Digital Aesthetics: The Everyday and Yesterday. In J. Marchessault & S. Lord (Eds.), *Fluid Screens, Expanded Cinema* (pp. 145–159). Toronto, Buffalo, and London: University of Toronto Press.
Flaxman, G. (2010). The Subject of Chaos. In P. Gaffney (Ed.), *The Force of the Virtual: Deleuze, Science, and Philosophy* (pp. 191–210). Minneapolis and London: University of Minnesota Press.
Fontanille, J. (2011). *Corps et Sens*. Paris: Presses Universitaires de France.
Foucault, M. (2013). *Surveiller et punir*. Paris: Gallimard.
Freud, S. (1970). Sostituti inadeguati dell'oggetto sessuale: il feticismo. In S. Misura (Ed.), *Figure del feticismo* (pp. 3–5). Torino: Einaudi. 2001.
Freud, S. (1973). *Introduzione al Narcisismo*. Torino: Bollati Boringhieri.
Freud, S. (2001). Per la genesi del feticismo. In S. Misura (Ed.), *Figure del feticismo* (pp. 6–18). Torino: Einaudi.
Freud, S. (2015). *L'avvenire di un'illusione*. Torino: Einaudi.
French, S., & Krause, D. (2006). *Identity in Physics: A Historical, Philosophical, and Formal Analysis*. Oxford: Oxford University Press.
Friedler, J. (1995). *Psychanalyse et neurosciences: La légende du Boiteux*. Paris: Presses Universitaires de France.
Friedman, M. (2016). Torus and Identification: The Beginning of Lacanian Mathematics. In M. Friedman & S. Tomšič (Eds.), *Psychoanalysis: Topological Perspectives* (pp. 153–190). Bielefeld: Transcript.
Galloway, A. (2013). The Poverty of Philosophy: Realism and Post-fordism. *Critical Inquiry, 39*, 347–366.
Garcia, T. (2014). *Form and Object: A Treatise on Things*. Edinburgh: Edinburgh University Press.
Gedo, J. E. (1991). *The Biology of Clinical Encounters: Psychoanalysis as a Science of Mind*. Hillsdale: The Analytic Press.
Gibson, J. (2015). *The Ecological Approach to Visual Perception*. New York: Psychology Press.
Glynos, J. (2002). Psychoanalysis Operates Upon the Subject of Science: Lacan Between Science and Ethics. In J. Glynos & Y. Stavrakakis (Eds.), *Lacan & Science* (pp. 51–88). London: Karnac.
Golse, B. (2008). Les Signifiants Formels Comme un lointain écho du bébé que nous avons été. In D. Anzieu et al. (Eds.), *Didier Anzieu: le Moi-peau et la psychanalyse des limites* (pp. 103–122). Paris: ERES «Le Carnet psy».
Gould, S. J., & Vrba, S. (2008). *Exaptation: Il bricolage dell'evoluzione*. Torino: Bollati Boringhieri.

Gramsci, A. (2014). *Quaderni del Carcere*. Torino: Einaudi.

Gratton, P. (2014). *Speculative Realism: Problems and Prospects*. London and New York: Bloomsbury.

Grosz, E. (1994). *Volatile Bodies: Toward a Corporeal Feminism*. Bloomington and Indianapolis: Indiana University Press.

Hägglund, M. (2011). The Arche-Materiality of Time: Deconstruction, Evolution and Speculative Materialism. In J. Elliott & D. Attridge (Eds.), *Theory After Theory* (pp. 265–277). London and New York: Routledge.

Hallward, P. (2010). You Can't Have It Both Ways: Deleuze or Lacan. In L. De Bolle (a cura di) (Ed.), *Deleuze and Psychoanalysis: Philosophical Essays on Deleuze's Debate with Psychoanalysis*. Leuven: Leuven University Press.

Harman, G. (2009). *Prince of Networks: Bruno Latour and Metaphysics*. Melbourne: re.press.

Hegel, G. F. (1981). *Scienza della logica*. Roma-Bari: Laterza.

Iacono, A. M. (2001). L'ambiguo oggetto sostituto. Il feticismo di Marx e Freud. In S. Mistura (Ed.), *Figure del feticismo* (pp. 35–59). Torino: Einaudi.

Johnson, X. (1990). *The Body in the Mind: The Bodily Basis of Meaning, Imagination, and Reason*. Chicago and London: University of Chicago Press.

Johnston, A. (2005). *Time Driven: Metapsychology and the Splitting of the Drive*. Evanston: Northwestern University Press.

Johnston, A. (2010). *Irrepressible Truth: On Lacan's 'The Freudian Thing'*. New York: Palgrave Macmillan.

Johnston, A. (2013). *Prolegomena to Any Future Materialism: Volume One—The Outcome of Contemporary French Philosophy*. Evanston, IL: Northwestern University Press.

Johnston, A. (2014a). *Adventures in Transcendental Materialism: Dialogues with Contemporary Thinkers*. Edinburgh: Edinburgh University Press.

Johnston, A. (2014b). On Deep History and Lacan. In L. Chiesa (Ed.), *Lacan and Philosophy: The New Generation* (pp. 63–83). Melbourne: re.press.

Johnston, A. (2015). Lacking Causes: Privative Causality from Locke and Kant to Lacan and Deacon. In F. Gironi (Ed.), *Speculations VI* (pp. 19–62). Brooklyn and New York: Punctum Books.

Johnston, A., & Malabou, C. (2013). *Self and Emotional Life: Phylosophy, Psychoanalysis, and Neuroscience*. New York: Columbia University Press.

Julien, P. (2008). Du Nom-du-Père au Père-du-Nom comme sinthome. In P. Julien (Eds.), *Psychose, Perversion, névrose: La lecture de Jacques Lacan* (pp. 67–77). Toulouse: ERES.

Kafka, F. (2017). Il Tormento del Capofamiglia. *La Metamorfosi e altri racconti* (pp. 130–132). Milano: Garzanti.

Kant, I. (2004). *Critica della Ragion Pura*. Milano: Bompiani.

Kant, I. (2006). *Prolegomeni ad ogni futura metafisica*. Bari: Laterza.

Kant, I. (2011). *Critica della facoltà di giudizio*. Torino: Einaudi.

Khandker, W. (2014). *Philosophy, Animality and the Life Sciences*. Edinburgh: Edinburgh University Press.

Kiarina Kordela, A. (2007), *$urplus: Spinoza, Lacan*. Albany: State University of New York Press.

Kiarina Kordela, A. (2017). *Essere, Tempo, Bios: Capitalismo e ontologia*. Verona: ombre corte.

Koyré, A. (2000). *Del mondo del pressappoco all'universo della precisione*. Torino: Einaudi.

Lacan, J. (Unpublished Typescript). Le Séminaire de Jacques Lacan, Livre XIX: …ou pire, 1971–1972.

Lacan, J. (Critic Transcription). *Séminaire Livre XII: Problèmes cruciaux pour la psychanalyse (1964–1965)* (P. Valas, Reconstructed Text). See http://www.valas.fr/Jacques-Lacan-Problemes-cruciaux-pour-la-psychanalyse,255.

Lacan, J. (Critic Transcription). *Séminaire Livre XV: L'Acte Psychanalytique (1967–1968)* (P. Valas, A. Porge, & J.-G. Godin, Reconstructed Text). See http://www.valas.fr/Jacques-Lacan-L-acte-psychanalytique-1967-1968,136.

Lacan, J. (Critic Transcription). *Séminaire Livre IX: L'identification (1961–1962)* (P. Valas, Reconstructed Text). See http://www.valas.fr/IMG/pdf/S9_identification.pdf.

Lacan, J. (1978). Del discorso psicoanalitico. *Lacan in Italia, En Italie Lacan* (pp. 40–51). La Salamandra: Milano.

Lacan, J. (1986). Il mito individuale del nevrotico. In D. Ciaccia (Ed.), *Il mito individuale del nevrotico* (pp. 13–29). Roma: Astrolabio.

Lacan, J. (1992). *The Seminar of Jacques Lacan: Book VII the Ethics of Psychoanalysis (1959–1960)* (D. Porter, Trans.). New York and London: Norton.

Lacan, J. (2001). *Il Seminario Libro XVII: Il rovescio della psicoanalisi (1969–1970)*. Torino: Einaudi.

Lacan, J. (2002). *Scritti*. Torino: Einaudi.

Lacan, J. (2003). *Il Seminario Libro XI: I quattro concetti fondamentali della psicoanalisi (1964)*. Torino: Einaudi.

Lacan, J. (2004). *Il Seminario Libro V: Le formazioni dell'inconscio (1957–1958)*. Torino: Einaudi.

Lacan, J. (2006a). *Il Seminario Libro II: L'io nella teoria di Freud e nella tecnica della psicoanalisi (1954–1955).* Torino: Einaudi.
Lacan, J. (2006b). *Le Séminaire Livre XVI: D'un Autre à l'autre (1968–1969).* Paris: Seuil.
Lacan, J. (2006c). *Il Seminario Libro XXIII: Il Sinthomo (1975–1976).* Roma: Astrolabio.
Lacan, J. (2006d). *Dei Nomi-del-Padre.* Torino: Einaudi.
Lacan, J. (2007). *Il Seminario Libro X: L'angoscia (1962–1963).* Torino: Einaudi.
Lacan, J. (2008). *Il Seminario Libro VII: L'etica della psicoanalisi (1959–1960).* Torino: Einaudi.
Lacan, J. (2010). *Il Seminario Libro III: Le psicosi (1955–1956).* Torino: Einaudi.
Lacan, J. (2011a). *Le Séminaire Livre XIX: …ou pire (1971–1972).* Paris: Seuil.
Lacan, J. (2011b). *Il Seminario Libro XX: Ancora (1972–1973).* Torino: Einaudi.
Lacan, J. (2013). *Altri scritti.* Torino: Einaudi.
Lacan, J. (2014a). *Il Seminario Libro I: Gli scritti tecnici di Freud (1953–1954).* Torino: Einaudi.
Lacan, J. (2014b). *Il mio insegnamento e Io parlo ai muri.* Roma: Astrolabio.
Lacan, J. (2016). *Il Seminario Libro VI: Il desiderio e la sua interpretazione (1958–1959).* Torino: Einaudi.
Ladyman, J., & Ross, D. (2007). *Every Thing Must Go: Metaphysics Naturalized.* Oxford: Oxford University Press.
Lafrance, M. (2012). From the Skin Ego to the Psychic Envelope: An Introduction to the Work of Didier Anzieu. In S. Cavanagh, A. Failler, & R. Hurst (Eds.), *Skin, Culture and Psychoanalysis* (pp. 16–44). New York: Palgrave Macmillan.
La Mantia, F. (2017). L'altro e l'uncino. Su un aspetto del pronome "Tu" in Lacan. *La psicoanalisi, 62*, 88–104.
Laplanche, J., & Pontalis, J.-B. (2010). *Enciclopedia della psicoanalisi.* Roma-Bari: Laterza.
Latour, B. (2013). *An Inquiry into Modes of Existence: An Anthropology of the Moderns.* Cambridge and London: Harvard University Press.
Le Gaufey, G. (2012). *L'objet a: Approches de l'invention de Lacan.* Paris: EPEL.
Lew, R. (2013). Identité de structure entre le schématisme de Marx et celui de Freud. In S. Lippi & P. Landman (Eds.), *Marx, Lacan: L'Acte révolutionnaire et l'acte analytique* (pp. 131–150). Paris: ERES.
Leclaire, S. (1971). *Démasquer le réel: Un essai sur l'objet en psychanalyse.* Paris: Seuil.
Lezra, J. (2018). *On the Nature of Marx's Things: Translation as Necrophilology.* New York: Fordham University Press.

Ligotti, T. (2017). *Nottuario*. Milano: Il Saggiatore.

Lippi, S. (2016). *La decisione del desiderio: Etica dell'inconscio in Jacques Lacan*. Milano and Udine: Mimesis.

Lippi, S. (2018). *Sigmund Freud*. Milano: Feltrinelli.

Lunbeck, E. (2014). *The Americanization of Narcissism*. Cambridge and London: Harvard University Press.

Maitre, A. (2010). Identifications et destins des identifications. *Analyse Freudienne Presse, 17*(1), 131–138.

Marrou, É. (2016). La bouche qui dit «Nous»: De l'intentionnalité collective à l'autorité en première personne du pluriel. In *Klesis, 2016*(34), 14–37.

Marx, K. (2013). *Il Capitale: Libro primo*. Torino: UTET.

McDowell, J. (2013). The Myth of the Mind as Detached. In J. K. Schear (Ed.), *Mind, Reason and Being-in-the-World: The McDowell-Dreyfus Debate* (pp. 41–58). London and New York: Routledge.

Means, D. (2016). *Hystopia: A Novel*. New York: Macmillan.

Meillassoux, Q. (2008). *After Finitude: An Essay on the Necessity of Contingency*. London and New York: Continuum.

Meillassoux, Q. (2013). *Tempo senza divenire*. Milano and Udine: Mimesis.

Meillassoux, Q. (2017). Metafisica, Speculazione, Correlazione. In D. Sanctis (Ed.), *I Nuovi Realismi* (pp. 61–86). Milano: Bompiani.

Menninghaus, W. (2013). *La promessa della bellezza* (S. Tedesco, Ed.). Palermo: Aesthetica Edizioni.

Mercier, C. (2012). L'intimité des diagrammes. *L'Unebévue, 29*, 179–206. Paris: L'unebévue.

Miller, J. A. (1984). Schede di lettura lacaniana. In D. Ciaccia (Ed.), *Il mito individuale del nevrotico* (pp. 73–105). Roma: Astrolabio.

Miller, J. A. (2000). Biologia lacaniana ed eventi di corpo *e* L'esperienza del reale nella cura analitica. *La Psicoanalisi, 28*, 14–100. Roma: Astrolabio.

Miller, J. A. (2003). La teoria del partner. *La Psicoanalisi, 34*, 22–83. Roma: Atrolabio.

Miller, J. A. (2006). *Pezzi staccati: Introduzione al seminario XXIII "Il sinthomo"*. Roma: Astrolabio.

Miller, J. A. (2012). Il reale nel XXI secolo. In *La Psicoanalisi, 52*, 13–22. Roma: Astrolabio.

Miller, J. A. (2014). Il filo del fantasma. In *La Psicoanalisi, 55*, 19–33. Roma: Astrolabio.

Miller, J. A. (2017). La signature des symptômes. In *La Cause Du Désir, 2*(96), 112–120.

Miller, J. A., et al. (2004). *Lakant*. Roma: Borla ed.
Milner, J.-C. (1995). *L'Œuvre claire: Lacan, la science, la philosophie*. Paris: Le Seuil.
Morton, T. (2018). *Noi, esseri ecologici*. Roma and Bari: Laterza.
Neill, C. (2011). *Lacanian Ethics and the Assumption of Subjectivity*. New York: Palgrave Macmillan.
Nietzsche, F. (2018). *Genealogia della morale: Uno scritto polemico*. Milano: Adelphi.
Noys, B. (2012). *The Persistence of the Negative: A Critique of Contemporary Continental Theory*. Edinburgh: Edinburgh University Press.
Nunes, R. (2015). Ancestrality. In P. Gratton & P. J. Ennis (Eds.), *The Meillassoux Dictionary* (pp. 22–24). Edinburgh: Edinburgh University Press.
Perniola, M. (2004). *Il Sex Appeal dell'Inorganico*. Torino: Einaudi.
Pessoa, F. (1984). *Una sola moltitudine* (II ed.). Adelphi: Milano.
Pirard, R. (2010). La Chose publique: pas-toute. In R. Pirard (Eds.), *Le sujet postmoderne entre symptôme et jouissance* (pp. 159–168). Toulouse: ERES.
Platone. (2011). *Menone*. Roma and Bari: Laterza.
Pragier, G., & Faure-Pragier, S. (2007). Métaphores du changement. *Repenser la psychanalyse avec les sciences* (pp. 53–83). Paris: Presses Universitaires de France.
Rastier, F. (2003). *Arti e scienze del testo: Per una semiotica delle culture*. Roma: Meltemi.
Réage, P. (2014). *Histoire d'O*. Milano: Bompiani.
Robertson, B. (2015). *Lacanian Antiphilosophy and the Problem of Anxiety: An Uncanny Little Object*. Basingstoke and New York: Palgrave Macmillan.
Roudinesco, É. (1995). *Jacques Lacan: Profilo di una vita, storia di un sistema di pensiero*. Milano: Raffaello Cortina.
Rousselle, D. (2018). *Lacanian Realism*. London: Bloosmbury.
Smail, D. (2017). *Storia profonda*. Torino: Bollati Boringhieri.
Sasso, G. (1999). *Struttura dell'oggetto e della rappresentazione*. Roma: Astrolabio.
Schuster, A. (2016). *The Trouble with Pleasure: Deleuze and Psychoanalysis*. Cambridge and London: MIT Press.
Sebold, R. (2014). *Continental Anti-realism: A Critique*. London and New York: Rowman & Littlefield.
Sechaud, É. (2008). Didier Anzieu: penser les pensée. In D. Anzieu, et al. (Eds.), *Didier Anzieu: le Moi-peau et la psychanalyse des limites* (pp. 11–30). Paris: ERES «Le Carnet psy».
Serres, M. (2007). *The Parasite*. Minneapolis and London: University of Minnesota Press.

Shaviro, S. (2014). *The Universe of Things: On Speculative Realism*. Minneapolis and London: University of Minnesota Press.

Shepherdson, C. (2008). *Lacan and the Limits of Language*. New York: Fordham University Press.

Skriabine, P. (2004). Clinic and Topology: The Flaw in the Universe. In E. Ragland & D. Milovanovic (Eds.), *Lacan: Topologically Speaking* (p. 81). New York: Other Press.

Soler, C. (2016). *Gli affetti lacaniani*. Milano: FrancoAngeli.

Tomšič, S. (2015). *The Capitalist Unconscious: Marx and Lacan*. London: Verso books.

Toscano, A. (2011). Against Speculation, or, a Critique of the Critique of Critique: A Remark on Quentin Meillassoux's After Finitude (After Colletti). In L. Bryant, N. Srnicek, & G. Harman (Eds.), *The Speculative Turn: Continental Materialism and Realism* (pp. 84–91). Melbourne: re.press.

Tyszler, J. J. (2013). Le fantasme pour la psychanalyse ou comment le corps se sexualise. In H. Guilyardi (Ed.), *Qu'est ce que le corps dans la psychanalyse?* (pp. 259–278). Association Psychanalyse et Médecine «Hors Collection».

Van Haute, P. (2002). *Against Adaptation: Lacan's "Subversion" of the Subject* (P. Crowe & M. Vankerk, Trans.). New York: Other Press.

Vigano, C. (2009). Réalité virtuelle et réalité sexuelle. *La Cause Freudienne, 73*(3), 37–41.

von Uexküll, J. (2010). *Ambienti animali e ambienti umani: Una passeggiata in mondi sconosciuti e invisibili*. Macerata: Quodlibet.

von Uexküll, J. (2013). Come vediamo la natura e come la natura vede se stessa? In A. Pinotti & S. Tedesco (Eds.), *Estetica e science della vita, A* (pp. 39–81). Milano: Raffaello Cortina.

Watson, J. (2009). *Guattari's Diagrammatic Thought: Writing Between Lacan and Deleuze*. London and New York: Continuum.

Wiener, S. (2001). Le tatouage, de la griffe ordinaire à la marque subjective. *Essaim, 2*(8), 35–49.

Worringer, W. (1997). *Abstraction and Empathy: A Contribution to the Psychology of Style* (M. Bullock, Trans.). Chicago: Elephant Paperbacks.

Žižek, S. (2018). Marx Reads Object-Oriented-Ontology. In *Reading Marx*. Cambridge: Polity Press.

Zupančič, A. (2011). *Ethics of the Real: Kant and Lacan*. London: Verso.

Zupančič, A. (2014). Realism in Psychoanalysis. In L. Chiesa (Ed.), *Lacan and Philosophy: The New Generation* (pp. 21–33). Melbourne: re.press.

Zupančič, A. (2017). *What Is Sex?* Cambridge and London: MIT Press.

Index

Y. Di Liberto, *Being and Contemporary Psychoanalysis*, The Palgrave Lacan Series, https://doi.org/10.1007/978-3-030-18476-6

S

T

U

V

The manufacturer's authorised representative in the EU is Springer Nature Customer Service Centre GmbH, Europaplatz 3, 69115 Heidelberg, Germany. If you have any concerns regarding our products, please contact ProductSafety@springernature.com

Printed and bound by CPI Group (UK) Ltd, Croydon, CR0 4YY
22/09/2026
02221067-0005